The Environment

VICTORIA BISHOP · ROBERT PROSSER

Series editor:
ROBERT PROSSER

COLLINS INSIGHT GEOGRAPHY

COLLINS
EDUCATIONAL

CONTENTS

Glossary words are highlighted in SMALL CAPITALS in the text the first time they appear in any Unit.

Location of case studies

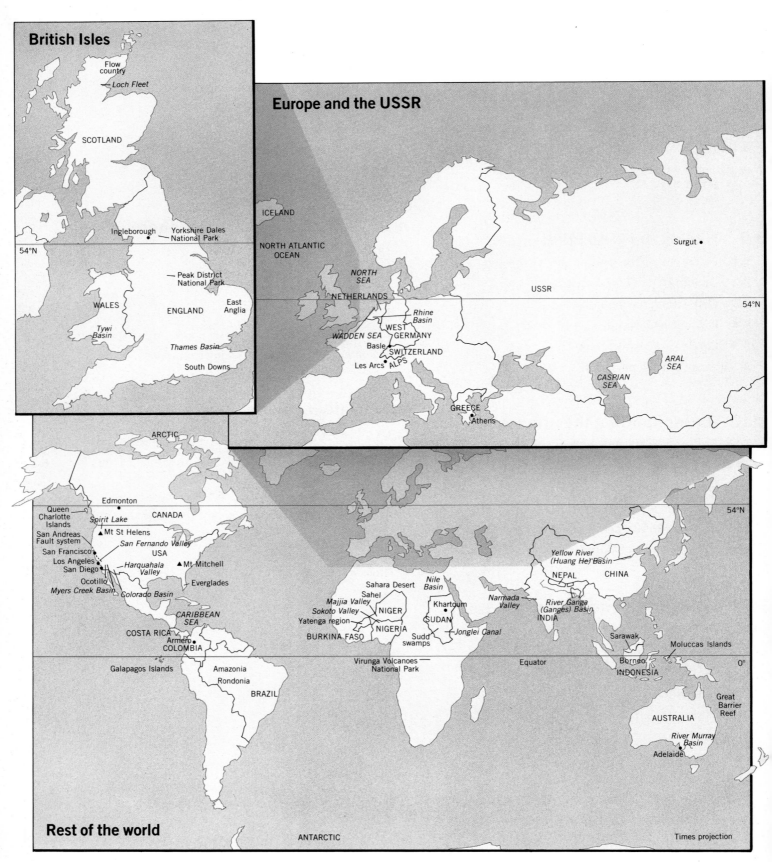

British Isles

Flow country
— Loch Fleet
SCOTLAND

54°N

Ingleborough • • Yorkshire Dales National Park

— Peak District National Park

WALES

ENGLAND

East Anglia

Tywi Basin

Thames Basin

South Downs

Europe and the USSR

ICELAND

NORTH ATLANTIC OCEAN

NORTH SEA

NETHERLANDS

Rhine Basin

WEST GERMANY

WADDEN SEA

Basle •
SWITZERLAND

Les Arcs • ALPS

Surgut •

USSR

54°N

ARAL SEA

CASPIAN SEA

GREECE
• Athens

Rest of the world

ARCTIC

Edmonton •
CANADA

Queen Charlotte Islands

Spirit Lake

San Andreas Fault system

▲ Mt St Helens

San Fernando Valley

San Francisco •
Los Angeles •
San Diego •
USA

Harquahala Valley

▲ Mt Mitchell

Ocotillo
Myers Creek Basin

Colorado Basin

— Everglades

CARIBBEAN SEA

COSTA RICA

Armero •
COLOMBIA

Galapagos Islands

Amazonia
Rondonia

BRAZIL

Sahara Desert
Sahel
Majjia Valley

Nile Basin

Sokoto Valley
Yatenga region

NIGER

Khartoum •
SUDAN

BURKINA FASO

NIGERIA

Sudd swamps

Jonglei Canal

Narmada Valley

Yellow River (Huang He) Basin

NEPAL

CHINA

River Ganga (Ganges) Basin
INDIA

Sarawak

Moluccas Islands

Virunga Volcanoes — National Park

Equator

Borneo
INDONESIA

0°

Great Barrier Reef

AUSTRALIA

River Murray Basin

Adelaide •

54°N

ANTARCTIC

Times projection

ENVIRONMENTAL SYSTEMS

Giant Californian redwoods, USA

Introducing systems

This book is about ENVIRONMENTAL SYSTEMS. In it you will learn how environments are made up of a set of parts which work together and depend on each other. We call such a working structure a SYSTEM.

UB40

Mountain environment, Switzerland

Work with a partner.
1 Look at Source A.
   a) What would happen if one of the microphones stopped working?
   b) What would happen if the drummer did not turn up to play?
2 From the definition of a system, name one way in which the Californian redwood forest (p. 1) and the mountain environment (Source B) are similar to the pop group (Source A).
3 Make a list of all the *parts* in the mountain environment (Source B). Think of the plants, what is around them, on them and what goes into them. Each choose one of the parts and describe it to your partner, explaining the job it does in the environmental system.
4 This book looks at:
   ● environments and the way they work,
   ● how humans make, change and destroy environments,
   ● why it is important for us to understand how environments work.
   Decide which of these key understandings match each of the headlines in Source C.

Thousands dead in Armenian earthquake

Deforestation may make 6000 species extinct by the year 2000

Three million trees needed to halt soil erosion in Nepal

A new reserve set up to save gorillas

Introducing ecosystems

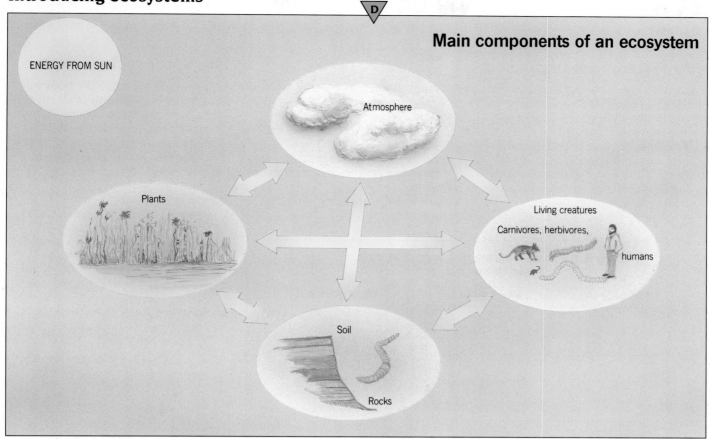

Main components of an ecosystem

ENERGY FROM SUN

Atmosphere

Plants

Living creatures
Carnivores, herbivores, humans

Soil

Rocks

Your list of parts in the mountain environment (question 3), should contain two types: living and non-living. An environment which is made up of a set of living elements plus the non-living parts needed by the living things is called an ECOSYSTEM. (See Source D above.)

The two ecosystems shown in Source E are quite close to each other in southern England. The obvious difference is that one is *natural* and the other has been created by humans (it is *artificial*).

5 Work in a small group.
   a) Using Source D to help you, list the components of the two ecosystems in Source E.
   b) Describe the job done by each component on your two lists.
   c) What changes have farmers made, and why?
   d) In which component have the changes been the greatest, and why?

Ripe wheat crop, Berkshire

Deer in the New Forest

1.2 STORES AND CYCLES

How systems are organised

In your discussions about the examples on pages 1–3, you may have discovered several important features of environmental systems:

- First, they are made up of *materials* and *energy* in a variety of forms.
- Second, these materials and energy are kept or *stored* in the components of the system.

- Third, materials and energy *move* in circular routes or pathways, which we call CYCLES.
- Fourth, while in the STORES or moving through the *cycles*, the *materials* and *energy* are used and changed by *processes* at work in the system.

All these features are summarised in Source A.

The water cycle

As case studies through the book will show, water is a vital part of all environments. Source B shows where it is stored and how it moves through the HYDROLOGICAL CYCLE or water cycle. Follow the arrows in Source B to see how the cycle works.

Work with a partner.

1. Using Source B list the places where water is stored.
2. Describe any *two* routes a water droplet could take as it moves through the hydrological cycle in Source B. You start from the * and go right round the whole cycle.
3. Suggest ways in which people can alter or control this natural hydrological cycle.

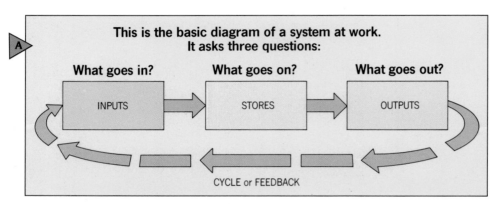

A

This is the basic diagram of a system at work. It asks three questions:

What goes in?	What goes on?	What goes out?
INPUTS	STORES	OUTPUTS

CYCLE or FEEDBACK

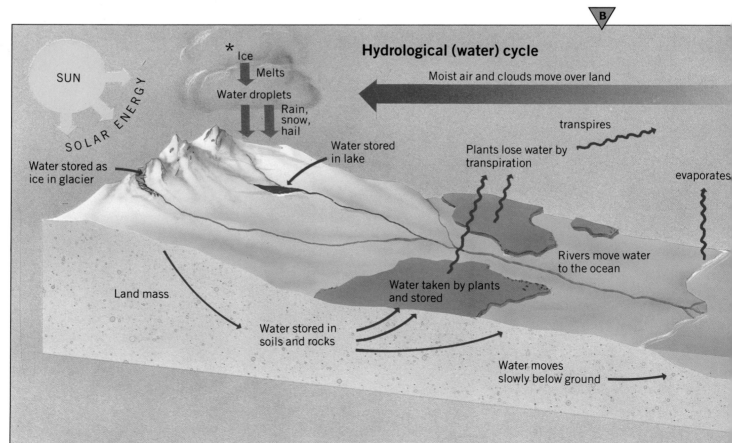

B

Hydrological (water) cycle

SUN

SOLAR ENERGY

* Ice

Melts

Water droplets

Rain, snow, hail

Moist air and clouds move over land

Water stored as ice in glacier

Water stored in lake

Plants lose water by transpiration

transpires

evaporates

Land mass

Rivers move water to the ocean

Water taken by plants and stored

Water stored in soils and rocks

Water moves slowly below ground

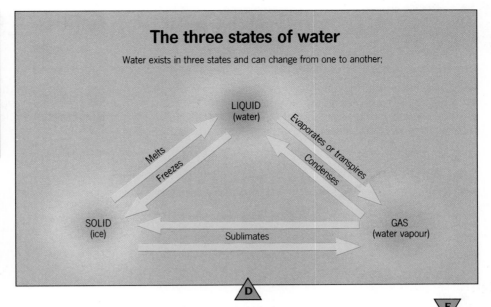

The three states of water

Water exists in three states and can change from one to another;

LIQUID (water)

Melts / Freezes

Evaporates or transpires / Condenses

SOLID (ice)

Sublimates

GAS (water vapour)

D

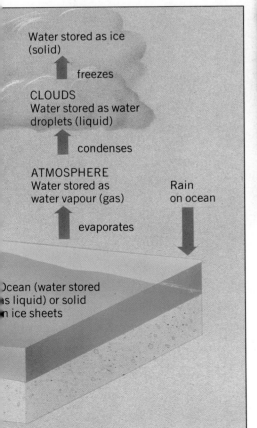

Water stored as ice (solid)

↑ freezes

CLOUDS
Water stored as water droplets (liquid)

↑ condenses

ATMOSPHERE
Water stored as water vapour (gas)

Rain on ocean

↑ evaporates

↓

Ocean (water stored as liquid) or solid in ice sheets

C

Where in the world is all the water?

Of every 100 litres, 97 are stored in the oceans. The remaining 3 litres are stored:

77% in ice caps and glaciers
22.5% in soils and rocks;
0.45% in rivers, lakes and swamps
0.05% in the atmosphere

4 Using Source C draw two pie graphs:
a) one to show the ocean store (97 litres out of 100) and the rest (3%);
b) one to show the remaining 3 litres divided into percentages. Why is it difficult to draw a clear graph of (b)?

5 As Sources B and D show, water or moisture exists in three states and can change from one to another. Identify in what state water is through each part of the hydrological cycle.

6 The names along the arrows in Source D are the processes which change moisture from one state to another. For each process, name one place in the hydrological cycle (Source B) where it occurs.

Messing about with natural cycles

E

Why is the Caspian Sea dying?

POLLUTION and increasing concentrations of salt are destroying fish stocks in the Caspian Sea, according to a recent report on Moscow Radio. In the past decade, catches have fallen by up to four-fifths in the world's largest inland lake.

Hydroelectric projects, and schemes for irrigating the dry farmland around the sea, have disrupted the rivers which feed it. Each year, some 40 cubic kilometres of water are taken from these rivers, destroying the freshwater spawning ground of the fish. Two-thirds of the water from the rivers Terek and Kura, for instance, never reach the sea but are diverted to agriculture and industry. The result has been an increasingly salty sea.

Then there is pollution. The water authorities of the southern republics of Azerbaijan, Dagestan, Turkmenia and Kazakhstan calculate that in 1985, industrialists dumped some 10,200 tonnes of oil products into the sea along with 104,200 tonnes of sewage.

In Baku Bay, oil pollution is 10 times more than the official upper permitted limits. The seabed is so polluted that if discharges ceased immediately, the water would still contain five times the permitted limit at the end of the century. Each year, Baku discharges more than 300 million cubic metres of pollutants into the sea.

The river waters that flow into the sea are also polluted. Harmful metals and oil products in the Terek and Kura rivers exceed the permitted limit by up to 30 times.

New Scientist, 5 May 1988

Read the newspaper extract and study the map (Source E). The Caspian Sea acts as a *store* in the hydrological cycle. Working in small groups, answer the following questions:

7 Which rivers provide *inputs* of water to the Caspian Sea store?

8 Where does the water from the Caspian Sea store go, i.e. what are its outputs and what processes allow this to happen? (Use Source B to help you.)

9 How has human activity affected the input of water to the Caspian Sea?

10 What new input is there to the Caspian Sea due to human activity?

11 The inputs have changed: the store has changed. So what has happened to the outputs?

12 Copy Source A and label it for the Caspian Sea system:
a) under natural conditions.
b) the system today (you may need to add extra arrows and boxes).

Water does two vital jobs as it 'cycles' through an ecosystem:
● it provides the moisture that plants and animals need;
● it carries the NUTRIENTS (food) that they need.
One such nutrient is CARBON. The energy which drives the

cycles comes from the sun. Source A shows how the water and carbon cycles work in a woodland ecosystem typical of much of Britain. Follow the arrows through the two cycles.

The natural cycles

A

Carbon dioxide (CO_2)
stored in atmosphere

SUN

SOLAR ENERGY

Water stored
in atmosphere

CO_2 taken into
leaves and carbon is
fixed in the plant
by photosynthesis

CO_2 released
by plant

Water transpires
from plant

Some CO_2
in raindrops

Rain and snow

Water stored
in the plant

Carbon stored
in the plant

Water evaporates
from surface

Dead matter containing
carbon falls to the ground

WATER
CYCLE

CARBON
CYCLE

Carbon stored
on surface

Water stored on surface

Water stored
in the soil

Water taken up
by plant roots

Carbon compounds dissolved
in water and taken into
plant roots

Carbon set free as
dead matter breaks
down and is stored
in the soil

Other important
nutrients

Nitrogen   Phosphorus   Potassium   Calcium   Magnesium   Sodium

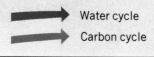

Water cycle

Carbon cycle

Work with a partner.
1 Study Source A. What are the two ways that carbon gets into plant tissues?
2 In which parts of the carbon cycle does water carry the carbon?

3 How many stores of carbon are there in the ecosystem? Name them.
4 What is likely to happen to the water and carbon cycles in a DROUGHT year?

Energy flows and stores

Life in an oak wood

A food web (with many chains):

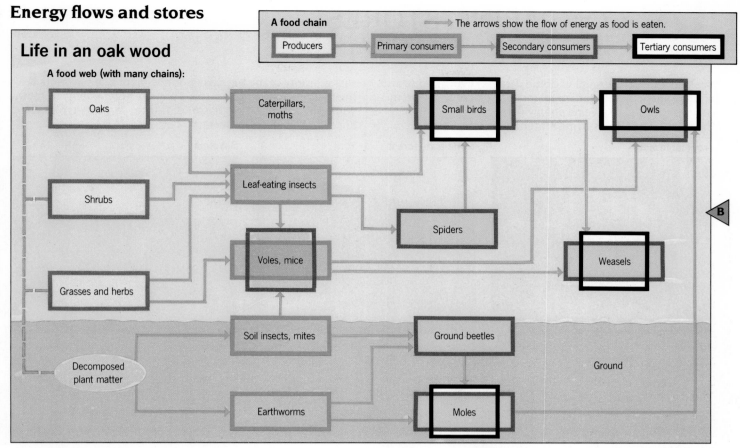

A food chain → The arrows show the flow of energy as food is eaten.

Producers → Primary consumers → Secondary consumers → Tertiary consumers

B

C

5 Source B shows that there is a SUC-CESSION OF FEEDING. It goes from PRODUCERS to TERTIARY CONSUMERS. Name one producer, one PRIMARY and one SECONDARY CONSUMER.

6 Look at Source B, a FOOD WEB.
a) What do spiders and beetles depend on?
b) What threatens beetles and spiders?

7 Suppose a forester sprays chemicals on the oak trees to wipe out leaf-eating insects. What effect does this have on the woodland? Think of both the vegetation and the animal life.

8 As part of the European Year of the Environment (1987–8), oak trees were planted by school children in Britain. In groups, discuss whether this was a good idea. Give reasons for your answer. Why was this project necessary?

9 Study Source C. List the four things that soil is made of.

10 Draw a labelled inputs → store → outputs diagram to show what is happening in Source C.

11 If the vegetation were removed, what would happen to the soil and the cycle of material through it?

The soil, cycles and stores

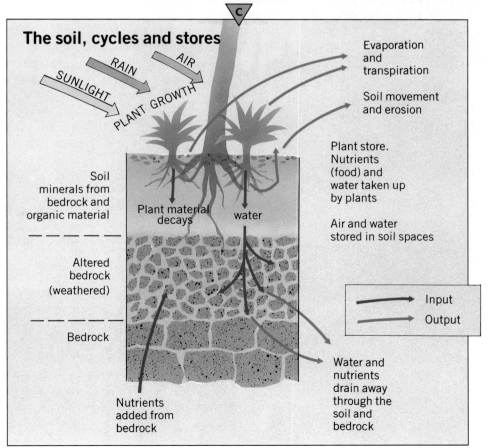

1.4 COMPARING STORES

In all ecosystems (except extreme deserts) living plants and animals are a major store of material and energy. (Remember: we eat food to give us energy – the energy is stored in the food.) We call this living material BIOMASS. The vast majority of the biomass is made up of plants. Plants are the first link in the FOOD CHAIN. They use solar energy to grow and so increase the biomass. For this reason, green plants are called primary producers.

Tropical forest

Temperate forest

Savanna

A

Temperature
Range 1.5°C

Manaus, Brazil

Temperature
Range 13.5°C

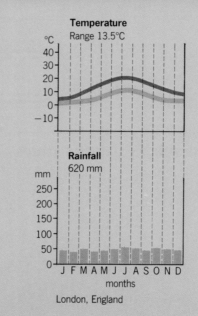

London, England

Temperature
Range 2°C

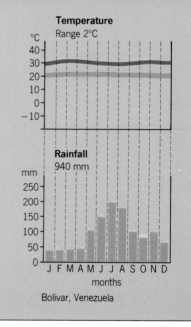

Bolivar, Venezuela

Rainfall 1800 mm

Rainfall 620 mm

Rainfall 940 mm

months

months

months

━━━ Monthly means of daily maximum temperature

━━━ Monthly means of daily minimum temperature

From these we can determine monthy actual temperature

B

Size and production rates of biomass stores

| Ecosystem | Biomass store | | Weight added each year | |
	Range (grams/m²)	Mean	Range (grams/m²)	Mean
Tropical forest	6,000–80,000	45,000	1,000–5,000	2,000
TEMPERATE FOREST	6,000–200,000	30,000	600–3,000	1,300
SAVANNA	200–15,000	4,000	200–2,000	700
TUNDRA	100–3,000	600	10–400	140

The four photographs in Source A show that natural ecosystems vary widely in the size of their biomass stores. Source B tells us just how different the biomass stores are.

Working in pairs, answer the following questions:

1 Is the biomass of a tropical forest *always* larger than that of a temperate forest? (Use Source B.)
2 In which of the ecosystems would you expect to find
   a) the most living creatures?
   b) the fewest living creatures? Why?
3 a) Use a world vegetation map in an atlas to find out the LATITUDES of each of the four ecosystems.
   b) Use a political map to name the main countries where they are found.

Work in a small group.

4 Use the graphs in Source A to describe the climate in each of the four ecosystems.
5 Look at Source C and describe the characteristics of each ecosystem. For instance, it is very hot and wet in areas where there are tropical rainforests.
6 Rank the ecosystems according to:
   a) the amount of solar energy available (use temperatures);
   b) the amount of moisture available. (The graphs of Source A show PRECIPITATION, which is moisture falling as rain, snow, sleet, hail.)
7 For most plants, active growth starts at 6°C. In which of these ecosystems will there be growth all year and which will be seasonal?
8 Plants also need moisture. They may store moisture, but their growth (adding to the biomass store) usually slows and stops in dry periods.
   a) What does Source D tell us about the relationship between rainfall and growth?
   b) In which months are the moisture inputs greatest for each ecosystem? (Use the precipitation figures given in the graphs for Source A.)
9 Use the photographs in Source A to draw four large labelled sketches showing the features of the vegetation (the biomass store), e.g. height, layers, density, types and shapes of plants. Under each sketch, say how the climatic characteristics help to explain the features you have identified.

Tundra

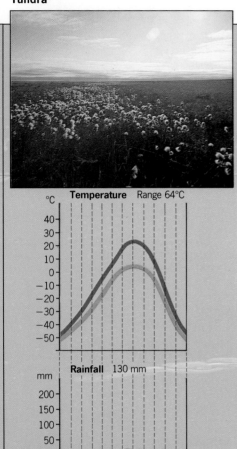

Temperature   Range 64°C

°C
40
30
20
10
0
−10
−20
−30
−40
−50

Rainfall   130 mm

mm
200
150
100
50
0
J F M A M J J A S O N D
months
Verkhoyansk, USSR

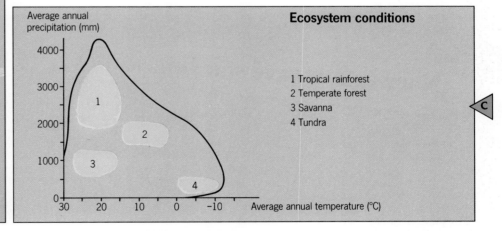

Ecosystem conditions

Average annual precipitation (mm)
4000
3000
2000
1000
0

30 20 10 0 −10   Average annual temperature (°C)

1 Tropical rainforest
2 Temperate forest
3 Savanna
4 Tundra

C

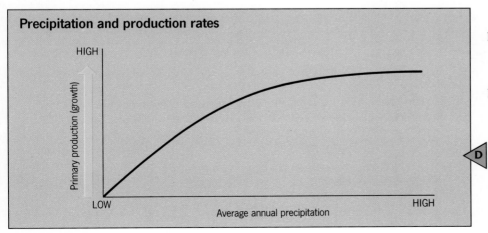

Precipitation and production rates

HIGH

Primary production (growth)

LOW   HIGH
Average annual precipitation

D

10 What factors other than temperature and precipitation may affect the biomass store and production rates?
11 How could people improve ecosystem production (i.e. increase the amount of plant growth each year)?

Coping with change

Any ecosystem has a set of conditions which suit it best, and which allow it to be as productive as possible (Source A). Also, any plant or animal has an ideal set of conditions for living.

When temperatures and water supply are good, soils are not being ERODED, there is plenty of space and food, and an ideal, balanced state is achieved. This is shown in Source A by Zone 1.

- As conditions move away from Zone 1, life becomes harder. Plants and animals can adapt, and all species have a RANGE OF TOLERANCE to change.
- But finally, one or more species cannot cope, and change becomes more rapid. This is the THRESHOLD in Source A. Some species will disappear, and change will spread through the rest of the environment.

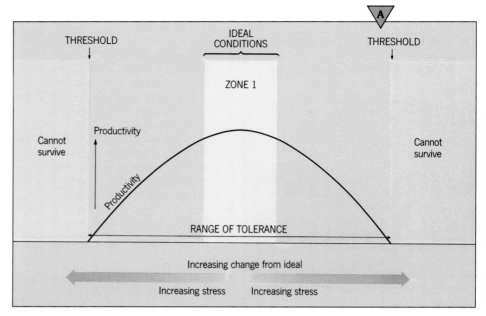

For example, an oak woodland can stand some dry or cold years, but if this happens too often, trees will start to die, and the ecosystem may begin to break down. If foresters cut down too many of the oaks, the effect may be the same.

A case study from the North Atlantic Ocean

Norwegians save starving seals

In June 1988, the headline appeared in a British newspaper. It seems to show that people do care about other species: helping hungry seals. But why are these thousands of seals starving? Why does the vast Atlantic Ocean not provide enough food? Follow the story below and find out what many scientists believe.

Until 1940s		Seals hunt and eat fish. Seals help to control the fish population. Food supply of fish helps to control seal numbers.
		Traditional fishing and seal hunting methods do not take out more animals than are born.
1940s–1970s		Larger modern fleets catch more fish. Fish populations decline.
		Less food for seals, and more seals caught. Seal populations decline.
1970s		High-technology fishing fleets catch still more fish. Fish populations continue to decline as fishing spreads farther and farther across the ocean.
		Seal hunting declines because of protest campaigns by conservationists over 'cruel' methods of killing.
1980s		Modern fishing fleets continue to make large catches. Fish populations decline, so there is less food for seals.
		Seals are protected, fewer are hunted and seal populations grow.
1988		Fish supplies continue to decline. Many seals starve. The hungry seals drift on to the coasts of Norway.
		Rescue operation by the Norwegians to save the stranded seals.

Saving the seals?

The case study in Source B shows how people can influence a major ocean ecosystem.

Work with a partner.
1. Study Sources A and B. In the case study from the North Atlantic Ocean, why did the fishing and seal hunting not affect the ecosystem seriously before the 1940s?
2. **a)** Why did the seal population decline from the 1940s?
   b) What has helped the seal population since the 1970s?
   c) Why has this help not completely solved the problem?
3. List different ways of restoring the North Atlantic ecosystem to a state of balance.
4. Explain how this example shows what is meant in Source A by *range of tolerance* and *threshold*.

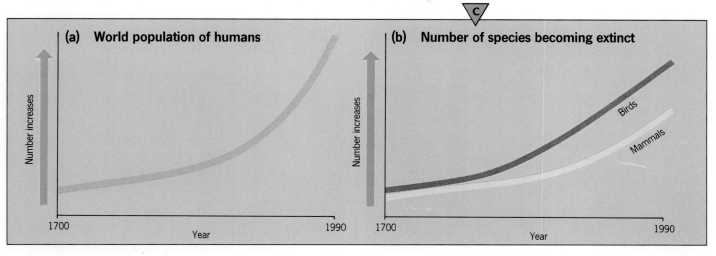

(a) **World population of humans**

Number increases

1700   Year   1990

(b) **Number of species becoming extinct**

Number increases

Birds

Mammals

1700   Year   1990

C

How much should we value planet Earth?

We could find stories like the one in Source B in every ocean and on every continent – even Antarctica. Many stories have even sadder endings: the graphs in Source C (**a** and **b**) show that more and more species are becoming extinct as human populations increase. Is there a connection?

5. The key question is: now that there are so many more people on Earth, all with increasing demands, and with such incredible technology, how ought we to behave towards planet Earth? Use the viewpoints in Source D as a basis for discussion in small groups.

6. *Something to bear in mind:*
   When you come to the end of this book, discuss the two viewpoints in Source D again, and see if your opinions and attitudes are the same.

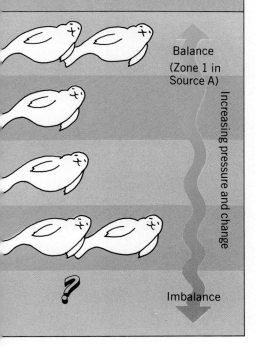

UPDATE

Later in 1988 thousands of seals throughout the North Sea died from a mystery disease. Scientists believe it is a new virus carried from the Arctic Ocean. They think pollution may have put North Sea seals more at risk.

Balance (Zone 1 in Source A)

Increasing pressure and change

Imbalance

D

"Things have always changed. Evolution is all about survival of the fittest, and some things must disappear. We humans are now the fittest and strongest and so have the right to use all the world resources for our benefit. We need the space and we have to change environments. If some plants and animals suffer, hard luck."

"All living things have an equal right to life on planet Earth. If we humans are the most powerful species then it is our duty to help and protect the weaker species. To do this, we need to conserve the habitats they need to survive. We must see ourselves as guardians of planet Earth."

1 THE WATER CYCLE

Draw simple line sketches of the photographs in Sources A and B.

1. On each sketch, add labels to show the water (*hydrological*) cycle. Use boxes to show where water is stored and arrows to show movement and processes. Look again at Source B on page 4 and Source A on page 6.
2. In a different colour add labels to show how people have altered the water cycle (think of stores and routes).

Llyn Brianne reservoir, Dyfed

Cultivated field, Hampshire

Sioux Indians hunting buffalo

2.1 ECOSYSTEMS AT WORK

Natural ecosystems

All living things must have food. So, *feeding* is one of the main activities of the living components of any ECOSYSTEM: plants feed on nutrients from the soil; creatures eat plants and each other. This is how matter and energy move through ecosystems in cycles (called FOOD CHAINS), as we saw in Unit 1. The second essential is to be able to *reproduce*; all plants and creatures die, and so they must be able to replace themselves.

A **Food chains on an African savanna**

Savanna grass

Wildebeest grazing

Bee-eater with dragonfly. The bird also eats other insects

Flies on a lion's nose

Lion with its kill

Vultures and hyena feeding

Buffalo carcass

The ecosystem is in balance, but:
1. Why could the lions not survive without the wildebeest?
2. What would happen if all the lions in a district died? (Follow the cycle both ways from the middle photo.)
3. What might happen if the numbers of wildebeest doubled?
4. Could the vultures survive without the lions?
5. **a)** Name a PRIMARY and a SECONDARY CONSUMER in Source A. (See p. 7.)
   b) Where might humans fit into that chain?

Adding humans to ecosystems

Using an ecosystem for food

B

INPUTS Water, sunlight, plant foods, seeds	→	STORE OR FACTORY Plant growth	→	OUTPUTS = FOOD Edible fruit, seeds, leaves, roots

← FEEDBACK ←

D

Harvesting in a Russian wheatfield

E

Comparing natural and farming ecosystems as food producers

The most productive land ecosystem is tropical rainforest. If we say that an area of rainforest the size of a football pitch produces 100 units of BIOMASS a year, then we can compare it with other ecosystems.

Natural		Farming	
Tropical rainforest	100	Rice	5
English woodland	35	Maize	4
STEPPE grassland	5	Prairie wheat	3.5
Desert	0.5	Intensive wheat with fertiliser	15
		Irrigated vegetables in hot deserts	4

Look at Source B. If we take more of the OUTPUTS than the 'factory' is producing, then eventually the SYSTEM will break down. For example, if we take *all* the seeds, there will be none left to germinate and provide new plants. So, we can take less from the natural system, or we can change it. If we change it, we have two choices: (a) change the INPUTS, or (b) encourage only those plants we want to grow and get rid of all the others.

6 Look at the images on page 13. *A resource is anything which is felt to be useful.*
   a) What could the cartoon man be seeing as resources?
   b) Why are the Indians hunting?

Humans may be bad for ecosystems, and may destroy them. But is this necessarily true? Take the example of food: the simplest way we can obtain food is to pick what an ecosystem produces, as in Source B.

7 Look back at pages 8–9 and suggest reasons why the natural ecosystems of Source C (below) produce different amounts of growth.

C

Average growth a year in kilograms on one square metre of land	
Tropical rainforest	2.5
Marsh and swamp	2.0
Oak and beach woodland	1.2
Tropical SAVANNA	1.0
Coniferous forest	0.8
Prairie (TEMPERATE GRASSLAND)	0.6
Arctic TUNDRA	0.15
Semi-desert SCRUB	0.1

8 For the ecosystem in Source D list the inputs and outputs:
   a) that we control and
   b) that we do not control.
9 Are farming ecosystems more productive than natural systems? (Consider Source E.)
10 Why do we go to all the effort of making farming ecosystems?
11 Humans now go beyond changing ecosystems: they create them. Describe a greenhouse environment and what it aims to do.

15

2.2 PROFIT AND LOSS IN BRITISH FARMING

The explosion in Britain's farm production

1 Draw bar graphs for Source A.
2 Productivity has risen, and Britain is now self-sufficient in many of our main foods. There are even surpluses, e.g. beef 'mountains'. Use the figures and your graphs to support the claim that British farming has been a success story.
3 With a partner, define what you mean by 'success'; 'productivity' and 'self-sufficiency'.
4 Work with a partner. Make a list of ways you could measure 'success' in farming, without using 'productivity'.

Farm produce	1948	1968	1978	1985
Wheat output (tonnes/hectare)	2.2	3.9	4.7	7.7
Barley output (tonnes/hectare)	2.2	3.6	4.0	5.6
Potato output (tonnes/hectare)	17.2	24.9	27.3	37.0
Milk output (litres/cow/year)	2400	3700	4400	4710
Egg output (eggs/hen/year)	114	211	240	269

A

A second agricultural revolution

B

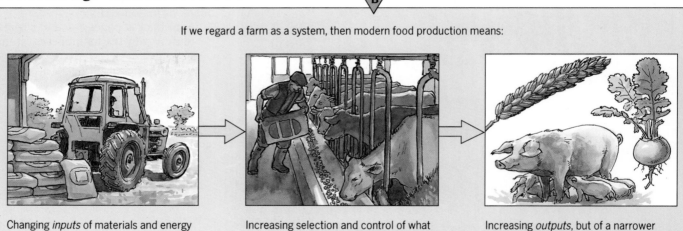

If we regard a farm as a system, then modern food production means:

Changing *inputs* of materials and energy

Increasing selection and control of what lives and grows (we change the *stores* – animals and plants are stores of matter and energy. We control *processes* by irrigation, temperature control etc.)

Increasing *outputs*, but of a narrower range of things.

Changes to farming in the UK

	1954	1959	1964	1969	1974	1979	1984
Number of tractors (thousands)	400	454	482	444	480	486	480
Full-time workers (thousands)	583	493	389	308	230	187	160
Crop area (million hectares)	4.7	4.3	4.5	4.4	4.8	5.0	5.2
Use of nitrate fertilisers (thousand tonnes)	290	340	570	840	1000	1180	1330

C

*A tractor today does five times the work of a tractor in the 1950s.

5 Look at Sources A, B and C. What have been the main changes in British farming in terms of:
   a) *Inputs:* what goes into food production,
   b) *Processes:* how the land is worked and animals reared,
   c) *Outputs:* what is produced?
6 How have the changed outputs of Source A been achieved by the changing inputs of Source C?
7 Source C shows how important nitrates have become. Use library books to find out how nitrates help the farmer.

Changing landscapes – changing attitudes

D

Lowland farming in 1936

Lowland farming in 1986

Variety or monotony?

The changes in our countryside are the results of decisions – by governments and individual farmers. Governments and the EEC have encouraged farmers to grow more food by using modern methods and equipment. Just as factories are redesigned when new techniques are introduced, so the layout of farms has had to change.

Changes have been enormous but opinions vary as to whether it has all been worth it.

For example: one way of measuring the richness of an ecosystem is by the number of plants, insects, birds and animals that live in it. A hectare of hedgerow might support 50 pairs of blackbirds, but hedgerows are an obstacle to large tractors and combine harvesters. So, hedgerows are ripped out.

A hectare of natural meadow may contain 40 types of wildflower and 12 species of butterfly. When farmers plough the meadow, they will sow one species of grass, say ryegrass. Butterflies do not like ryegrass. So what do you think will happen to them?

8 Look at the photos in Source D. List what you think are the three main differences between the farming landscapes. Compare your list with that of a partner, and explain why you chose your three items.
9 Why are modern farming ecosystems becoming simpler, and what do we mean by 'simpler'?
10 Read the two extracts in Source E.

What changes in *land features* and *attitudes to the land* are suggested?
11 In groups, discuss why farmers and conservationists often hold opposing views about our countryside ecosystems.

E

A writer in 1943

66 Our countryside is like a multi-coloured chequerboard. Its chief characteristic is its attractive patchwork appearance, with an infinite variety of small, odd-shaped fields of brown ploughland or green pasture bounded by twisting hedges, narrow winding lanes, small woodlands and copses and isolated trees and hedgerow timber. 99

G.M. Young,
Country and Town, 1943

A conservationist in 1980

66 A new agricultural revolution is underway. If allowed to proceed unhindered, it will transform the face of England. Already a quarter of our hedgerows, 24 million hedgerow trees, thousands of acres of down and heathland, a third of our woods and hundred upon hundred of ponds, streams, marshes and flower-rich meadows have diasppeared. 99

Marion Sheard,
The Theft of the Countryside, 1980

The growing problem of soil erosion

All over the world, one of the major problems caused by farming is soil EROSION. Soil is the thin store of plant foods (nutrients) and water upon which all agriculture depends. *Soil erosion* is the removal of some of this precious store by wind and water. All parts of Britain suffer from soil erosion. Just look at the muddy colour of rivers after rain storms.

But it is only in certain regions that erosion has become a serious problem. The materials on these pages help you to answer the question: Is farming to blame?

1   Use Source A and an atlas to name the counties which suffer most from soil erosion.
2   Describe the main types of farming found in the counties you have named.

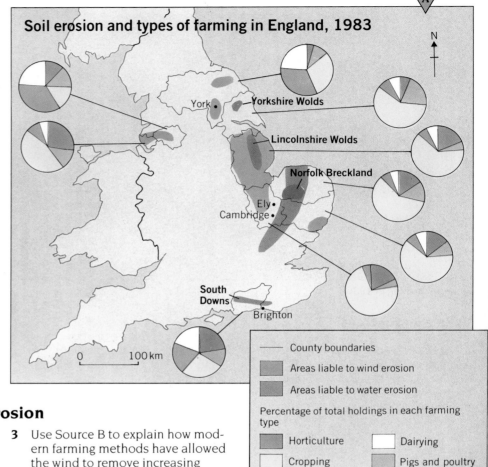

A

Soil erosion and types of farming in England, 1983

York •
Yorkshire Wolds
Lincolnshire Wolds
Norfolk Breckland
Ely •
Cambridge •
South Downs
Brighton •

0   100 km

—— County boundaries

Areas liable to wind erosion

Areas liable to water erosion

Percentage of total holdings in each farming type

Horticulture   Dairying

Cropping   Pigs and poultry

Cattle and sheep

Looking for causes: wind erosion

At least 10 mm of the rich top soil of these Fenlands in East Anglia are being blown away each year. Over large areas, the soil is less than half the depth it was after being drained from peaty wetlands in the 17th century.

3   Use Source B to explain how modern farming methods have allowed the wind to remove increasing amounts of soil in the last 30 years.

B

Sunny spells dry out the surface

Land lies bare for several months

All land is used for arable crops

Monoculture (same crop each year) breaks down soil structure

Chemicals are sprayed to remove weeds

Flat land – hedges removed, so few windbreaks

Machines break the soil to fine particles.

Artificial fertilisers break down the soil structure

Looking for causes: water erosion

Erosion on the South Downs

The photograph in Source C was taken in December. The field was planted with barley seed in the autumn (it is called winter barley). The surface of the field will be largely bare until the plants grow in the spring. The ploughing and seed drilling run directly downslope, as the lines down the field show.

The soil is a LOAM: a mixture of clay and silt, plus larger sand particles. Soil dries out after heavy rain, and this can cause a surface crust to form. This happens most often when farmers work the soil into a fine texture. The old field boundary shown on the map in Source D shows up on the photograph as the line dividing paler soil on the upper half from darker soil on the lower half.

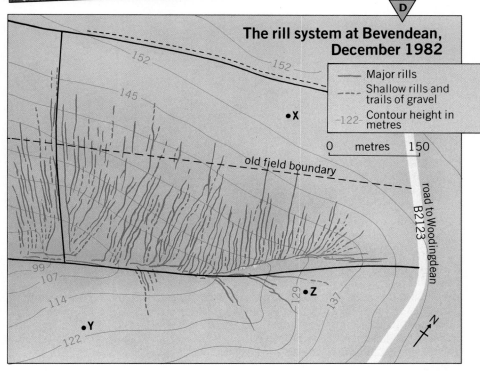

Bevendean on the South Downs in East Sussex. Rills running down the slopes show worrying evidence of soil erosion

The rill system at Bevendean, December 1982

— Major rills
---- Shallow rills and trails of gravel
-122- Contour height in metres

0 metres 150

old field boundary

road to Woodingdean B2123

•X
•Z
•Y

4   The photograph in Source C shows part of the area in Source D. Locate, on the map, where the photographer was standing (at X, Y or Z?). Give the reasons for your choice.

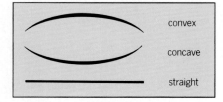

convex
concave
straight

5   Which of the three shapes in the box above fits the slope at Bevendean best?

6   Describe the pattern of gullies and deposits at Bevendean, and suggest reasons for their distribution.

7   The main reasons scientists give for the sudden spread of soil erosion on the South Downs are listed in Source E. Use the list to explain the erosion of the field at Bevendean.

8   Use the information about both wind and water erosion to make two lists: one of natural causes, and one of causes due to human activity. Do you think farming is to blame for erosion?

Reasons for the sudden spread of soil erosion on the South Downs

● Grassland for sheep grazing used to dominate the rolling Downs. In the last 40 years, 80% have been ploughed up for arable crops.
● Many field boundaries have been removed. This leaves long, open slopes and areas for water to collect.
● Land is often ploughed directly downslope, even on quite steep slopes.
● Convex slopes collect water on their flatter upper sections. This water gains speed as it runs to the steeper, lower sections.

● Since 1978, EEC policy has made it more profitable for farmers to grow winter barley rather than spring-sown crops. Autumn-sown crops leave largely bare surfaces through the winter.
● Crusts develop on the surface of many Downland soils because of raindrop impact. The crust is IMPERMEABLE.
● Autumn 1982 was wetter than average, with more heavy storms than normal.

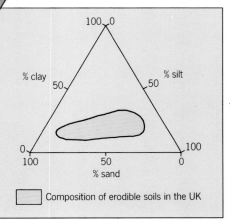

% clay
% silt
% sand

Composition of erodible soils in the UK

Farming in the Sokoto Valley, Northern Nigeria

All over the world, farmers organise their lives and environments around the water supply, especially when there is a long dry season. This case study shows you how skilfully traditional farmers adapt to rhythms of water supply, and how modern technology may *not* improve their lives.

The villagers of the floodplain of the River Sokoto live off the crops they grow, the fish they catch, the cattle and goats they rear. From the map (Source A) you can see that the floodplain begins when the river leaves the hills through which it cuts its upper course.

1 In what direction is the river flowing?
2 How long is this section of the river on the map?
3 How many villages are there?

The problem to be solved

The Hausa farmers depend upon the input and THROUGHPUT of water, from rainfall and the river: how much water is available; when it is available; where it is available; who controls its use. The problem for these farmers is shown by the two graphs in Source C – the inputs of water to the floodplain environment are *highly seasonal*.

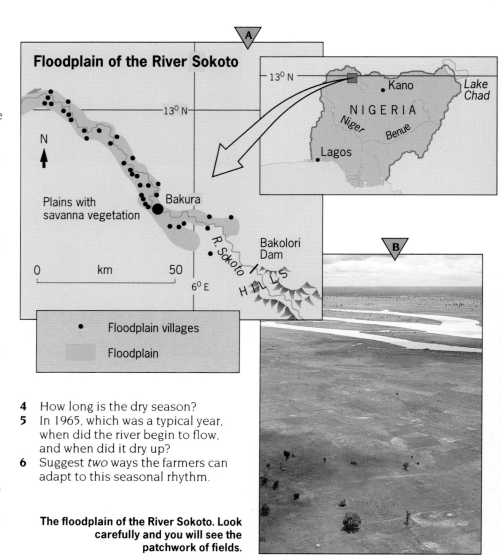

Floodplain of the River Sokoto

Plains with savanna vegetation

Bakura

R. Sokoto HILLS

Bakolori Dam

- Floodplain villages
- Floodplain

4 How long is the dry season?
5 In 1965, which was a typical year, when did the river begin to flow, and when did it dry up?
6 Suggest *two* ways the farmers can adapt to this seasonal rhythm.

The floodplain of the River Sokoto. Look carefully and you will see the patchwork of fields.

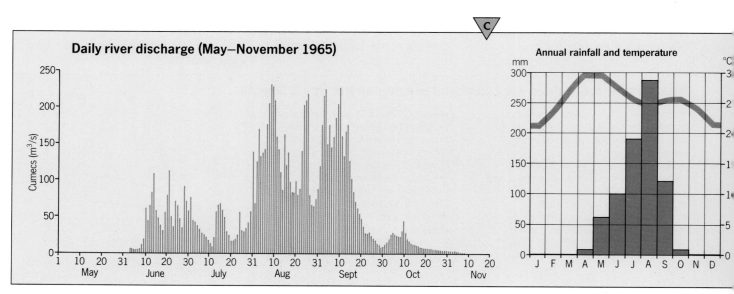

Daily river discharge (May–November 1965)

Cumecs (m³/s)

Annual rainfall and temperature

Learning about the water

Over many centuries, the farmers have learned about the river and their land:

- The river floods across the flood-plain each year some time in August and September.
- Even slight differences in the level of the land affect which parts flood and for how long.

- Water is stored in the soil, and the longer the floods last, the longer this soil water will last.
- The floodwaters deposit fresh silt each year, which helps to keep up soil fertility.

7 Using Sources D and E, describe the movements of water:
   a) during the wet season
   b) during the dry season.
8 In 1972 and 1973, the annual rainfall was only half of the average. What happened to the water stores in those years?

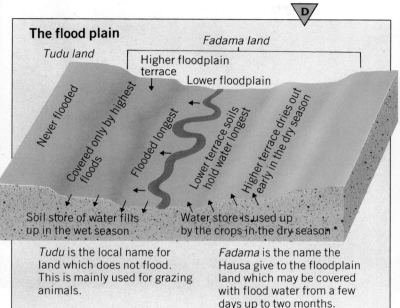

D

The flood plain

Tudu land · Fadama land

Higher floodplain terrace · Lower floodplain

Never flooded

Covered only by highest floods

Flooded longest

Lower terrace soils hold water longest

Higher terrace dries out early in the dry season

Soil store of water fills up in the wet season

Water store is used up by the crops in the dry season

Tudu is the local name for land which does not flood. This is mainly used for grazing animals.

Fadama is the name the Hausa give to the floodplain land which may be covered with flood water from a few days up to two months.

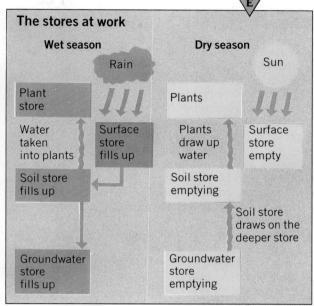

E

The stores at work

Wet season

Rain

Plant store → Water taken into plants → Soil store fills up → Groundwater store fills up

Surface store fills up

Dry season

Sun

Plants → Plants draw up water → Soil store emptying → Groundwater store emptying

Surface store empty

Soil store draws on the deeper store

Solving the problem

The Hausa farmers have become skilled in making best use of the water. As the floods spread across the *fadama*, the farmers plant crops which need most water, on land which floods most easily. Rice is most important.

Through July and August they INTER-PLANT sorghum and millet (interplanting means mixing different crops on the same plot). As the floods subside and on land which has little flooding, they interplant a second crop of sorghum and millet with sweet potatoes, beans, tomatoes, peppers and cotton.

By the time the dry season begins, the rice becomes ready for harvest, and the second crops use up the water in the soil store. After the crops are harvested, animals are grazed on many of the plots.

Notice three important things:
- The timing and sequence of planting.
- The use of so many types of seed

closely adjusted to water and soil conditions, e.g. the Hausa farmers use at least 20 varieties of rice.
- The growth and harvest are extended as far as possible into the dry season.

9 How do the graphs for the three main food crops (Source F) show that:
   a) Rice has the greatest need for water?

b) Millet can be grown on the land which has little flooding?
c) Sorghum can be used to cut down risks to the farmer because it can stand both flooding and dry conditions?
10 Copy the block diagram in Source D. On this diagram:
   a) shade the areas which flood most easily;
   b) label where rice, sorghum, millet are most likely to be planted.

F

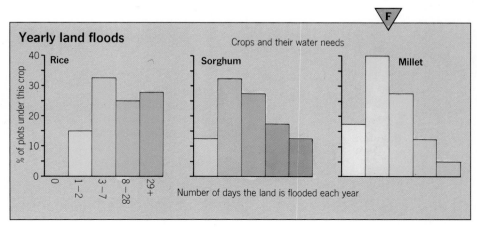

Yearly land floods

Crops and their water needs

% of plots under this crop

Rice — Sorghum — Millet

Number of days the land is flooded each year: 0, 1–2, 3–7, 8–28, 29+

2.5 CHANGING THE WATER CYCLE

Building a dam

The Bakolori Dam is a Nigerian Government project completed in 1976. Its main purpose is to store water in a reservoir, and to control the release of this water to irrigate 30,000 ha of the Sokoto Valley.

At least 6000 people live in the 90 km stretch of floodplain shown on the map on page 20. Within 35 years, there may be twice as many people, so you would expect the communities to be happy that the dam is providing water for extra land. But many farmers are complaining. The materials on these pages show you why Sokoto farmers see themselves as being worse off since the coming of the dam.

Complaint 1:

The irrigation scheme does help to solve the problem of population growth, by allowing new land to be cultivated, and new villages to be built. The farmers of most of the 30 older villages complain they are outside the scheme, and so do not benefit.

1 Copy the map from page 20 (Source A) and add to it, as accurately as possible, the information from the map from Source B.
2 How does your map back up the farmers' complaint?

A The Bakolori Dam, northern Nigeria

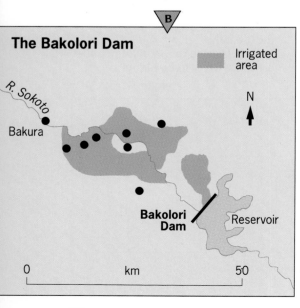

B

The Bakolori Dam

Irrigated area

R. Sokoto
Bakura
Bakolori Dam
Reservoir
N
0 km 50

Birnin Tudu village and ifs *fadama* (flooded land)

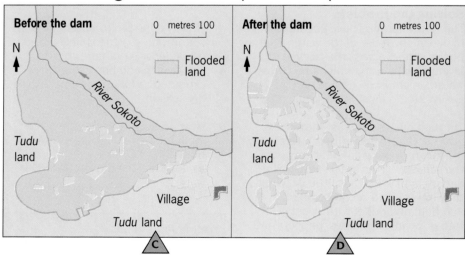

Before the dam
0 metres 100
N
Flooded land
River Sokoto
Tudu land
Village
Tudu land

C

After the dam
0 metres 100
N
Flooded land
River Sokoto
Tudu land
Village
Tudu land

D

Complaint 2:

The farmers in many older villages complain that less of their *fadama* (floodplain) land now floods.

3 Look at Sources C and D. With a partner work out the approximate proportion of the *fadama* which was flooded *before* the dam and *since* the dam. How much land has been lost? (For the 30 older villages, the area flooded is less than half of what it was.)
4 Can you suggest why the annual floods have been reduced since the dam was built?

Complaint 3:

Because less of their *fadama* is flooded, and the floods last for fewer days (Source H), the farmers complain that their skilful sequence of wet season and dry season crops is badly affected (look again at pages 20–1). Source E shows just what these changes have been for one village.

5 Before the dam, 66% of all the farming plots were planted with rice. What has happened to rice growing since then? (See Source E.)
6 What are the two main changes in the wet season agriculture?
7 Why is the reduction of the rice area so important?
8 Vegetables grown in the dry season have always been important items of the villagers' diet. What has happened to these crops since the dam?

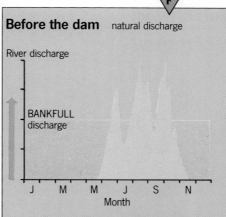

E

How crops changed after the dam
The figures show the % of the total number of agricultural plots used for a crop

	Before the dam	After the dam	Av. yield per hectare (kilograms)
Wet season crops (Growing during the flood period)			
Rice	66	14	180
Sorghum	41	75	56
Millet	35	61	45
Beans	22	37	60
Dry season crops (Growing after the floods have gone)			
Sweet potatoes	52	23	100
Cassava	42	32	100
Peppers and tomatoes	40	23	225
All plots with *any* dry season crop	80	50	not known

How the dam changes the water cycle

In systems terms, a dam adds a new *store* to the environment (it makes a reservoir). Water is released (*output* from the store) through pipes and gates in the dam, when the farmers need it. So, the *throughput* of water in an environment is controlled by the water engineers at the dam.

Sources F and G show the differences between natural and controlled throughputs of water in regions where rainfall is seasonal and irregular.

9 Copy the graph in Source F and then add the discharge line from the graph in Source G.
   a) Shade in red the times when natural discharge is higher than controlled discharge.
   b) Shade in blue the times when the controlled discharge is greater than the natural discharge.
10 Describe briefly:
   a) the differences between the two discharges,
   b) why these differences happen.
11 Can you explain the sudden change of discharge at X on the graph in Source G?
12 In groups, discuss what it would be like to be a farmer of a floodplain village. Then, individually, write a letter to your district councillor, stating what has happened to your food supply since the throughput of water has been controlled by the engineers at the dam. Use Source H to help you.

F

Before the dam   natural discharge

River discharge

BANKFULL discharge

J M M J S N
Month

Bankfull discharge = when river channel is full. Floods begin above this line

- Highly seasonal
- High, short-lived flood levels
- Too much water at times, too little water at other times
- Fresh silt spread across the floodplain each year, which helps maintain soil fertility

G

After the dam   controlled discharge

River discharge

X

BANKFULL discharge

J M M J S N
Month

- Controlled flows through the year
- Lower flood levels
- Water released to make growing season longer
- Less water wasted, athough evaporation from the reservoir may be high
- Most silt is deposited on the bed of the reservoir, and within 100 years will have filled it in

Floods are lower, shorter, narrower

H

	Average height of floods (metres)	Average number of days land is flooded each year	Percentage of farming plots flooded each year
Before the Bakolori Dam	4	23	88
After the dam was built	3	6	25

THE FARM AS A SYSTEM

Farming uses natural ecosystems to produce food for humans. The environmental system is changed and managed by people. We can still consider the farm as a system – with inputs, processes, stores, outputs and feedback (Source A).

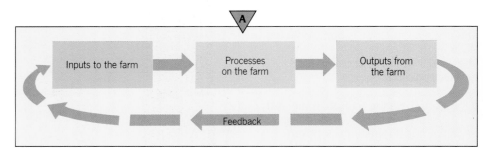

A

Inputs to the farm → Processes on the farm → Outputs from the farm

Feedback

1 Select a farm in your local area, or while you are on a field trip. Alternatively, you could use a textbook. Instead of just collecting facts, arrange the information into a systems diagram such as the one in Source B. These questions will help you study the farming system:
a) Which are natural inputs?
b) Which are inputs added by people?

c) How have the outputs changed from being inputs?
d) What passes along the pathways in the farming system?
e) Are the natural inputs/outputs from the system the most important to the farmer, or are other factors more important? (E.g. government or EEC policy.)

2 On your diagram indicate the *stores* in the farming system. Remember that the stores may be natural or made by people. Include both energy and matter.
3 With a partner, discuss whether this is the best type of diagram for showing the farming system. If not, design your own systems diagram.

A diagram to show an agricultural system

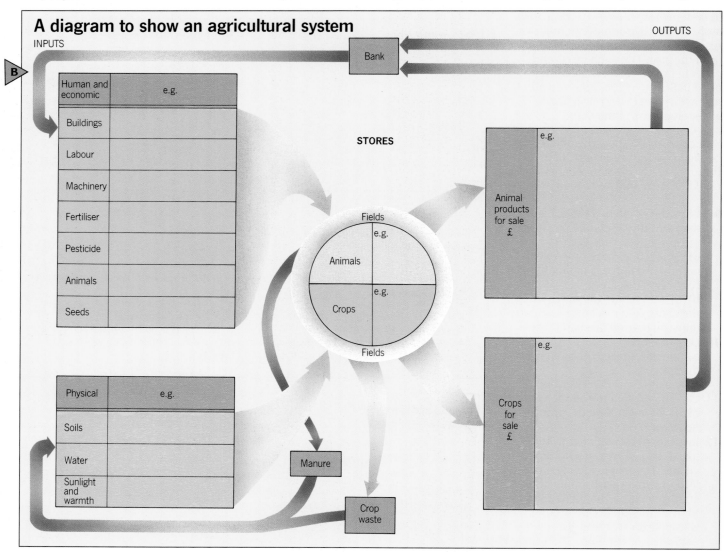

INPUTS   OUTPUTS

B

Bank

Human and economic	e.g.
Buildings	
Labour	
Machinery	
Fertiliser	
Pesticide	
Animals	
Seeds	

STORES

Fields / Animals / Crops / Fields (e.g.)

Animal products for sale £ (e.g.)

Crops for sale £ (e.g.)

Physical	e.g.
Soils	
Water	
Sunlight and warmth	

Manure

Crop waste

Logging in British
Columbia, Canada

Forest resources

It is not surprising that, for many thousands of years, humans have lived in forests, depended on them and chopped them down. Nor is it surprising that some of the most important environmental issues today are about forests. How should they be used? Can they be saved? Who should decide? This unit helps you to understand how TEMPERATE FORESTS work. Temperate forests are found in regions of mild temperature, between the tropics and the polar circles. Unit 4 looks at tropical forests.

Forests are:
- the most extensive ECOSYSTEMS. Even though half of all natural forests have been cut down, they cover almost one-third of the land of planet Earth. (See Source A.)
- the longest-living of all organisms.
- the most complex of all ecosystems: most species, most variety.
- the most energetic of all ecosystems (the giant sequoia trees of California (see page 1) are the world's largest living things).
- the most productive of all ecosystems: tropical rainforests produce more weight of growth in a year than any other ecosystem.
- the source of more products useful to humans than any other ecosystem.

World forest cover, 1985 (million hectares)

| | Forest with full canopy (CLOSED FOREST) | | | | |
	(a) BROADLEAVED	(b) CONIFEROUS	(c) OPEN FOREST	(d) Total	(e) % of land area
World total	1,720	1,140	1,280	4,140	32
Developed world					
N. America	170	300	210	680	37
Europe	65	90	20	175	37
USSR	150	650	130	930	41
Other countries (1)	50	20	70	140	15
Developing world (2)					
Africa	220	2	500	722	24
Latin America	670	30	250	950	46
Asia (not China)	320	30	80	430	26
China	100	25	15	140	15

(1) Includes Japan, Australia, New Zealand, Israel, South Africa.
(2) In addition, there are 1000 million hectares of SCRUB and SECONDARY FOREST lying FALLOW (resting) following cultivation.

World Resources, 1986

Working in groups, take part in the following activities to produce wall displays from Source A.

1   *How much forest of each type is there in each of the eight major areas of the world, and what are the totals?*
   Show your answer as a set of eight pie graphs. Use column (d) to decide the size of each circle. Use columns (a)–(c) to work out the 'slices' of the circle.
   N.B. Draw your graphs large enough for display. You may be able to attach them to a wall map of the world. Remember to add titles and labelling. (A question: Where will you attach your 'Other Countries' graph?)

2   *Where are the three types of forest found?*
   Draw three graphs (columns (a)–(c) large enough to display. This time, *you* decide what will be the best style of graph and most effective display.

3   *How much of the various areas of the world are forested?*
   Draw a set of bar graphs from column (e) and make up a display.

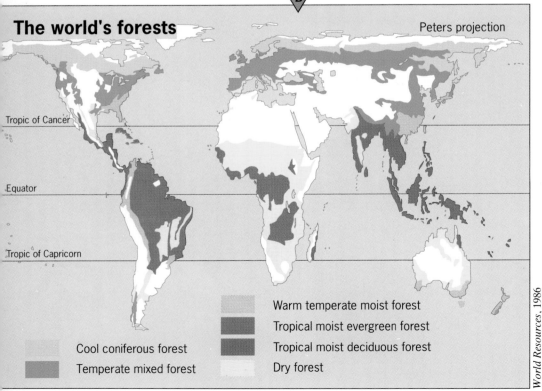

The world's forests

Peters projection

Tropic of Cancer

Equator

Tropic of Capricorn

Cool coniferous forest
Temperate mixed forest
Warm temperate moist forest
Tropical moist evergreen forest
Tropical moist deciduous forest
Dry forest

World Resources, 1986

Are the forests under threat?

The dilemma

For the Haida people of the Queen Charlotte Islands, British Columbia, Canada, the coniferous forest is the centre of their lives and their religion. They skilfully carve totem poles (like those shown above) and build their houses from wood. For hundreds of years they have lived in the forest and from it. They have conserved it: they know they depend on its riches and it is their home.

The ecosystem is in balance – with humans occupying a NICHE within it.

Commercial logging companies see the forests differently: as a rich resource of valuable timber. They want to fell the trees and destroy the habitats of hundreds of species of plants, animals, birds, insects, fishes – and the home and livelihood of the Haida.

New forests can be planted, but in huge blocks of single species. They would be harvested in perhaps 50 years, and the cycle begun again. They would not provide a home for many plant or animal species, nor a home for the Haida. Some Haida people might be able to stay on as workers for the logging companies.

How much wood is the world using?

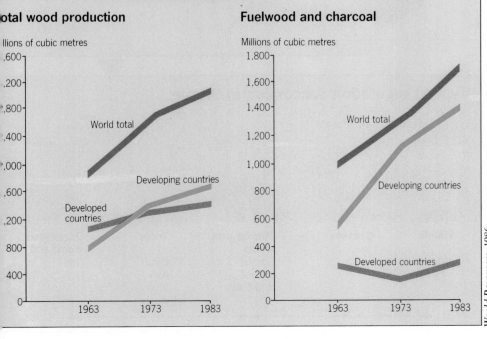

World Resources, 1986

4 Work with a partner. Use Source B and your graphs for questions 1–3 to write a brief statement about world forests.

5 Working with a partner, each take the role of the Haida people and the loggers in turn (use page 25 and Source C). Give your reasons for and against the felling of the trees.

6 What do the figures in Source D tell us about the chances of survival for forest ecosystems?

3.2 BRITAIN SHOULD BE WOODED

1 For your own district, assume that you can persuade:
  ● a farmer to stop using her land
  ● a City Parks Department to abandon a large park
  ● the owners of a golf course to close it.
  You may also assume that you have the power to stop anyone else from using these open spaces.
  In groups, make a forecast of the changes in the vegetation and wildlife you might find after:
  ● 1 year
  ● 20 years
  ● 100 years

In your group, you have been exploring a very important idea about ecosystems: that of SUCCESSION. This key idea states that in any environment, following a major disturbance, or change of conditions, there will be a sequence of changes in the vegetation until a new balance occurs. You have caused a major disturbance to your three environments: you have stopped INPUTS of energy and materials by the farmer, the park-keeper and the golf course ground staff. Make a list of what they will not be supplying to the environment.

Only the natural inputs of the sun's energy, water, soil nutrients, seeds, etc., remain. As Source A shows, across most of Britain, the vegetation will slowly change to become DECIDUOUS BROADLEAVED FOREST. This is made up of trees which shed their leaves each autumn. The typical succession from farmland, park or golf-course is shown in Source B.

The end-product of the succession is the CLIMATIC CLIMAX VEGETATION. This is the vegetation assembly best suited to the environmental conditions: CLIMATE, soils, rocks, NUTRIENTS. For most of you, the climatic climax vegetation of your district would be oak-beech-ash-elm woodland, similar to that shown in Source B.

2 Use the map in Source A to find out what the climax vegetation of your district would be if the people left, and the natural succession of vegetation took over. Remember, this is a very generalised map. There will be local variations to suit different conditions, e.g. river valleys, hill slopes; so, research the library for more detailed maps.

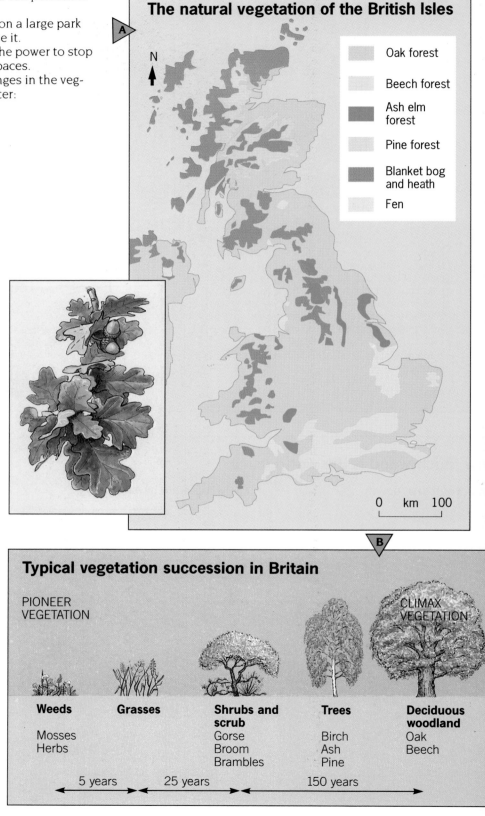

A

The natural vegetation of the British Isles

N

Legend:
- Oak forest
- Beech forest
- Ash elm forest
- Pine forest
- Blanket bog and heath
- Fen

0   km   100

B

Typical vegetation succession in Britain

PIONEER VEGETATION

CLIMAX VEGETATION

Weeds	**Grasses**	**Shrubs and scrub**	**Trees**	**Deciduous woodland**
Mosses Herbs		Gorse Broom Brambles	Birch Ash Pine	Oak Beech

5 years ← → 25 years ← → 150 years

How much woodland is left?

When you take trips into the countryside, see if you can find any 'natural' forests (use a tree identification book to help you). The map in Source C shows just how little of the forest cover is left, so you may be unlucky. Today, Britain is one of the least wooded countries in Europe as you can see by comparing the pie charts in Source D.

3 Collect a selection of leaves from the school grounds, on your way home, from the park or your garden. Use reference books to identify the trees they have come from. Note which are 'native' to the British Isles and which have been introduced ('exotic').

4 Study Source C.
   a) Where are the most densely wooded counties?
   b) Where are the least densely wooded counties?
   c) Can you suggest any reasons for this pattern?

Woodlands are owned either by private individuals and companies or by the Forestry Commission (FC). The FC is the government agency concerned with British forests.

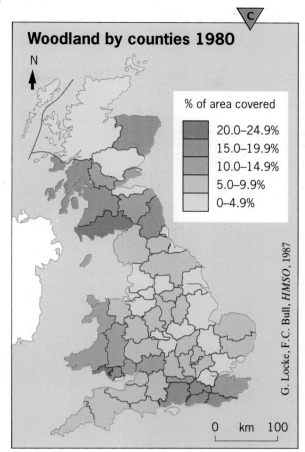

Woodland by counties 1980

N

% of area covered
- 20.0–24.9%
- 15.0–19.9%
- 10.0–14.9%
- 5.0–9.9%
- 0–4.9%

G. Locke, F. C. Bull, *HMSO*, 1987

0 km 100

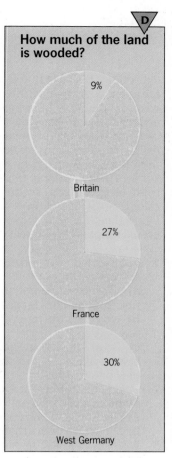

How much of the land is wooded?

9%
Britain

27%
France

30%
West Germany

Who own British woodlands (in 1000 hectares of full woodland)

	1950 Private	FC	Total	1980 Private	FC	Total
Deciduous	340	40	380	510	54	564
Coniferous	196	200	396	500	819	1319

**Four main species of trees in 1986
Deciduous and coniferous (thousand hectares)**

	Private		Forestry Commission	
Deciduous	1 Oak	153.5	1 Beech	20
	2 Ash	57	2 Oak	19
	3 Birch	64	3 Birch	4
	4 Beech	54	4 Ash	2.9
Coniferous	1 Sitka spruce	147	1 Sitka spruce	379
	2 Scots pine	135	2 Scots pine	106
	3 Jap larch	48	3 Lodgepole pine	101
	4 Norway spruce	45	4 Norway spruce	71

5 Draw graphs from the figures in Source E to show the changes in the ownership of woodlands in Britain since 1950.

6 What have been the three main changes?

7 What are the main similarities and differences between private and FC forests?

8 Study Source F. The deciduous species are mostly native to Britain, but most of the CONIFEROUS species (those which bear cones) have been introduced. Look at their names. Where do you think they have come from?

9 Most coniferous trees are EVERGREEN (which means they do not shed their foliage as deciduous trees do). Pine and fir trees are conifers. Just look at their foliage. How is it different from that of deciduous trees like oaks?

3.3 FOREST RHYTHMS

One of the special features of temperate forest ecosystems is their strong *seasonal rhythms*. Trees have large appetites and thirsts. However, they can draw water and nutrients from the soil and up through their tissues only if they are making energy by PHOTOSYNTHESIS. To do this, most trees need mean temperatures of more than 6°C, called the CRITICAL GROWTH THRESHOLD. Below this threshold, growth stops, even if water is available in the soil.

1. Look at Source A and discuss the following with a partner:
   a) What is happening to this oak tree through the seasons?
   b) Why does the tree behave in this way?
   c) Do all the tree species you see behave like this? If not, how are they different?

2. Study Source B. What is the length of the growing season likely to be in
   a) the English lowlands?
   b) the Welsh or Scottish uplands?

3. Water from winter rain and snow is stored in the soil. Some is lost by evaporation or by seepage below the ground (see Unit 1). What remains can be drawn on by the trees and other plants in the summer. From Source C work out
   a) how much water each square metre of soil a Somerset woodland uses during a growing season.

A | Seasonal rhythms

SPRING
Tree reacts quickly to sunlight so that young leaves with green chlorophyll can begin photosynthesis, i.e. make energy for the tree.

SUMMER
Leaf area is greatest, so photosynthesis is greatest. Nutrients and water move vigorously through the tree. The tree grows: BIOMASS increases.

WINTER
The tree is DORMANT. No leaves, so no photosynthesis. Low food demands, little TRANSPIRATION (loss of water).

AUTUMN
Chlorophyll is being lost from the leaves (they turn brown) so photosynthesis slows, as does the tree growth. Dead leaves fall off.

b) how much of the winter store of moisture in the soil is used between April and September. (Use the 'water deficit' columns.)
c) what might happen if there was a very dry winter.

4. Study Source D.
   a) What is the length of the growing season in Somerset?
   b) If all of the rain and snow of the no-growth period was stored in the soil, how much would be available for next summer?

B | The growing season (Britain)

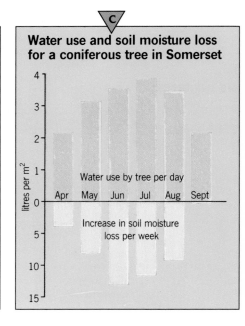

GROWTH

6°C
a
b

NO GROWTH

J F M A M J J A S O N D

Model to show monthly variations in growth above and below the *critical growth threshold* (6°C) for (a) lowland Britain and (b) upland Britain

C | Water use and soil moisture loss for a coniferous tree in Somerset

litres per m²

Water use by tree per day

Apr May Jun Jul Aug Sept

Increase in soil moisture loss per week

D | Mean temperature and rainfall, (Somerset)

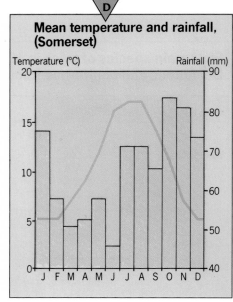

Temperature (°C)   Rainfall (mm)

J F M A M J J A S O N D

Adapting to survive

To survive the cold, all living things have to adapt. They try to behave in a way which uses least energy, so that they need to take in less heat and food. What tactics for survival are being used in the photographs in Source E taken in and around British woodlands?

5 As a *research project* choose *one* type of animal or bird found in British woodlands and find out how it survives the winters. What conditions could threaten its life during winter?

E

Soils: a healthy food store

F

Brown forest earth: typical soil under a deciduous hardwood forest

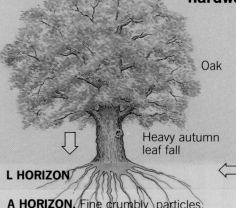

Oak

Heavy autumn leaf fall

L HORIZON

A HORIZON. Fine crumbly particles. Thick humus horizon: dark brown in colour

Many air spaces

B HORIZON. Pale brown colour because there is less humus. Sandy and some stones

Many air spaces

C HORIZON. Pale yellowish grey. Parent material is weathered

SOLID BEDROCK This weathers to form the parent material of the soil.

85% of the biomass of the whole ecosystem is in the main trees, especially the trunks. Trees live up to 1,000 years, so it may be a very long time before the trunk falls and is decomposed; but leaf fall occurs every autumn.

THICK LITTER LAYER (dead leaves and other plant matter). DECOMPOSERS, mainly bacteria, break down the litter to HUMUS which provides the organic nutrients for plants.

Soil animals, e.g. earthworms, carry humus deeper into the soil.

All layers (horizons) are well drained. Some nutrients are carried away (leached) into the groundwater.

Roots from the plants penetrate all horizons. The tree roots go down to the C horizon.

Soils found under oak, ash and beech woodlands are famous for their FERTILITY. Why is this so? A soil is said to be fertile when it stores a large supply of plant foods: MINERAL and ORGANIC NUTRIENTS (see Unit 2).

Study Source F.
6 a) What are the main features of a BROWN FOREST EARTH?
  b) How can you tell that this type of soil is fertile?
7 Why is the seasonal rhythm of deciduous trees vital to this fertility?
8 Does the character of the soil STORE help to explain why so much of Britain's native deciduous woodland has been cleared away?
9 What is likely to happen to the soil after the forest has been removed? (What inputs will have changed?)

Scientists call the different layers in a soil HORIZONS. The 'brown forest earth' shows four separate horizons.

3.4 CONIFEROUS FORESTS

Surviving severe cold

One of the great forests of the world is the TAIGA of the USSR. This is the belt of coniferous forests that covers 30% of that huge country.

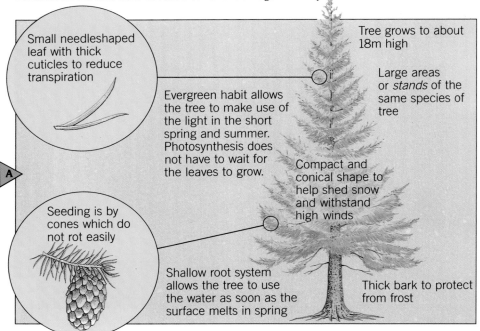

A

Small needleshaped leaf with thick cuticles to reduce transpiration

Evergreen habit allows the tree to make use of the light in the short spring and summer. Photosynthesis does not have to wait for the leaves to grow.

Seeding is by cones which do not rot easily

Shallow root system allows the tree to use the water as soon as the surface melts in spring

Tree grows to about 18m high

Large areas or *stands* of the same species of tree

Compact and conical shape to help shed snow and withstand high winds

Thick bark to protect from frost

B

The taiga in winter, USSR

C **Mean temperature and precipitation, Surgut (61°N and 73°E), USSR**

	J	F	M	A	M	J	J	A	S	O	N	D
Temperature (°C)	−25	−19	−13	−6	3	11	16	13	8	−3	−10	−21
Rain and snow (mm)	13	11	11	11	30	63	63	75	50	35	22	20

1 Study Sources A and B. What are the main features of coniferous trees? Think in terms of things like the shape of the tree and leaf size.

2 List *three* ways in which conifers differ from deciduous trees (pages 30–1).

3 The weather station in Source C lies in the heart of the Russian taiga. Locate Surgut in an atlas and describe its location.

4 Draw a graph similar to the mean temperature and rainfall graph for Somerset (Source D, p. 30).

5 Compare the environmental conditions for plant growth at the two weather stations, Somerset and Surgut.
   a) What are the three most important differences in climate?
   b) What effect might the differences have upon the vegetation? Compare the graph in Source D with the graph showing the growing season in Britain (Source B, p. 30).

6 The critical features of this climate are the long severe winters with heavy snowfall and short summer growth period. How have conifer trees adapted to these conditions?

7 Use Source D below and Source B on p. 30 to compare how altitude affects the length of the growing season. Do you think that Surgut is a lowland or an upland area?

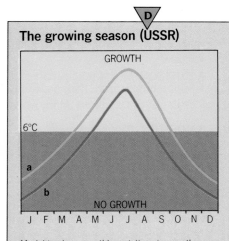

D

The growing season (USSR)

GROWTH

6°C

a

b

NO GROWTH

J F M A M J J A S O N D

Model to show monthly variations in growth above and below the *critical growth threshold* (6°C) for continental areas for (a) lowland and (b) upland

32

Soils under coniferous trees

A soil type very common under coniferous woodland is the PODSOL. Podsols are normally less fertile than the 'brown forest earths' which develop under deciduous forests. They are a limited food store.

8 a) From Source E make a list of the main features of a podsol. Compare this soil profile with the one on p. 31.
b) Suggest the differences which make the podsol less fertile than the brown earth.

9 a) Why is the podsol less fertile?
b) Is it true that conifers will grow on poorer soils than deciduous hardwoods?

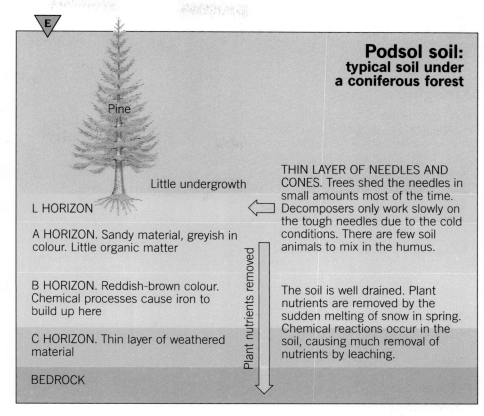

E

Podsol soil: typical soil under a coniferous forest

Pine

Little undergrowth

L HORIZON

A HORIZON. Sandy material, greyish in colour. Little organic matter

B HORIZON. Reddish-brown colour. Chemical processes cause iron to build up here

C HORIZON. Thin layer of weathered material

BEDROCK

Plant nutrients removed

THIN LAYER OF NEEDLES AND CONES. Trees shed the needles in small amounts most of the time. Decomposers only work slowly on the tough needles due to the cold conditions. There are few soil animals to mix in the humus.

The soil is well drained. Plant nutrients are removed by the sudden melting of snow in spring. Chemical reactions occur in the soil, causing much removal of nutrients by leaching.

Changing forests

All forests change through time, even without human interference. *As woodlands mature, a process of natural thinning takes place. As the trees increase in size, so they decrease in number.* Study Sources F and G. Neither woodland has been thinned by humans. The changes take place because of competition (the strongest trees survive) and natural disturbances, e.g. droughts, gales, disease. Woodland ecosystems are dynamic: they change through time.

10 In pairs, use the key idea in italics to describe and explain what is happening in the Scots pine plantation (Source F) and Lady Park Wood (Source G).

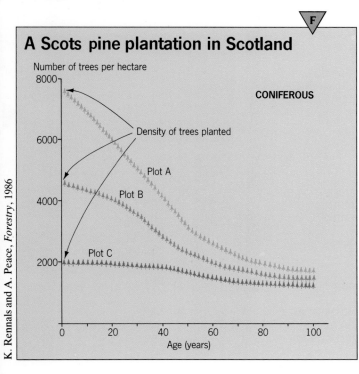

F

A Scots pine plantation in Scotland

Number of trees per hectare

CONIFEROUS

Density of trees planted

Plot A

Plot B

Plot C

Age (years)

K. Rennals and A. Peace, *Forestry*, 1986

G

Deciduous forest
Changes in Lady Park Wood, Monmouth 1945–1983
(Number of trees in a 35 hectare wood)

Species	1945	1955	1977	1983
Ash*	151	131	93	78
Beech	239	242	160	132
Elm	13	11	7	0
Lime	89	97	56	51
Maple*	56	29	10	6
Oak	58	56	37	36
Birch*	30	43	6	1
Total	616	509	368	298
Basal area of trees per hectare	20	25	32	29

*Pioneer species in this succession
1970s: Spread of Dutch elm disease.   1976: Severe summer drought.
1981–2: Severe gales.

Peterken, G.F. & Jones, E.W. (*J. of Ecology*, 75(2), June 1987, 477–51)

3.5 WHAT TYPE OF FOREST?

Managing a forest

If you own the wood in Source A or have the job of managing it, you have some power to control the way the eco-system works, what lives there and how it changes.

> " Hmmm....there's so much competition for space in this crowded country. So why should I keep the land under trees? "

> " The problem is – I need to make a profit, to earn a living. If I grow native oak or beech, it will be 100 years before they are big enough – and will anyone buy them? With these foreign softwoods, like the sitka spruce from Canada, I could be felling them, and getting my money back, within 40 years. "

A

1 In a small group, discuss
   a) What factors will affect the decisions you take.
   b) How your decisions will affect the woodland ecosystem.
2 Make a chart to compare the two types of forest in Sources B and C under the following headings: visual appearance, growth rate, range of habitats for wildlife, undergrowth and other plants, soil, disease resistance.

3 **a)** In your group, decide which sort of forest you would grow if your priority was *profit* (making money).
   b) Now list four reasons why it might be better to grow the *other* sort of forest.

B

Native deciduous hardwoods

Many people regard them as beautiful

A mixture of species, textures and colours

Trees grow slowly - it is said that an oak takes 40 years to grow, 40 years to spread and 40 years to mature

Limited uncertain market

A rich, varied ecosystem

Varied wildlife

Part of the country's heritage

Variety and species richness give resistance to disease

The natural habitat of most animals, birds and insects native to Britain. Many species cannot live in any other home

Rich ground and understorey vegetation

RICH, BASIC LITTER LAYER

Fertile brown forest soils - large humus and mineral nutrient store, usually 'basic' soils (high pH)

C

Exotic coniferous softwoods

Often planted as large single species blocks

Monotonous appearance, dark colours, similar textures

Large market

Trees grow quickly; most are mature within 60 years

Narrow range of wildlife

All but the Scots pines are 'exotic'

Single species plantations are prone to disease

Few native animals, birds make homes here

A constricted ecosystem with a narrow range of species

Species can be chosen to suit different climatic, soil and slope conditions

PINE LITTER IS ACID AND PERMITS LITTLE GROUND VEGETATION

Acid podsol soils (pH 4-5): thin humus horizon, much leaching of nutrients, poor fertility store

Conifers rule – OK?

The figures for British forests on page 29 have told us of the huge increase in coniferous woodlands, by private landowners and the Forestry Commission. This is because conifers are profitable and the government has given grants, subsidies and tax relief to encourage people to grow these. Since 1950, three-quarters of all conifers planted have taken over non-wooded habitats, mainly in upland parts of Britain. When these areas are planted with trees, the habitats of animals, birds, insects, fishes, plants – and people – are destroyed and replaced by a new ecosystem. This issue is looked at in more detail on pages 96–7.

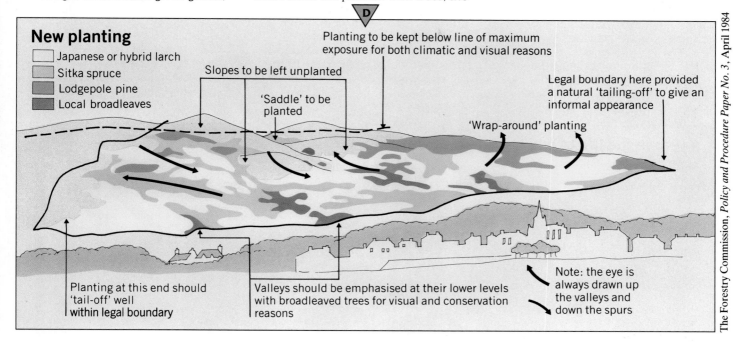

D

New planting

- ☐ Japanese or hybrid larch
- ▧ Sitka spruce
- ▨ Lodgepole pine
- ▩ Local broadleaves

Planting to be kept below line of maximum exposure for both climatic and visual reasons

Slopes to be left unplanted

'Saddle' to be planted

Legal boundary here provided a natural 'tailing-off' to give an informal appearance

'Wrap-around' planting

Note: the eye is always drawn up the valleys and down the spurs

Planting at this end should 'tail-off' well within legal boundary

Valleys should be emphasised at their lower levels with broadleaved trees for visual and conservation reasons

The Forestry Commission, *Policy and Procedure Paper No. 3*, April 1984

Can management of coniferous forests reduce their impact on the landscape?

The diagrams in Sources D and E show how the Forestry Commission aims to manage planting and harvesting (felling) of trees in upland areas.

4 How does the type of conifer planted vary with the RELIEF OF THE AREA? (See Source D.)

5 Which areas have been left unplanted, and why? (See Source D.)
6 How does the planting vary with how we 'view' the landscape? i.e. our eyes tend to be drawn up the valleys and down the spurs.
7 When the trees are harvested how can careful management reduce the impact on the landscape? (See Source E.)

In groups, discuss the following, using what you have learned in this Unit:
8 Do you think that native deciduous hardwood ecosystems will be found only where the priorities are to *conserve* the ecosystem and provide an *amenity* for recreation?
9 How might forests be managed to *successfully* combine conservation and amenity with financial profit?

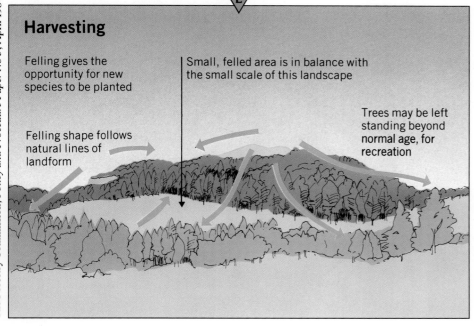

E

Harvesting

Felling gives the opportunity for new species to be planted

Felling shape follows natural lines of landform

Small, felled area is in balance with the small scale of this landscape

Trees may be left standing beyond normal age, for recreation

The Forestry Commission, *Policy and Procedure Paper No. 3*, April 1984

3 A YEAR IN THE LIFE OF ONE HECTARE OF SCOTS PINE

Source A shows where nutrients and water are stored, and how they move through a forest ecosystem. The information in the diagram can be used to explore the forest SYSTEM at work. Here are some possible activities.

1 Use the information in the diagram to show how a forest system works. Make use of diagrams and brief written statements to show

inputs–stores–OUTPUTS, THROUGH-PUTS and pathways. Throughputs are nutrients, water and energy which move along the pathways through the system, or from one part of the system to another.

2 Construct a labelled chart to show how material (e.g. water and nutrients) is CYCLED through the forest ecosystem.

3 Investigate FEEDBACK: the effects of changed inputs of any materials; changes in the nature of individual stores; changes in demands made on the ecosystem. For example:
a) What will be the effect of a dry year throughout the system in terms of stores and cycles?
b) What will be the effect of a cold year when the growing season is reduced to only 200 days?

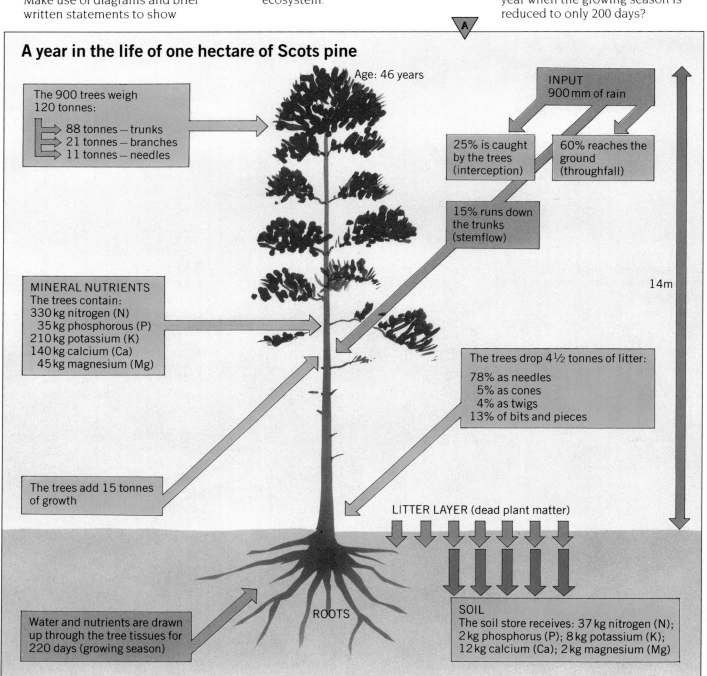

A year in the life of one hectare of Scots pine

Age: 46 years

The 900 trees weigh 120 tonnes:

88 tonnes – trunks
21 tonnes – branches
11 tonnes – needles

INPUT
900 mm of rain

25% is caught by the trees (interception)

60% reaches the ground (throughfall)

15% runs down the trunks (stemflow)

14m

MINERAL NUTRIENTS
The trees contain:
330 kg nitrogen (N)
35 kg phosphorous (P)
210 kg potassium (K)
140 kg calcium (Ca)
45 kg magnesium (Mg)

The trees drop 4½ tonnes of litter:

78% as needles
5% as cones
4% as twigs
13% of bits and pieces

The trees add 15 tonnes of growth

LITTER LAYER (dead plant matter)

ROOTS

Water and nutrients are drawn up through the tree tissues for 220 days (growing season)

SOIL
The soil store receives: 37 kg nitrogen (N); 2 kg phosphorus (P); 8 kg potassium (K); 12 kg calcium (Ca); 2 kg magnesium (Mg)

Sarawak, East Malaysia:
Forest nomads
barricaded roads in an
effort to stop logging
companies from cutting
down the rainforests,
their home

RAINFORESTS – WHOSE ARE THEY ANYWAY?

This unit looks at the speed with which tropical rainforests are being chopped down or burned. Rainforests are EVER-GREEN forests with rain in all months.

An important question arises: is the destruction of rainforests a problem, and for whom?

Conflict in Sarawak

Sarawak is an East Malaysian state on the north side of Borneo (Source A).

Work with a partner. Look at Source B and answer these questions:
1 Who is attempting to destroy the forests, and why?
2 Who is fighting to keep the forests, and why?

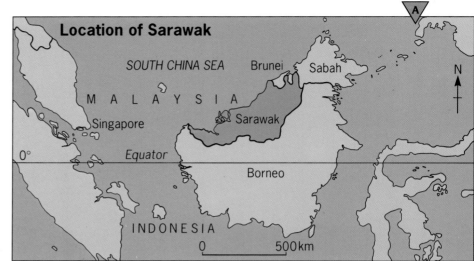

A

Location of Sarawak

SOUTH CHINA SEA — Brunei — Sabah

MALAYSIA

Singapore

Sarawak

0° — Equator

Borneo

INDONESIA

0 — 500km

N

3 What damage has been done to the environment?
4 Are we told who 'owns' the forest?

5 What do you think the Malaysian government should do to settle the conflict in Sarawak?

B

Battle lines in the jungle

The attackers: international timber companies

There is a small Dayak village on the River Baram called Uma Bawang. Across the river lies a logging camp of the Marabong Lumber Co. It is deserted except for a watchman. No-one has worked on the camp since March. When you ask why, he points to a muddy track. The track bears the marks of tractors that dragged out the felled logs – the mahogany, the teak, the damar – the Sarawak woods that end with the house builders, furniture makers and chopstick factories of Yokohama and Tokyo. And the wooden loo-seat manufacturers of upwardly mobile London. These days the track goes nowhere, for the Dayaks have built a crude barrier.

Barricade against advancing loggers in the Sarawak rainforest

The defenders: people who live in the forest

The Dayaks are farming people who have lived in the Sarawak jungle for many centuries.

'We are here to make sure no logging continues in our forest' says their leader, a young, well-educated English speaker named Francis. 'You see what it has done. Our jungles cut down, our rivers polluted, our animals dead, our fish gone. And these are *our* jungles, *our* rivers. They have been for many hundreds of years. Now these greedy people want them. These dirty politicians are giving our lands away. And now we are fighting back.'

The Punan are nomadic hunters and collectors. Like the Dayaks their home has always been the rainforest. The Punan chiefs made this statement:

'We see with sorrow the logging companies entering our country. In these areas where timber is extracted there is no more life for us nomadic people. Our natural resources like wild fruit trees, sago palms, wood trees for blow-pipe, dart-poison will fall. Animals like wild boar, our daily food, and deer will flee. Rivers will be polluted and over-fished. So now we declare our wood reserved. We forbid any working by use of tractors. We don't sell the lands of our fathers'.

A pioneer in Costa Rica

Costa Rica is a small country in Central America (Source C).

Lupe Barrantes' story (Source D) is told by a visitor to Costa Rica. The story could in fact be set in any country with a rainforest.

Read Source D and answer the questions:

6   Why did Lupe move into the forest? What did he do before his move?
7   What scheme made it possible for him to move into the forest?
8   How does he use the land?

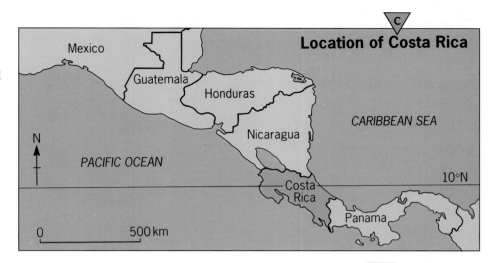

Location of Costa Rica

Mexico

Guatemala

Honduras

Nicaragua

CARIBBEAN SEA

PACIFIC OCEAN

N

Costa Rica

Panama

10°N

0   500 km

Forests are precious, but we need homes and food

Lupe Barrantes is taking us up the mountain to see his parcelito *of two hectares, a little piece of Central American rain forest he began clearing of trees three years ago to build a home and grow coffee beans.*

The clearing, half a kilometre across, sprouts haphazard rows of coffee bushes between rotting hulks of giant trees collapsed where Lupe had felled them.

Above: Lupe Barrantes, a pioneer in Costa Rica, Central America

Lupe Barrantes' two-hectare *parcelito* has been partly cleared and planted with coffee, but flowering weeds are spreading.

Right: Lupe's wife, Anna, cooks tortillas on a wood-burning stove in the dirt-floored kitchen next to their four-room house.

It took him a month, working alone with his machete and a small petrol chainsaw to flatten the clearing, planting coffee as he went along. Later he put in a little corn to feed his animals, and sugar cane and bananas.

Lupe is fulfilling his lifelong dream of becoming a *patron*, a landowner, master of his own fate. That is why he cuts trees. Before he obtained his *parcelito* from land grants during Costa Rica's land-reform programme of 1969, he was a day-labourer, building roads and other people's houses. 'I had nothing', he says, 'no future, no life.'

The Smithsonian, 1986

WHERE AND WHAT ARE TROPICAL RAINFORESTS?

Huge areas of evergreen forest

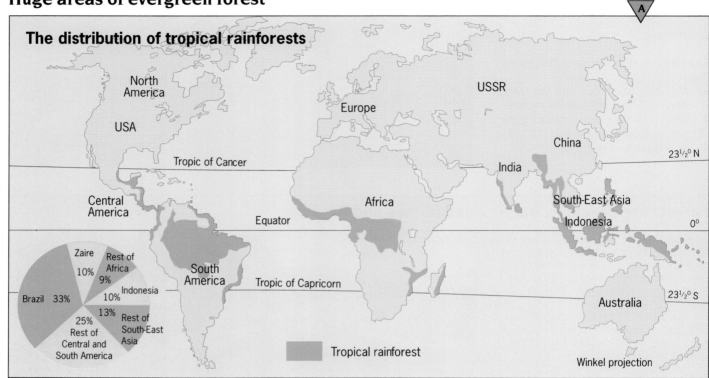

A

The distribution of tropical rainforests

North America

USA

USSR

Europe

China

India

Tropic of Cancer

23½° N

Central America

Africa

South-East Asia

Equator

Indonesia

0°

South America

Tropic of Capricorn

23½° S

Australia

Winkel projection

Tropical rainforest

Pie chart:
- Brazil 33%
- Zaire 10%
- Rest of Africa 9%
- Indonesia 10%
- Rest of South-East Asia 13%
- Rest of Central and South America 25%

Source A shows the world distribution of tropical rainforests. Although 70 countries possess rainforests, three countries between them own more than one-half of the total area. The scale of the forests in some areas is difficult to imagine: the River Amazon in Brazil is 6,000 km long, and throughout this distance it is surrounded for hundreds of kilometres by forests.

1 How many days would it take you to cross the Brazilian rainforest *non-stop* down the Amazon, by boat, if you could travel at an average speed of 10 km an hour?

2 Look at Source A. Which continent has most of the world's rainforests?

3 Which three countries have most of the world's rainforests?

4 Between which LATITUDES do the forests lie?

What is happening to the forests?

Two hundred years ago, rainforests covered 1,500 million hectares, an area 1½ times the size of Europe. Today they are down to 900 million hectares. This is still a huge area, but every minute 40 hectares (the size of 80 hockey or football pitches) are felled or burned. This is called DEFORESTATION.

5 Study Source B.
a) What is happening to the percentage of world's land which is covered by rainforests?
b) What percentage of rainforests do we estimate will be left by the year 2000 if something is not done?

6 Study Source C.
a) For the five years 1981–85, work out how many million hectares each continent has lost.
b) Which continent has lost the largest area of forests?

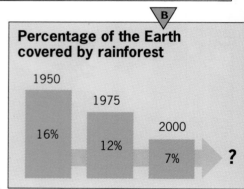

B

Percentage of the Earth covered by rainforest

- 1950 — 16%
- 1975 — 12%
- 2000 — 7% ?

c) Which continent has the fastest *rate* of deforestation – i.e., which one is losing the biggest proportion of its forests each year?

How much forest is lost each year?

C

Continent	Area of rainforest and deciduous forest, 1986 (million hectares)	Area lost each year 1981–5 (%)
Africa	216	3.7
Asia	317	2.0
Central and South America	650	6.0

World Resources, 1986 and 1987

Very special ecosystems

Study the information in Source D carefully and write a statement on each of these questions.

7 In what ways are rainforests so special?

8 Do you think that we should conserve them? Why?

● The richest store in the world:

Tropical rainforests are very special ECOSYSTEMS. They are home to at least 50% of the world's species of plants and animals – more than two million species. If you take a count of a hectare of European beech or oak wood, you would find at most ten tree species. Compare this to the figure for rainforests given in the graph opposite.

Madagascar, one island in the Indian Ocean, has 13 000 plant species. Britain has 1430 species of flowering plants; West Africa has 7000; Brazil 4000. The Amazon basin has more than 600 species of birds, and on a single hectare you might find 40 000 species of insect. In Central America, a scientist counted 950 kinds of beetle on one tree. Clusters of one species of tree are rare. You may find only one specimen of, say, teak, in a hectare. This rich bank of species may be vital for the future of life on planet Earth.

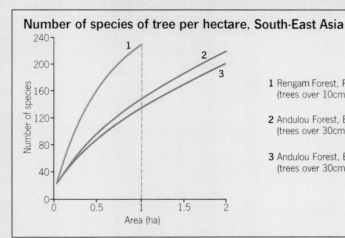

Number of species of tree per hectare, South-East Asia

(graph: y-axis "Number of species" from 0 to 240; x-axis "Area (ha)" from 0 to 2; curves labelled 1, 2, 3)

1 Rengam Forest, Peninsular Malaysia (trees over 10cm in diameter)

2 Andulou Forest, Borneo (valley bottom) (trees over 30cm in diameter)

3 Andulou Forest, Borneo (ridge) (trees over 30cm in diameter)

● There is much about rainforests that we do not know:

Only 10% of plant species have been fully studied and more plants and animals are being discovered every year. Already many substances are used in medicines: curare, a poison used on arrow tips by Amazonian Indians is used in surgery to relax muscles before an operation.

Many plants are very productive and may prove useful sources of food. For example, the peach palm of Brazil produces twice the volume of fruit that banana palms produce. In Indonesia, one type of Calliandra tree grows five metres a year, provides up to 100 cubic metres of firewood from a hectare each year, and cattle love the leaves and fruit. Could there be others?

Left: A quetzal with wild avocado fruit for nestlings, in Costa Rica

Above: A lantern bug with waxy tail, one of the Amazon's 40,000 species of insect.

Below: A margay in the Belize rainforest

Below, right: A red uakari, one of the endangered rainforest primates

● The forest is a home for many rare creatures.

An amazing variety of creatures live and feed side-by-side in a rainforest, but a surprising number of species consist of only a small number of individuals – they are rare. For example the Sumatra rhinoceros and margay of Central America are animals which have a very specialised way of life. They live in a special HABITAT and occupy a narrow NICHE or place in the ecosystem.

4.3 A VERY ENERGETIC ECOSYSTEM

The inputs: solar energy and moisture

One of the most important things we have already learned about ecosystems is that growth (OUTPUT), is determined largely by the INPUTS of SOLAR ENERGY and moisture.

Use Sources A and B to complete the following:

1 Draw a climate graph for Kuching in Sarawak (Source A).
2 How organically productive are rainforests? (Source B.)
3 From Source B, work out the proportions of organic matter stored in:
   a) the living plants and trees,
   b) the litter layer,
   c) the soil.
   Draw two pie charts (for tropical and TEMPERATE FORESTS) to show your results.
4 What is distinctive about the way rainforests store their organic matter?
5 How does the data help to explain why tropical rainforests are the most productive ecosystems on Earth?

Average temperature and rainfall in Kuching, Sarawak (1°N)

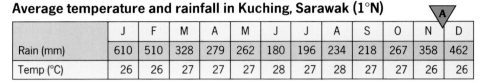

	J	F	M	A	M	J	J	A	S	O	N	D
Rain (mm)	610	510	328	279	262	180	196	234	218	267	358	462
Temp (°C)	26	26	27	27	27	28	27	28	27	27	26	26

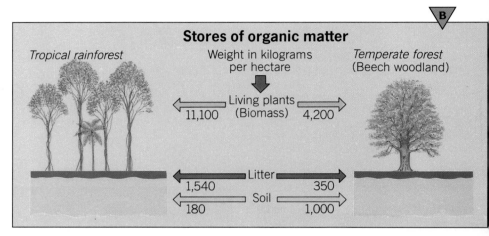

Stores of organic matter

Tropical rainforest   Weight in kilograms per hectare   *Temperate forest (Beech woodland)*

Living plants (Biomass)
11,100   4,200

Litter
1,540   350

Soil
180   1,000

6 In addition to heat and water, what else do plants need for rapid growth?

The result: a luxuriant gallery structure

7 Study Source C. Why is the forest made up of several layers? (Think in terms of competition between plants for the water and light they need to grow.)

a) Why is there very little growth on the forest floor?
b) Name two unusual types of plants in the forest. How have they adapted themselves to reach the light and water?
c) How does the forest structure help to explain the great variety of animal life found in the forest ecosystem?

Structure of evergreen tropical forest

Forest layers

The crowns of the trees are covered in *epiphytes*, plants which use the trees as a place to grow to the light

Woody climbers called *lianas* root themselves in the ground and climb through the trees to the light and rain

EMERGENTS. Tall trees grow through the canopy layers. There are usually 1 or 2 per hectare

CANOPY LAYER. A dense continuous layer about 10m thick. This blocks out 95% of the sunlight and 8 out of 10 raindrops

LOWER CANOPY LAYER. The trees are shaped like candle flames and struggle towards the light

GROUND LAYER. Dark and gloomy. Little vegetation between the trees

Rapid cycling and storing

Source D shows how nutrients and water move rapidly through the ecosystem from one STORE to another. For example, the various trees have different patterns of dropping their leaves through the year. So, there is a constant supply to the litter store. Bacteria and fungi work so vigorously in the hot, moist conditions that a leaf may decompose in a week, compared with several months in an oak woodland in Britain. Once it is decomposed, the organic matter is in a form which can be absorbed by the hungry and thirsty plants.

8 a) What is by far the largest store of nutrients in the rainforest?
b) Why are the litter and soil stores so small?
c) Explain why the decomposition and NUTRIENT CYCLE in the forest can be described as 'energetic'.

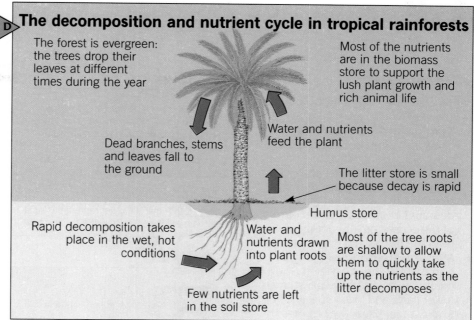

D ## The decomposition and nutrient cycle in tropical rainforests

The forest is evergreen: the trees drop their leaves at different times during the year

Most of the nutrients are in the biomass store to support the lush plant growth and rich animal life

Dead branches, stems and leaves fall to the ground

Water and nutrients feed the plant

The litter store is small because decay is rapid

Humus store

Rapid decomposition takes place in the wet, hot conditions

Water and nutrients drawn into plant roots

Most of the tree roots are shallow to allow them to quickly take up the nutrients as the litter decomposes

Few nutrients are left in the soil store

The soil store

The traditional agriculture in rainforests is SHIFTING CULTIVATION or slash-and-burn. Clearing the forest takes enormous effort (see Source F), yet forest peoples are forced to do this every three or four years because their crop yields fall so low on their existing plots. The people on pages 38–9 are shifting cultivators defending the large areas they need to live in.

A SOIL PROFILE consists of a series of layers, or HORIZONS. The upper horizons of rainforest soils – that is, where roots are concentrated – tend to be highly LEACHED. They have lost most of the minerals valuable to plants. As with organic nutrients, a high proportion of the mineral foods available is stored in the living plants themselves.

9 Why do shifting cultivators need a large area of rainforest to support them?
10 a) Use Source E to describe the structure of rainforest soils.
b) Why are rainforest soils so infertile yet are able to support such luxuriant vegetation?

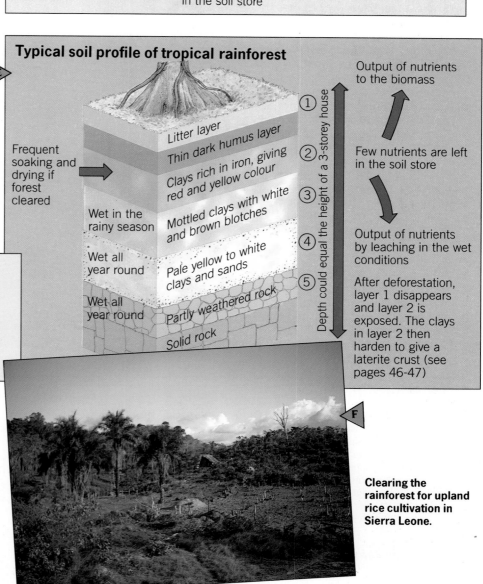

E **Typical soil profile of tropical rainforest**

Frequent soaking and drying if forest cleared

Wet in the rainy season

Wet all year round

Wet all year round

Litter layer

Thin dark humus layer

Clays rich in iron, giving red and yellow colour

Mottled clays with white and brown blotches

Pale yellow to white clays and sands

Partly weathered rock

Solid rock

① ② ③ ④ ⑤

Depth could equal the height of a 3-storey house

Output of nutrients to the biomass

Few nutrients are left in the soil store

Output of nutrients by leaching in the wet conditions

After deforestation, layer 1 disappears and layer 2 is exposed. The clays in layer 2 then harden to give a laterite crust (see pages 46-47)

F Clearing the rainforest for upland rice cultivation in Sierra Leone.

4.4 IF WE USE FORESTS, MUST WE DESTROY THEM?

Different users

Below are some statements about how people use the rainforest ecosystem.

- **Traditional forest dwellers** (humans, animals, birds, etc.) need, and help to support, richness and variety in the rainforest ecosystem. They do not take out more than is replaced. In systems language, the demands they make on the *outputs* of the ecosystem are not greater than the *inputs* and the *stores*.
- **Modern intruders** want only certain parts of the ecosystem. They create much simpler ecosystems: fewer parts and fewer species. In SYSTEMS language, they change the *inputs* and control the *stores* to get the *outputs* they want.
- To other users, **the forest is simply a nuisance**, so they destroy it. This creates a new but less productive ecosystem.
- Some users take out what they want and **do not return anything** to the ecosystem. *Outputs* go up, but *inputs* do not.

Work with a partner. Look at the main uses of the rainforest ecosystem (Sources A to G).

1. Match each of the uses to the statements above. Note that more than one statement may be relevant to some of the uses.
2. Rank the uses according to how much damage they cause. Put the most damaging at the top.
3. A *resource* is defined as anything that people find useful. Make a list of the tropical rainforest resources shown on these pages.

Ranching

Over one-quarter of the Amazonian rainforest that has been cleared is now used for large-scale cattle ranching. Trees are stopped from growing again, and the land is covered with grasses. However, grasses do not give much nutrient supply back to the soil. New grasses grow weaker and weaker. So, many ranches have failed, forcing their owners to move on to get more land. Most of the meat is sent to the USA for burgers.

C

Farming

The largest area of rainforests in the world is being cleared by settlers coming in from outside. Landless people set up farms in the hope of a new and better life. Huge areas of the Brazilian Amazon states of Rondonia and Acre are now being cleared for farming.

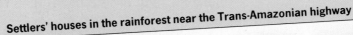

Settlers' houses in the rainforest near the Trans-Amazonian highway

A   **B**

Shifting cultivation

The Nuaulu people live in the Moluccan Islands, Indonesia. They live in villages scattered through the rainforest across an area as big as Leicestershire. Each village has about 200 people, and they live entirely from and in the forest. They are shifting cultivators: they clear new patches of land every three years or so, leaving the old plots fallow for about 15 years. This lets the soil fertility recover.

Each village has a network of forest paths that spread out for about 15 km all round it.

The Nuaulu use these paths to collect a wide variety of forest products for their needs.

However, health care and other services have begun to reach the Nuaulus, so their population has increased rapidly. The population of each village may double in 25 years. This could mean:

- Shortening the time when land lies fallow
- Growing crops on a larger area.
- Starting new villages.
- Growing crops or felling trees for sale to buy more food.

Uses of the forest by the Nuaulu

- Building materials
- Firewood (cooking)
- Transport—canoes
- Food
- Clothing (bark and leaf fibres)
- Wrapping materials
- Source of money
- Medicines
- Stimulants: drinks
- Ritual ornaments
- Musical instruments e.g. drums
- Tools
- Weapons e.g. spears, arrows
- Colouring
- Cosmetics
- Resins

Mining

Mining companies use the forest area to quarry minerals such as copper and iron ore. The companies fell trees and build roads.

D

Carajas iron ore mine, Brazil▶

E

Logging

International timber companies usually want only two or three species of tree from the hundreds available. So they fell only one or two trees per hectare, but in the process they can destroy or damage half of the remaining trees.

Logging is the second largest use of rainforests, after agriculture

F

Pulp mills for paper

G

Each year, an area of forest the size of a large town is felled to feed the pulp mill at Jari in Amazonia. The wood is pulped to make paper. When the forests have been cleared, new trees such as pimids may be planted, because they grow easily and quickly.

Plantations

It is not convenient for companies to have only a few teak or rubber trees per hectare. So, over vast areas of the Tropics, companies have planted huge areas of the trees they want. These areas are called PLANTATIONS. They give higher yields than natural rainforests because:

● Stands of trees are usually of one species and of the type wanted.
● Trees can be planted on the whole site and planting can be adjusted to varying conditions on the site.
● Trees can be thinned out and used at various stages of growth. Spraying and other measures can control disease and wipe out weeds, insects etc.
● Planting can be phased so that yields can be kept high over long periods.

Deforestation at work

Every minute of every day 40 hectares of tropical rainforest disappear. Newspapers, television and environmentalists sometimes blame the damage on logging and mining companies, large plantation and ranch owners, and governments who build huge dam and reservoir schemes. But the truth is that most clearance is by millions of people like Lupe Barrantes (pp. 38–9): poor families trying to make a living from their own piece of land. What happens when settlers clear the land shows how fragile the rainforest is when it is disturbed.

Look at Source A and you will see how a neighbour of Lupe Barrantes in Costa Rica is affecting the ecosystem.

A

The tree canopy has gone.

Soil is thinner and less fertile (fewer nutrients from the litter layer). Crops, such as these coffee bushes, yield less.

Thin litter layer means that fewer nutrients enter the soil.

Less dead vegetation falls to the surface (the vegetation contains nutrients).

Hard crust forms as the soil dries out. This infertile LATERITE crust lets less water INFILTRATE. Surface RUNOFF increases.

Trees no longer INTERCEPT the heavy rain. So raindrops fall directly on to the land surface.

Steep bare slopes are easily ERODED by rainstorms. Upper soil layers containing most nutrients are the first to be washed away.

More sediment and nutrients are washed into the streams.

Less water absorbed by vegetation and soil. More surface runoff directly into streams.

Floods downstream occur more often and more rapidly.

1 Source B sums up how the rich growth in a tropical rainforest is supported by the rapid cycling of nutrients. Use Source A to explain how deforestation affects this cycle.
2 Explain why deforestation:
   a) makes soils less fertile,
   b) makes floods more frequent.
3 A Costa Rican forestry official said: 'Topsoil is our largest export.' Explain what he meant by this.

4 Look back at the article about Lupe Barrantes on p. 39. With a partner discuss:
Should the government allow people like Lupe Barrantes to clear the forest? What alternative policies might the government follow?

B

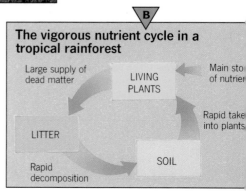

The vigorous nutrient cycle in a tropical rainforest

Large supply of dead matter

LIVING PLANTS

Main sto of nutrien

Rapid take into plants

LITTER

SOIL

Rapid decomposition

Rondonia, Brazil

The province of Rondonia lies on the southern edge of Amazonia (Source C). Since 1970 it has suffered some of the highest deforestation rates in Brazil. In 1986, the Governor said: 'We are facing a disaster.' Sources C–F will help you to understand what he meant.

C Location of Rondonia

ATLANTIC OCEAN

Equator

naus ● R. Amazon

B R A Z I L

DONIA

● Brasilia

N

● Rio de Janeiro

500 km

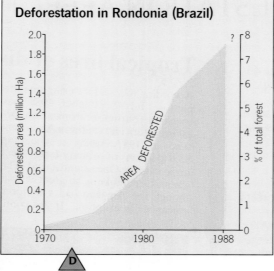

Deforestation in Rondonia (Brazil)

Deforested area (million Ha)

% of total forest

AREA DEFORESTED

?

1970   1980   1988

D

Population growth in Rondonia (Brazil)

1 million

500 000

100 000

1970   1980   1988

E

5 Use Sources D and E to describe what has been happening in Rondonia.

6 How do the three facts below help to explain the changes shown in Sources D and E?
- In other parts of Brazil, there are thousands of landless people.
- The government has encouraged the settlement of new areas.
- The government has built penetration roads into Rondonia.

7 The Brazilian government policy of making more land available seems a good one. So why does Rondonia's governor feel things have gone wrong? With a partner, follow the seven stages of Source F, then:
a) Describe what happened.
b) With the help of Sources A–F, suggest reasons why this happened.

F

Stage 1: Natural forest is inhabited by Indian tribes.

Stage 2: Penetration roads are built, to get to mines, for logging companies, to encourage settlers. Indians move deeper into the forest.

Stage 3: Settlers clear plots in the forest along the road. Ranchers clear large areas for cattle.

Stage 5: Ranchers take over the abandoned plots as the grasses fail on their own ranches.

By this time, many Indians have suffered and often died from diseases introduced by settlers.

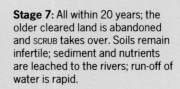

Stage 4: Crop yields fall and many settlers abandon their plots. On poor soils, 50% of settlers have moved on within five years. They then clear more land for cultivation.

Stage 6: Weeds, which the cattle cannot eat, kill off the grasses, and the cattle starve. Like the settlers, the ranchers have to give up, or move on and clear more forest.

Stage 7: All within 20 years; the older cleared land is abandoned and scrub takes over. Soils remain infertile; sediment and nutrients are leached to the rivers; run-off of water is rapid.

The photograph (Source A) on page 46 shows that deforestation has major environmental impacts. On these pages we will look at other important effects of deforestation on systems outside the forest area.

Fire!

1 What changes is burning the forests making:
   a) to the atmosphere (Source A)?
   b) to the world's climate? (Use the glossary and pages 170–1 to help you.)

Fewer trees, less moisture

Follow the arrows carefully through Source B.

2 Name the two stores which each provide 50% of the moisture for the atmosphere store.
3 Explain what is meant by the statement: 'One-half of all the rainfall comes from water cycling within the Amazonian system.'

What can happen without forest

● Up to 40% less rainfall, because farmland, grassland and scrub forest store much less water to release to the atmosphere.
● Daytime temperatures would be higher, because more solar radiation would reach the surface and in turn heat the air above.
● More moisture would be available in *other* parts of the Earth's atmosphere.

Tropical fires of disaster

According to scientists using satellite photos, July–September 1988 has seen more burning of tropical rainforest in eastern and southern Amazonia than in 1987, when a whopping 83,000 sq km of primary forest went up in smoke. One scientist said 'The amount of smoke is so great it is as though the Amazon had a hundred volcanoes in eruption'. If this continues, all Amazonia's forests could disappear in 30 years.

Trees are one half made up of carbon. So forest burning adds to the carbon dioxide in the atmosphere, and in turn to the *greenhouse effect*. Brazilian Amazonia is probably providing 700 million tonnes, or 10% of all the CO_2 added to the atmosphere by humans each year.

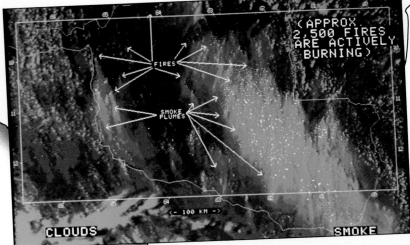

Adapted from *the Guardian*, 18 October 1988

The light and red spots on this satellite image are fires in the Brazilian Amazon. These occurred during several weeks in 1987 and have been put together in one image.

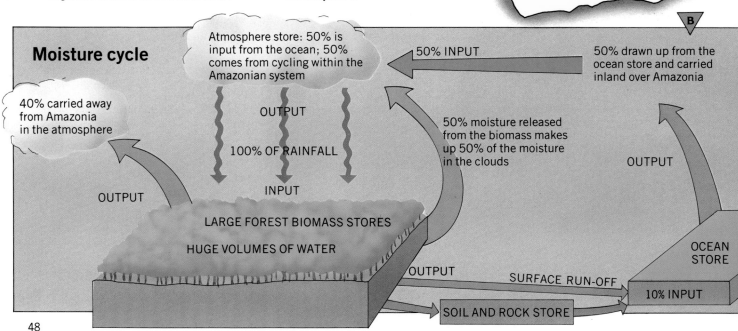

Moisture cycle

Atmosphere store: 50% is input from the ocean; 50% comes from cycling within the Amazonian system

40% carried away from Amazonia in the atmosphere

OUTPUT

100% OF RAINFALL

INPUT

OUTPUT

50% INPUT

50% drawn up from the ocean store and carried inland over Amazonia

50% moisture released from the biomass makes up 50% of the moisture in the clouds

OUTPUT

LARGE FOREST BIOMASS STORES

HUGE VOLUMES OF WATER

OUTPUT

SURFACE RUN-OFF

OCEAN STORE

10% INPUT

SOIL AND ROCK STORE

Few trees, more sediment downstream

C

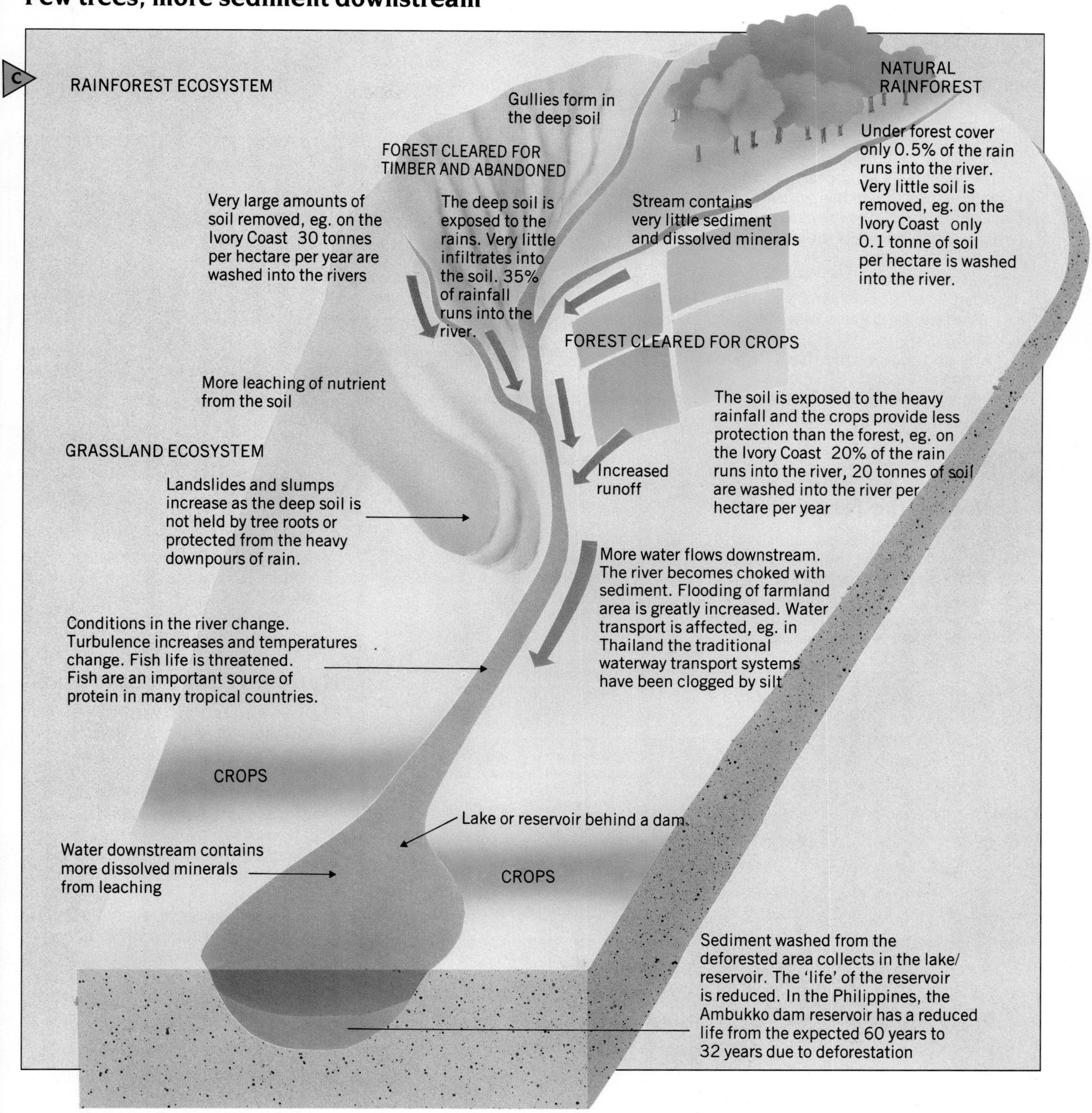

RAINFOREST ECOSYSTEM

NATURAL RAINFOREST

Gullies form in the deep soil

FOREST CLEARED FOR TIMBER AND ABANDONED

Under forest cover only 0.5% of the rain runs into the river. Very little soil is removed, eg. on the Ivory Coast only 0.1 tonne of soil per hectare is washed into the river.

Very large amounts of soil removed, eg. on the Ivory Coast 30 tonnes per hectare per year are washed into the rivers

The deep soil is exposed to the rains. Very little infiltrates into the soil. 35% of rainfall runs into the river.

Stream contains very little sediment and dissolved minerals

FOREST CLEARED FOR CROPS

More leaching of nutrient from the soil

The soil is exposed to the heavy rainfall and the crops provide less protection than the forest, eg. on the Ivory Coast 20% of the rain runs into the river, 20 tonnes of soil are washed into the river per hectare per year

GRASSLAND ECOSYSTEM

Landslides and slumps increase as the deep soil is not held by tree roots or protected from the heavy downpours of rain.

Increased runoff

Conditions in the river change. Turbulence increases and temperatures change. Fish life is threatened. Fish are an important source of protein in many tropical countries.

More water flows downstream. The river becomes choked with sediment. Flooding of farmland area is greatly increased. Water transport is affected, eg. in Thailand the traditional waterway transport systems have been clogged by silt

CROPS

Water downstream contains more dissolved minerals from leaching

Lake or reservoir behind a dam

CROPS

Sediment washed from the deforested area collects in the lake/ reservoir. The 'life' of the reservoir is reduced. In the Philippines, the Ambukko dam reservoir has a reduced life from the expected 60 years to 32 years due to deforestation

4 **a)** Study Source C. Compare the run-off and soil erosion rates under natural forest with areas that have been deforested.
b) What impacts does deforestation have on environments further downstream?

5 Use all the information on these pages to draw up a list of how deforestation can have consequences outside the forest ecosystem.

49

4 WHAT CAN BE DONE?

Getting the message – changing values

Burger King and Habitat have been successful at selling products which people want. Like all companies, they stay in business by making profits from popular products. Yet they are taking actions which may cost them money.

Look at Source A.

1 What have the companies and the international organisation decided to do?
2 Why do you think they have decided to do this?
3 Design a poster for Burger King or Habitat to put up in their shops. Show why they have taken the action described in Source A.

4 Conduct a survey in local shops to see what rainforest products are on sale. Do some library research first, to find out what products to expect.

A

'Cattle ranching is responsible for wiping out millions of hectares of forest. Because it takes five square metres to produce enough grazing for a single beefburger, at least 100 hectares of rainforest disappear every day.
   Faced with an environmental outcry, Burger King, the American-based fast-food chain, told its suppliers to stop buying meat from Central America last year.'

'The International Trade and Timber Organisation is to consider whether to put a tax on imports of tropical hardwood products and give the profits to reforestation schemes.
   Some retailers have already taken the lead. Habitat, the British high-street furniture chain, is banning the sale of all rainforest products.'

Imitating the forest

In many countries, people and governments are now using their common sense. They realise that the natural rainforest is a strong, productive ecosystem – so why not imitate it? Farmers can make an ecosystem that is useful to them and is similar in many ways to a forest. The example in Source B is called AGROFORESTRY, as it combines agriculture and forestry.

5 With a partner, study Source B.
   a) Describe the main features of agroforestry.
   b) List the ways it imitates the features of a natural forest.

National Rainforest Parks

Some countries, e.g. Cameroon, have set up National Rainforest Parks to protect areas of rainforest. The Korup NATIONAL PARK aims to protect 125,000 hectares of virgin forest. But economically developing countries badly need foreign currency from exporting forest products. They also need more land for their growing populations.

6 In a small group, discuss whether it is a good idea for economically developing countries to set up National Rainforest Parks. Who would be in favour, and who would be against the idea?

B

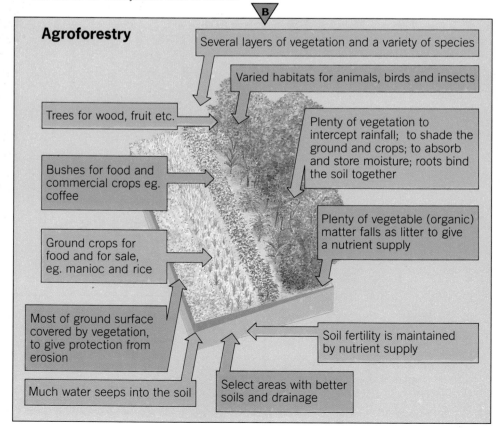

Agroforestry

- Several layers of vegetation and a variety of species
- Varied habitats for animals, birds and insects
- Trees for wood, fruit etc.
- Bushes for food and commercial crops eg. coffee
- Plenty of vegetation to intercept rainfall; to shade the ground and crops; to absorb and store moisture; roots bind the soil together
- Ground crops for food and for sale, eg. manioc and rice
- Plenty of vegetable (organic) matter falls as litter to give a nutrient supply
- Most of ground surface covered by vegetation, to give protection from erosion
- Soil fertility is maintained by nutrient supply
- Much water seeps into the soil
- Select areas with better soils and drainage

Train disaster caused by flooding of the River Tywi, Wales, in 1987 (see also pp. 124–5)

Water: a vital issue

One of the vital issues for the future of life on planet Earth is summed up in this equation:

More people + More water demanded by each person = Increased demands for the world's water

Unit 1 (pages 4–5) showed you that water is found in several STORES and moves between them by the HYDROLOGICAL CYCLE. This section of the book (Units 5 and 6) explores some of these stores and pathways on and below the surface. It also explores how people use them and are affected by them.

An exercise to set you thinking:
1   When you turn on a tap, where has the water come from? What are the stores and pathways it has followed to get to your tap?

2   If the taps failed, make a list of the places you would go to find water. (Be prepared to travel a long way and to purify the water you find.)
3   Look at Source A. Why does this Bushman girl of the Kalahari desert of south-western Africa know so much more about how to find water than we do?

A Bushman girl squeezes water from a desert root

The routes water takes

Look carefully at Source B and you will see a series of streams running down to join a main river. The area of land from which a river collects its water is called its CATCHMENT AREA and the boundary of the catchment area is the WATERSHED. The catchment area and the stream network make up the DRAINAGE BASIN, which is the most important geographical unit in studying how water affects our lives.

For example, the photograph on page 51 shows a serious flood on the River Tywi in Wales. Floods occur when the normal stores and pathways in a drainage basin cannot hold the INPUT of water, and so they overflow. The river floodplain becomes a temporary store.

Across the world, millions of people live on flat, fertile floodplains. This is why floods are so often disasters, with much loss of life and property.

4   Place a sheet of tracing paper over Source B. Draw in the stream network, the watershed, and shade the catchment area. Give the title to your diagram: 'Part of the drainage basin of the River Calder in North Wales.'

The disappearing Aral Sea, USSR

Changing the water balance

Drainage basins are like other ENVIRON-MENTAL SYSTEMS – they settle into a balanced state. They develop a set of pathways and stores that can normally cope with the input of water, move it through the SYSTEM and out to a lake, a sea, or sometimes a GROUNDWATER (underground) STORE.

Source C shows such a system at work, with the Aral Sea as the outlet store for two river basins. The Aral Sea is special, as it is an inland sea and its only large sources of water are the two rivers shown on the map.

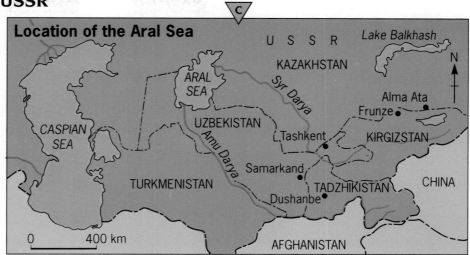

C

Location of the Aral Sea

0 ———— 400 km

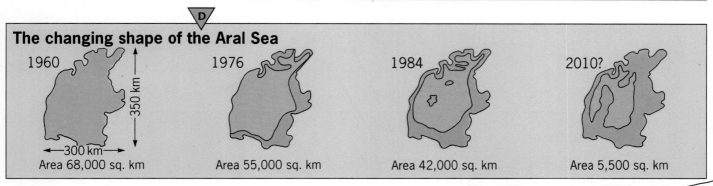

D

The changing shape of the Aral Sea

1960 — ↕ 350 km — ←300 km→ — Area 68,000 sq. km

1976 — Area 55,000 sq. km

1984 — Area 42,000 sq. km

2010? — Area 5,500 sq. km

The material on this page helps you to understand how quickly people can change a system which may have taken centuries to develop.

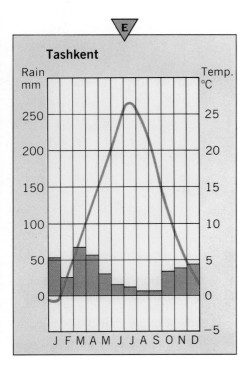

E

Tashkent

Rain mm / Temp. °C

J F M A M J J A S O N D

Use Sources, C, D, E and F:

5 **a)** Measure the N–S and E–W size of the Aral Sea in 1960 and 2010.
   b) How much smaller was the sea in 1984 than in 1960?
   c) Why does the Aral Sea depend so much on the two rivers?
   d) What has caused this sea to shrink?

6 The sea lies in a basin. How can you tell that the shallowest parts of the basin are in the east and south?

7 What is happening to the water and water life as the sea shrinks?

8 What is happening to the environments and the lives of the people around the sea?

9 Why is the CLIMATE becoming more 'extreme'? What does the scientist mean by 'extreme'?

10 Draw two labelled flow diagrams:
   a) For the natural hydrological cycle at work, i.e. before humans changed it.
   b) For the hydrological cycle today. Show and name the pathways, stores and, where possible, processes such as EVAPORATION, INFILTRATION. Use Sources B and D on pages 4–5 to help you.

F

Aral Sea doomed

THE ARAL Sea, located among the deserts of the southern Soviet Union, is doomed.

By early next century it will be only about 8 per cent of its size in 1960 and will be highly saline.

Salinity has more than doubled to 27 grams of salt per litre of water.

The shrinkage has been caused by water being siphoned off for irrigation from two rivers that feed the lake – the Amudar'ya and Syrdar'ya. Last year virtually no water from the rivers reached the lake. About 100 cubic kilometres of water is being taken from the rivers to irrigate eight million hectares of land in the Aral Sea Basin.

The area has become an environmental disaster. Excessive salinity has killed off all 20 species of fish in the lake and destroyed a fishing industry that employed 60000 people. Storms, heavily laden with dried salt, are dumping 43 million tonnes of salt annually on plants and pastures of over 200000 square kilometres of land surrounding the lake.

Residents near the lake are blaming an increase in cancer of the throat on the salt that they inhale.

The ecology of the large delta formed by the two rivers is threatened. Extremes of climate are now common because the moderating influence of the lake no longer exists. A shorter growing season caused by the climatic changes is damaging the growth of cotton.

New Scientist, 18 February 1988

Background

Before studying examples of rivers and drainage basins, we need to understand the processes which move the water through the system.

1 Use the glossary to find out what the terms in Source A mean.
2 Source B shows these processes in a British river basin. Follow the arrows through the system, and check that you have found a place for all the items in Source A. Notice too, how the OUTPUT from one part or store in the system becomes an input to the next. Give two examples of where this happens.

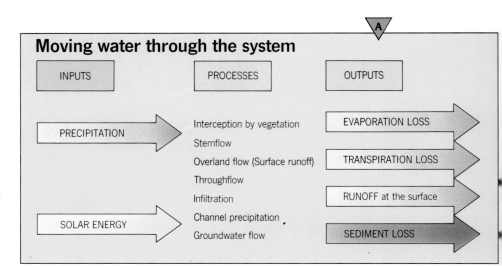

Moving water through the system

INPUTS	PROCESSES	OUTPUTS

PRECIPITATION

Interception by vegetation
Stemflow
Overland flow (Surface runoff)
Throughflow
Infiltration
Channel precipitation
Groundwater flow

EVAPORATION LOSS

TRANSPIRATION LOSS

RUNOFF at the surface

SEDIMENT LOSS

SOLAR ENERGY

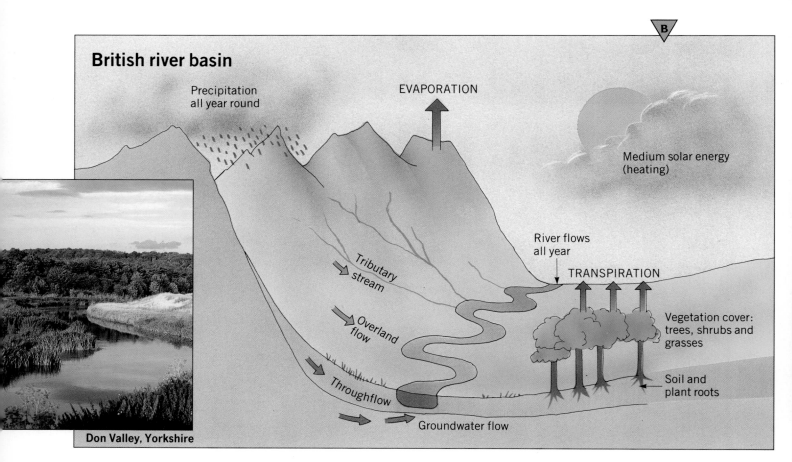

British river basin

Precipitation all year round

EVAPORATION

Medium solar energy (heating)

River flows all year

TRANSPIRATION

Vegetation cover: trees, shrubs and grasses

Tributary stream

Overland flow

Throughflow

Soil and plant roots

Groundwater flow

Don Valley, Yorkshire

3 **a)** The summer of 1989 was very dry in Britain, i.e. the PRECIPITATION input to environments like that in Source B was less than normal. Follow the hydrological cycle again and describe what might happen to each of the processes in such a dry spell.
b) In contrast, the summers of 1985 and 1986 were wetter than normal – what happens to the processes in such wet spells?

4 With a partner, each choose a part of the environment in Source B you think is likely to be affected by people. Explain your choice to each other.

Flows and stores in contrasting environments

How you think about the water cycle depends upon where you live. The diagram in Source C shows a hot desert – a very different environment from that in Source B.

5 Draw FLOW DIAGRAMS like that in Source A on p. 4 for each of these two environments. Make the size of the boxes (stores) and thickness of the arrows (processes and flows) vary, to show their importance in each environment. Work out a colour scheme for the arrows to make this clear.

6 List what you think are the two most important differences in the water cycle between the environments.

7 If you lived in each environment, would your main source of water be the same in each case? If not, why not?

C

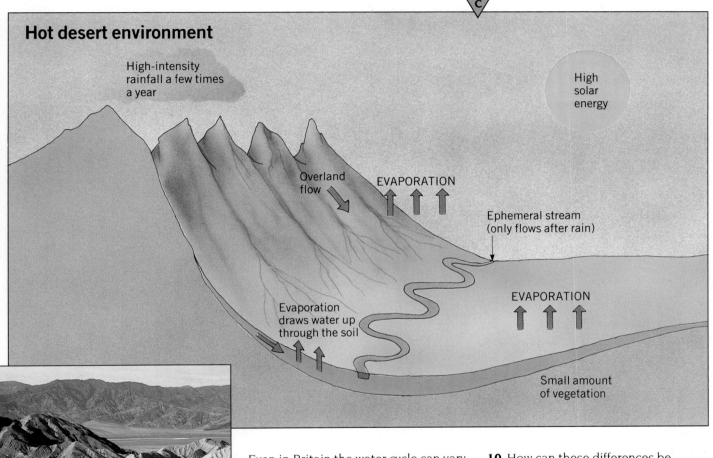

Hot desert environment

High-intensity rainfall a few times a year

High solar energy

Overland flow

EVAPORATION

Ephemeral stream (only flows after rain)

EVAPORATION

Evaporation draws water up through the soil

Small amount of vegetation

Death Valley, California, USA

Even in Britain the water cycle can vary a great deal. Source D shows figures for the River Ystwyth in Wales and the River Yare in East Anglia.

8 Locate the two rivers in Source D in an atlas.

9 How do the precipitation input, the outputs by surface runoff, and EVAPOTRANSPIRATION vary between the two stations?

10 How can these differences be explained? Why are the outputs so different? Discuss this with a partner. Think in terms of how the amount of cloud cover, temperatures and vegetation type may affect the processes in the water cycle.

D

	Precipitation input	Output by surface runoff	Output by evaporation and transpiration
River Ystwyth	1563 mm	1289 mm (82%)	274 mm (18%)
River Yare	739 mm	132 mm (18%)	607 mm (82%)

5.3 HOW THE PROCESSES WORK

The arrival of the water

If you are caught in a rainstorm, you may run for shelter under a tree. For the first few minutes, as you lean against the trunk, you may stay quite dry – then your back begins to feel wet, and water begins to drip on your head. Why?

A large tree in full leaf INTERCEPTS up to 8 out of every 10 raindrops. The surfaces and hollows of the leaves and branches store the water. When this vegetation store is full, the water runs down the trunk as STEMFLOW, and drips from the leaves – you get wet! So, trees and other vegetation delay the water reaching the ground.

On and under the land surface
In Source A three things are happening to the water:

- It lies on the surface as puddles.
- It flows as *surface runoff* and *overland flow*.
- It *infiltrates* into the ground and moves as *throughflow*.

1 On the photograph (Source A), identify places where each process seems to be happening.

A

The causes of overland flow

Surface storage (puddles) and overland flow occur when all of the input of water cannot infiltrate through the ground surface. Sources B and C show the two basic causes.

2 Look at Source B. What could cause this to happen? Think in terms of the nature of the surface or of the land uses which could encourage this to happen – e.g. refer back to Source A and think about *your* school grounds.
3 Now look at Source C.
 a) What could cause this to happen?
 b) Where on a slope is this most likely to be found? Why?

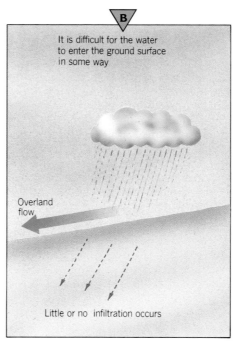

B

It is difficult for the water to enter the ground surface in some way

Overland flow

Little or no infiltration occurs

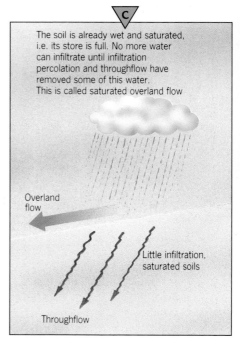

C

The soil is already wet and saturated, i.e. its store is full. No more water can infiltrate until infiltration percolation and throughflow have removed some of this water. This is called saturated overland flow

Overland flow

Little infiltration, saturated soils

Throughflow

Going down: infiltration and throughflow

MATCH CANCELLED
PITCH UNFIT

The person who looks after hockey, football or cricket pitches needs to know how well the soil drains. We mean by this: first, its INFILTRATION RATE (how quickly water passes through the soil) and, second, how much water the soil can hold or store (its storage capacity).

The close-up (Source D) shows that there are large numbers of tiny spaces within the soil. It is the number, size and pattern of these spaces which decide the infiltration rate. The amount of pore spaces in a soil is called its PO-ROSITY and is shown as a percentage of space within the total volume. Source D shows that water is likely to infiltrate less easily as it goes deeper in the soil. This causes water to move sideways, downslope as throughflow. The total volume which can pass through in a certain time is its INFILTRATION CAPACITY.

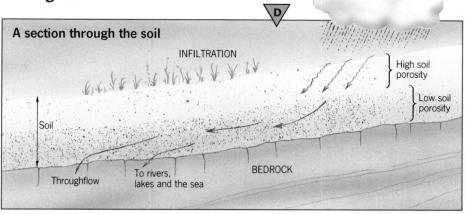

A section through the soil

INFILTRATION

High soil porosity

Low soil porosity

Soil

Throughflow

To rivers, lakes and the sea

BEDROCK

5 **a)** What causes the porosity to vary within the same soil?
   b) Why does infiltration rate generally decrease lower down in the soil?
6 The storage capacity of a soil (how much water it will store) is important for a good grass cover on a pitch. Why? (Think of what plants need.)
7 Why are soils which have high infiltration rates likely to have low storage capacities? (Think about the size and number of spaces and pathways for water to move or be held.)
8 Why do good sports pitches need soils which have a balance between infiltration rate and storage capacity?
9 In groups, discuss what effects these activities will have on infiltration capacity:
   a) trampling by animals,
   b) ploughing and cultivation,
   c) planting trees across grassland.

Hiding away: the groundwater store

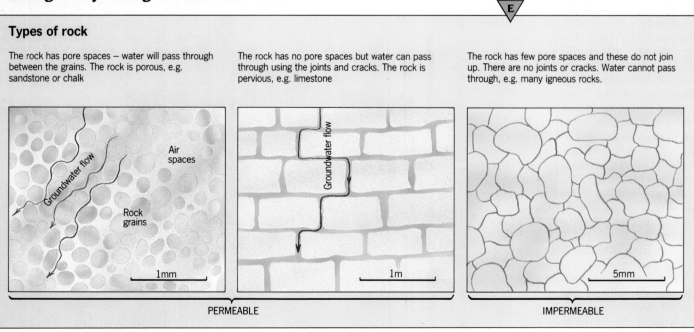

Types of rock

The rock has pore spaces – water will pass through between the grains. The rock is porous, e.g. sandstone or chalk

Groundwater flow

Air spaces

Rock grains

1mm

The rock has no pore spaces but water can pass through using the joints and cracks. The rock is pervious, e.g. limestone

Groundwater flow

1m

The rock has few pore spaces and these do not join up. There are no joints or cracks. Water cannot pass through, e.g. many igneous rocks.

5mm

PERMEABLE

IMPERMEABLE

Some water infiltrates through the soil and enters the rocks beneath. It moves as GROUNDWATER FLOW and is held as the groundwater store. Case studies in Unit 6 (pages 72–3) tell us how useful this store can be, so it is important to understand how rocks vary in their infiltration rate and storage capacity (Source E).

10 Look at Source E carefully. If you live in an area where all three types of rock lie below the surface, into which of them would you drill a well for water? Give your reasons.

The photograph in Source A shows a stream in the English Lake District. There has been no rain in the catchment area for two weeks, yet the stream has not dried up.

1 Use what you have learned about stores and pathways of water to explain where the supply (input) of water is coming from.

The low level of flow which survives dry spells is called the BASE FLOW of the stream. Source B explains how this base flow is supplied.

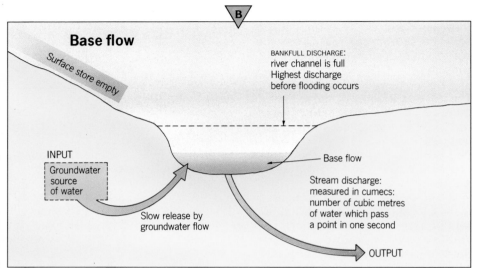

Base flow

Surface store empty

BANKFULL DISCHARGE: river channel is full Highest discharge before flooding occurs

INPUT
Groundwater source of water

Base flow

Slow release by groundwater flow

Stream discharge: measured in cumecs: number of cubic metres of water which pass a point in one second

OUTPUT

Keeping a watch on rivers

Rivers can be dangerous and it is useful for us to measure their DISCHARGE. The great rivers of the world have huge discharges: in the USA, the great Mississippi flood of 1973 took 24,000 cumecs past the city of St Louis. In Brazil, the average discharge of the Amazon as it enters the Atlantic Ocean is 130,000 cumecs (cubic metres per second). River discharges are measured by gauges set in the river channel, and then the measurements are plotted on a graph called a HYDROGRAPH. All rivers vary their discharge from day to day, and every river has its own, distinctive pattern or REGIME. The hydrograph is a diary of this regime (Source C).

2 How long after the rain stops does the peak discharge occur?
3 Why is there a time lag between peak rainfall and peak discharge in the river?
4 What are the three sources of supply to the river?
5 At what time does overland flow stop reaching the river?
6 Use Source C to say what these terms mean: time lag; peak discharge; rising limb; falling limb.

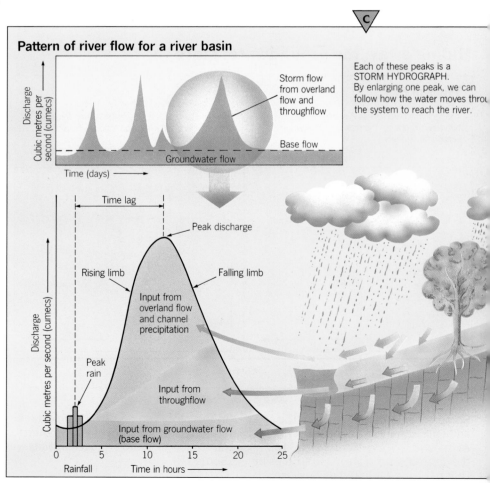

Pattern of river flow for a river basin

Storm flow from overland flow and throughflow

Base flow

Groundwater flow

Time (days)

Each of these peaks is a STORM HYDROGRAPH. By enlarging one peak, we can follow how the water moves throu the system to reach the river.

Time lag

Peak discharge

Rising limb

Falling limb

Input from overland flow and channel precipitation

Peak rain

Input from throughflow

Input from groundwater flow (base flow)

Rainfall   Time in hours ⟶

Can we forecast floods?

The hydrograph tells us how much water from a storm reaches the river, and how quickly it does so. It shows the response of the river to inputs of water into its catchment. Floods occur when more water arrives than the river channel can carry. So, the more rapid the build-up of water, the more likely the river is to flood, as the hydrographs of Sources D and E show. Two important factors which affect this build-up are *surface runoff* and the *infiltration capacity* of the soils in the catchment (see page 57).

The diagrams of Sources F, G and H show how the amount of precipitation, the time of year and the land use can affect surface runoff, infiltration and, in turn, stream discharge.

7   Study each set of conditions in Sources F, G and H and choose the storm hydrograph, Source D or E, likely to occur with each of the diagrams. Give your reasons.
8   There are two important elements of the environments missing in Sources F, G and H. These are *slope angle* (gradient) and *rock type*. Draw and label two pairs of diagrams to show what would happen when it rains:
   a) for steep and gentle slopes,
   b) for PERMEABLE and IMPERMEABLE rock types.
9   Work in a small group to prepare a brief report for the City Council of an imaginary city, who have asked for a forecast:

'For the main river in our city, what are the conditions and events within its drainage basin most likely to lead to serious flooding?'

Advice
You will need to start by deciding on what your drainage basin is like.

Write a description of it. Use the graphs on page 64 as well as the information on these pages.

Hydrographs

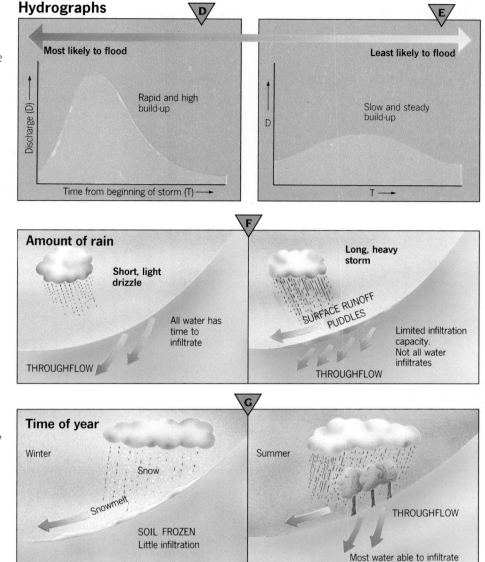

Vegetation cover

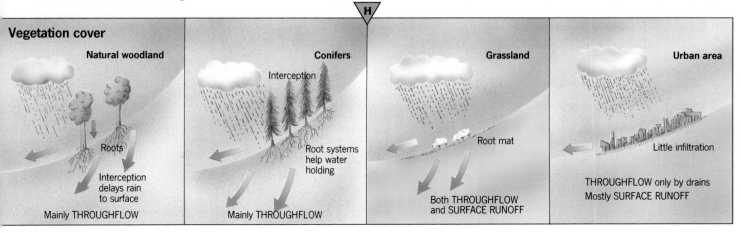

Reading hydrographs

On pages 58–9 we learned that the diary of a river's regime or discharge is usually shown as a hydrograph. The pattern of a hydrograph helps us to forecast how a river will behave and how likely it is to flood.

Two tributaries of the Thames

The information on these pages is for two tributaries of the River Thames with very different hydrographs (Sources A and B). The two hydrographs show the discharge in cumecs (see page 58) for each day of the water year 1979–80. The records were kept by the Thames Water Authority and, because English rivers usually have their lowest discharges in autumn, the Authority took its years from October to September.

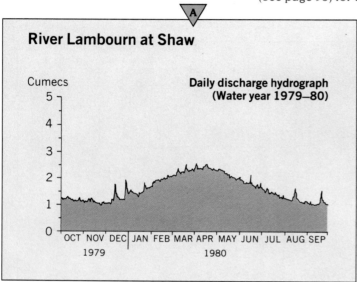

A

River Lambourn at Shaw

Cumecs

Daily discharge hydrograph
(Water year 1979–80)

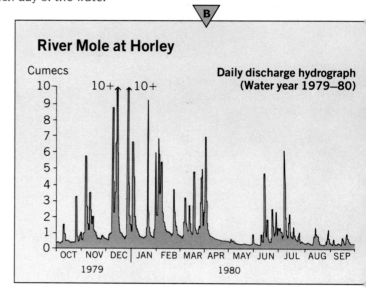

B

River Mole at Horley

Cumecs

Daily discharge hydrograph
(Water year 1979–80)

1 What are the main differences between the two hydrographs in Sources A and B? (Note the differences in the scales.)

2 Which river is the more likely to flood? Why?

3 Whether the bedrock is permeable or impermeable affects the amount of surface runoff which reaches a river. Use Source C to suggest how the geology of the area may influence a storm hydrograph for each river.

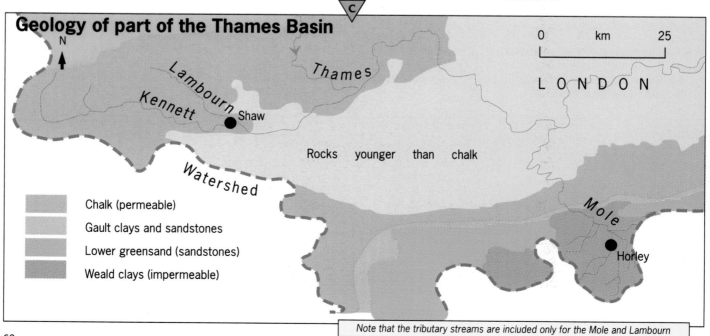

C

Geology of part of the Thames Basin

Chalk (permeable)
Gault clays and sandstones
Lower greensand (sandstones)
Weald clays (impermeable)

Note that the tributary streams are included only for the Mole and Lambourn

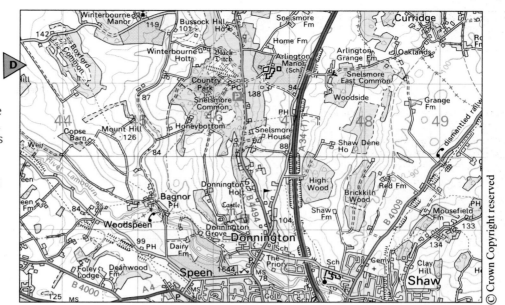

4 a) Use Sources D and E to describe the relief of the catchment area, e.g. steepness of slopes. Which river has the most tributaries?

b) How might the relief of the land and the number of tributaries affect the shape of the storm hydrographs?

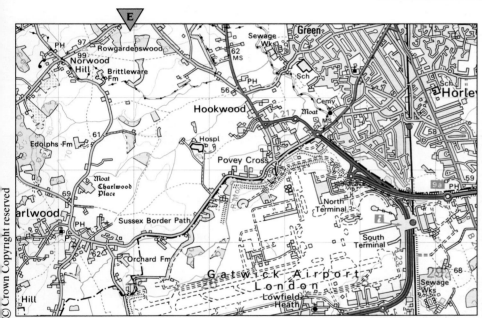

5 Using Source F, draw two graphs:
a) showing the monthly rainfall for each station,
b) showing the number of rain days each month for each station.
6 Describe the patterns shown on the graphs, and compare the two stations.
7 Which station has:
a) the greater total rainfall?
b) the larger number of rain days?
c) Do your answers suggest to you which catchment area has the more intense rainfall and so is more likely to flood?
d) Does your answer match with the pattern of the hydrographs (Sources A and B)?
8 Sum up the rainfall inputs for the two stations and suggest how these patterns influence the discharge.
9 From what you have learned, make a list of the factors which affect the way a river behaves.

Monthly rainfall and rain days

		Oct	Nov	Dec	Jan	Feb	Mar	Apr	May	Jun	Jul	Aug	Sep	Total
R. Lambourn (Shaw)	*Amount (mm)*	54	60	135	48	56	91	20	33	91	61	93	66	808
	No. of rain days	19	24	24	15	20	22	9	8	19	20	18	18	216
R. Mole (Horley)	*Amount (mm)*	42	76	145	59	65	85	22	20	129	81	57	51	832
	No. of rain days	14	22	20	16	16	20	10	6	17	20	12	15	188

5.6 RIVER CHANNELS

A simulation

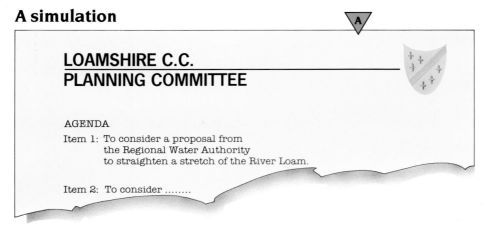

> ### LOAMSHIRE C.C.
> ### PLANNING COMMITTEE
>
> AGENDA
>
> Item 1: To consider a proposal from
> the Regional Water Authority
> to straighten a stretch of the River Loam.
>
> Item 2: To consider ....

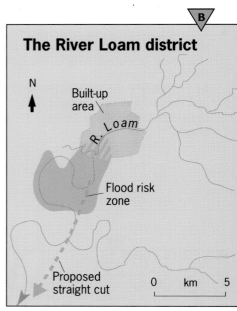

The River Loam district

N

Built-up area

R. Loam

Flood risk zone

Proposed straight cut

0   km   5

Background

There were a series of floods along one stretch of the River Loam. The floods damaged houses and farmland to the south of the town of Loamton. The Water Authority claimed that by straightening the course of the river they would be able to reduce this flooding (see the map in Source B). The local Conservation Society were opposed to the scheme (Source A), as they claimed it would damage the environment.

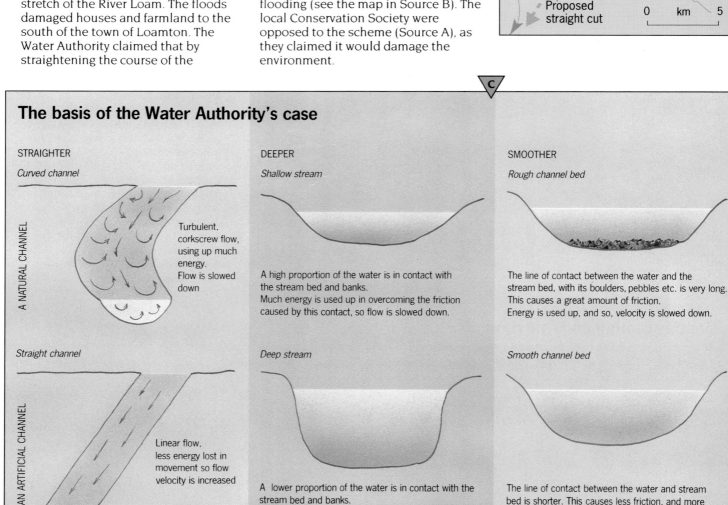

The basis of the Water Authority's case

STRAIGHTER

Curved channel

A NATURAL CHANNEL

Turbulent, corkscrew flow, using up much energy. Flow is slowed down

Straight channel

AN ARTIFICIAL CHANNEL

Linear flow, less energy lost in movement so flow velocity is increased

DEEPER

Shallow stream

A high proportion of the water is in contact with the stream bed and banks.
Much energy is used up in overcoming the friction caused by this contact, so flow is slowed down.

Deep stream

A lower proportion of the water is in contact with the stream bed and banks.
There is less friction, and so more energy is available to move the water. Velocity is increased.

SMOOTHER

Rough channel bed

The line of contact between the water and the stream bed, with its boulders, pebbles etc. is very long. This causes a great amount of friction.
Energy is used up, and so, velocity is slowed down.

Smooth channel bed

The line of contact between the water and stream bed is shorter. This causes less friction, and more energy is available to move the water.
So velocity is increased.

1 Study Sources A, B, C and D and write a statement for each side (the Conservation Society and the Water Authority) to present to the Planning Committee. You may find it helpful to work with a partner or in a small group. Remember, the issue is about *river channels*, and use other books to widen your understanding.

2 Having weighed up the advantages and disadvantages of each case, which of the alternatives do you think the Council chose and why?

▼ D

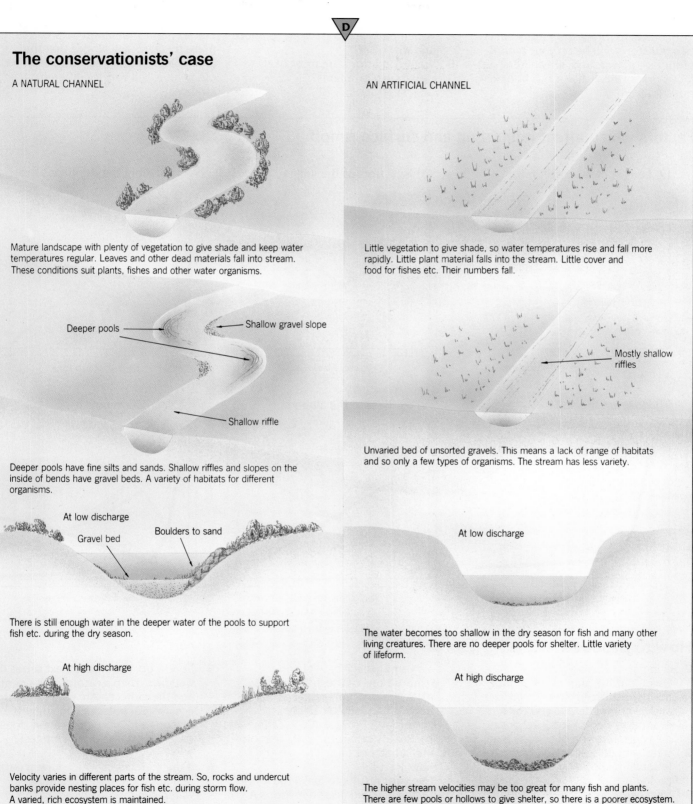

The conservationists' case

A NATURAL CHANNEL

Mature landscape with plenty of vegetation to give shade and keep water temperatures regular. Leaves and other dead materials fall into stream. These conditions suit plants, fishes and other water organisms.

Deeper pools
Shallow gravel slope
Shallow riffle

Deeper pools have fine silts and sands. Shallow riffles and slopes on the inside of bends have gravel beds. A variety of habitats for different organisms.

At low discharge
Gravel bed
Boulders to sand

There is still enough water in the deeper water of the pools to support fish etc. during the dry season.

At high discharge

Velocity varies in different parts of the stream. So, rocks and undercut banks provide nesting places for fish etc. during storm flow. A varied, rich ecosystem is maintained.

AN ARTIFICIAL CHANNEL

Little vegetation to give shade, so water temperatures rise and fall more rapidly. Little plant material falls into the stream. Little cover and food for fishes etc. Their numbers fall.

Mostly shallow riffles

Unvaried bed of unsorted gravels. This means a lack of range of habitats and so only a few types of organisms. The stream has less variety.

At low discharge

The water becomes too shallow in the dry season for fish and many other living creatures. There are no deeper pools for shelter. Little variety of lifeform.

At high discharge

The higher stream velocities may be too great for many fish and plants. There are few pools or hollows to give shelter, so there is a poorer ecosystem.

63

A FORECASTING EXERCISE FOR YOUR SCHOOL

Rainstorm damage

Your aim is to forecast what the effects of a rainstorm will be on your school grounds – playground, all-weather surfaces, grassy areas, fields etc. Your key questions are:

A Which parts are most likely to flood, and why?

B What conditions are most likely to cause such problems?

The six graphs (a–f) will help you to make this forecast. Notice that the graphs are generalised, and the *slope* of the lines will vary for different case studies.

Factors which affect infiltration and surface runoff

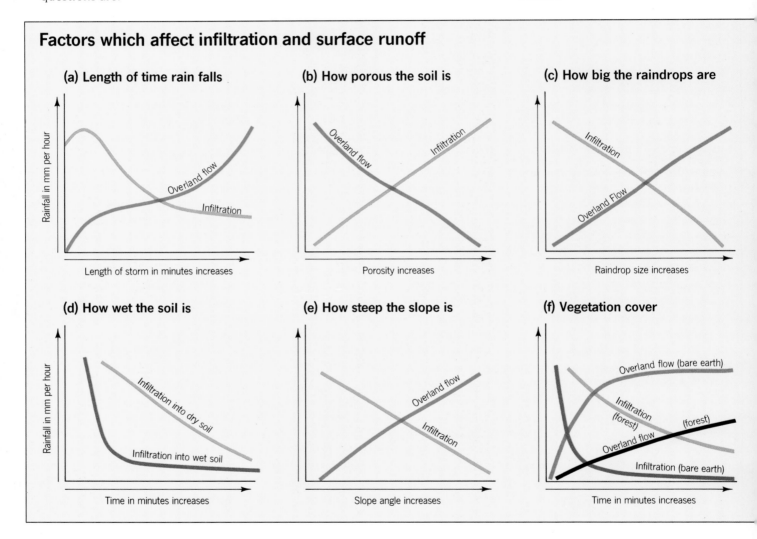

(a) Length of time rain falls

Rainfall in mm per hour

Overland flow

Infiltration

Length of storm in minutes increases

(b) How porous the soil is

Overland flow

Infiltration

Porosity increases

(c) How big the raindrops are

Infiltration

Overland Flow

Raindrop size increases

(d) How wet the soil is

Rainfall in mm per hour

Infiltration into dry soil

Infiltration into wet soil

Time in minutes increases

(e) How steep the slope is

Overland flow

Infiltration

Slope angle increases

(f) Vegetation cover

Overland flow (bare earth)

Infiltration (forest)

(forest)

Overland flow

Infiltration (bare earth)

Time in minutes increases

How to proceed

Work in pairs or small groups:

1 On an outline plan of the school, mark the different types of surface, and any other details you think relevant, e.g. slope. (Work out your own classification of surface types.)

2 Write a brief description of the relationship shown by each graph (a–f).

3 Use the information on the graphs to help you to forecast the effects of a storm on each type of surface. (Choose one of these situations:

a) A heavy storm lasting about an hour. It had rained heavily yesterday.

b) Steady drizzle for a whole morning. It had not rained for several days.)

4 Use your results to make the forecasts you need. (See questions **A** and **B** above.)

5 *Follow up:* During the next series of wet days, keep a record of the rains and their effects. Are your forecasts accurate? If not, can you suggest reasons why? On which areas does water lie on the surface longest? Why?

6 If there are areas which have a particular problem with standing water, suggest an answer to the problem.

Irrigation ditches
in Tanzania

MANAGING WATER

Myers Creek, California, USA

River basins come in all shapes and sizes, but they all behave as systems. So, if people come to live in them, they need to understand how they work. This case study about Myers Creek is a warning: it tells the story of careless decisions made by two different groups of people in the same river basin.

What did they do wrong? What can they now do? Work through the information and activities to help you decide.

The Myers Creek basin in Southern California is small: 85 km long and 20 km wide. In its natural state it is a simple SYSTEM, a typical hot desert basin. There are no permanent streams, and rain falls as occasional, intense storms.

Follow the routes of water through Source A. Source B shows that two important components have been added to this simple system: the small town of Ocotillo has grown since 1920, and in 1970 an interstate highway was built.

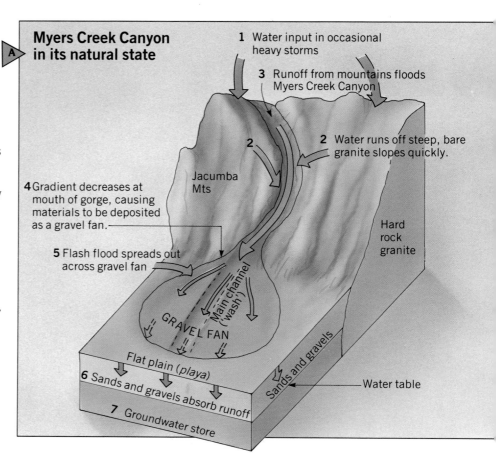

A **Myers Creek Canyon in its natural state**

1 Water input in occasional heavy storms

3 Runoff from mountains floods Myers Creek Canyon

2 Water runs off steep, bare granite slopes quickly.

Jacumba Mts

Hard rock granite

4 Gradient decreases at mouth of gorge, causing materials to be deposited as a gravel fan.

5 Flash flood spreads out across gravel fan

Main channel ('wash')

GRAVEL FAN

Sands and gravels

Flat plain (playa)

6 Sands and gravels absorb runoff

Water table

7 Groundwater store

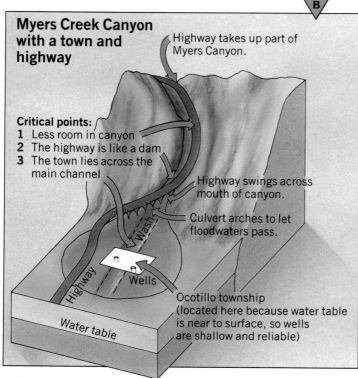

B **Myers Creek Canyon with a town and highway**

Highway takes up part of Myers Canyon.

Critical points:
1 Less room in canyon
2 The highway is like a dam
3 The town lies across the main channel

Highway swings across mouth of canyon.

Culvert arches to let floodwaters pass.

Wash

Highway

Wells

Water table

Ocotillo township (located here because water table is near to surface, so wells are shallow and reliable)

C

Ocotillo fan with the Jacumba Mountains in the background. Across the middle of the photograph, in front of the mountains, the gently sloping fan runs from right to left. The thin, pale line is the floodwash. The green patch across the wash is the trees and shrubs of Ocotillo township.

The 1976 Ocotillo flood

Rain began falling heavily about midnight on the 9th September and continued all morning. By 9.00 am, tropical storm Kathleen was still pouring her wrath along the mountain peaks just above the desert floor. 'Water was pouring off the canyon slopes like waterfalls' said Highway patrolman Rob Grossett, 'but what was most alarming were the rocks and boulders falling on the road.'

Myers Creek, normally a dry wash, had soon swollen to a raging river. The first of the four 14 × 21 ft arch culverts, which pass the creek beneath the freeway, had surging water backed up 20 ft above the arch. The water raced across the road, halting motorists going down the grade. One couple were waiting in their van on the shoulder of the roadway. Suddenly, water raced over the remaining arch culverts and smashed into the van, spinning and pushing it toward the raging creek. The couple were trapped for 20 minutes, as water continually battered against them. Never before in recorded history had this much water raced down Myers Canyon: 10–15 ft deep, 20–40 ft wide. The water's velocity was 25–30 mph, forcing huge boulders to tumble along, and the noise was deafening. A huge section of the roadway gave way: 'I couldn't believe it! That 50 ft high road and embankment just slipped into the creek,' said a maintenance worker.

In the desert town of Ocotillo, two miles downstream, no one was aware of what was about to happen. When the flood hit Ocotillo, the waters had joined to form a front 5 ft deep and a half-mile wide. Houses and trailers were torn off their foundations; vehicles overturned. 'After the wave went by,' said grocery store owner Richard Bell, 'you could see household stuff, refrigerators, trash barrels, furniture and gas tanks all floating by.'

El Centro Sentinel, 12 September 1976

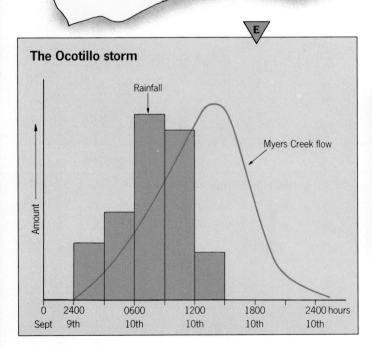

The Ocotillo storm

Rainfall

Myers Creek flow

Amount

| 0 | 2400 | 0600 | 1200 | 1800 | 2400 hours |
| Sept | 9th | 10th | 10th | 10th | 10th |

The flood poured across the alluvial fan from the mountains towards the township. Houses were very near the flood path.

1 Describe the pathways of storm water through the system *before* the highway was built. Use Source A.

2 How are the water pathways changed by the highway? Use Source B to help you.

3 What does Source E tell you about the timing of the storm and the RUNOFF in Myers Creek?

4 Why did the storm waters rise so quickly in Myers Canyon?

5 Imagine you live in a house in Ocotillo. Describe what you saw and heard as the 1976 flood happened. Read Source D to help you.

Work in a small group.

6 Discuss why Ocotillo was built where it was.

7 Why was Ocotillo so badly flooded in 1976 when, in a heavy storm in 1950, damage was slight?

8 Look at Source F. Who was to blame for the flood and damage in 1976?

9 How could further floods and damage be prevented?

6.2 TAMING THE WILD WATERS

Before and after the Colorado dams

In its natural state, the River Colorado had enormous power. It cut the Grand Canyon, 200 km long, up to 12 km wide and 1.5 km deep. Through this canyon the river used to carry 80 million tons of sediment each year. All is now changed: 19 dams control the flow, and less than 1% of the water reaches the delta in the Gulf of California, in Mexico.

The key questions for these pages are:
● Why has the river been controlled, and how does the system work?
● What are the differences between the natural system and the controlled system?

1 Using Source A, name the countries and states the Colorado flows through.
2 What distance in kilometres is each named dam from the mouth of the river? Include the dams on the tributary rivers of the Colorado. (It is easy to measure in a straight line, but try to follow the course of the river to get more accurate answers.)
3 a) Using Source A and your atlas name the mountains in which the Colorado rises.
b) Why are most of the tributaries in Arizona marked as 'non-permanent' in Source A?

The Hoover Dam and Glen Canyon Dam

The HYDROGRAPH (Source B) records the impact of the two main dams on the river DISCHARGE. It shows the natural system at work, before the first great dam, the Hoover Dam, was completed in 1935. Each year, there is a maximum and minimum discharge.

4 Describe the pattern of river discharge for the 1905–35 period. (Think in terms of the high and low points of the graph in Source B.)
5 Working in pairs, describe the changes caused by
a) the Hoover Dam,
b) the Glen Canyon Dam.

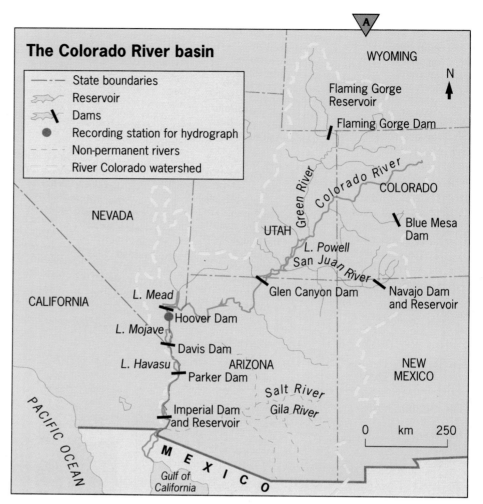

The Colorado River basin

- - - - State boundaries
Reservoir
Dams
● Recording station for hydrograph
- - - Non-permanent rivers
River Colorado watershed

WYOMING
Flaming Gorge Reservoir
Flaming Gorge Dam
Green River
Colorado River
COLORADO
NEVADA
UTAH
Blue Mesa Dam
L. Powell
San Juan River
Glen Canyon Dam
Navajo Dam and Reservoir
CALIFORNIA
L. Mead
Hoover Dam
L. Mojave
Davis Dam
NEW MEXICO
L. Havasu
ARIZONA
Parker Dam
Salt River
Gila River
PACIFIC OCEAN
Imperial Dam and Reservoir
0   km   250
M E X I C O
Gulf of California

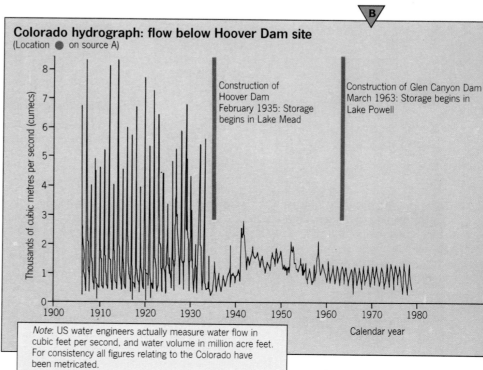

Colorado hydrograph: flow below Hoover Dam site
(Location ● on source A)

Construction of Hoover Dam February 1935: Storage begins in Lake Mead

Construction of Glen Canyon Dam March 1963: Storage begins in Lake Powell

Thousands of cubic metres per second (cumecs)

Calendar year

Note: US water engineers actually measure water flow in cubic feet per second, and water volume in million acre feet. For consistency all figures relating to the Colorado have been metricated.

How does the system work?

Source C is a simple model of a cascade of water through a controlled river like the Colorado. Notice it is a system, built of a series of INPUTS→ pathways→ STORES→ OUTPUTS. Only one dam and reservoir store is shown here to keep things simple, although the Colorado has a whole set. (Look at Source A.) Follow the numbers in Source C to understand the system, before answering the questions.

Use Source B and the model Source C to answer these questions:

6 The peaks on the hydrograph occur during June–August, while minimum discharges are in winter. Explain this pattern.

7 The River Colorado in its 'wild' or natural state had wide variations in flow, and floods were common.
   a) In which months would floods be most common, and why?
   b) How does the controlled system work to make floods less likely?

Model of the controlled Colorado cascade

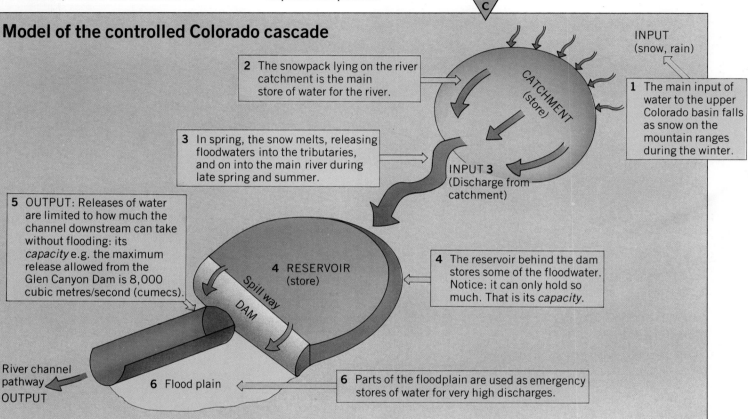

2 The snowpack lying on the river catchment is the main store of water for the river.

CATCHMENT (store)

INPUT (snow, rain)

1 The main input of water to the upper Colorado basin falls as snow on the mountain ranges during the winter.

3 In spring, the snow melts, releasing floodwaters into the tributaries, and on into the main river during late spring and summer.

INPUT **3** (Discharge from catchment)

5 OUTPUT: Releases of water are limited to how much the channel downstream can take without flooding: its *capacity* e.g. the maximum release allowed from the Glen Canyon Dam is 8,000 cubic metres/second (cumecs).

4 RESERVOIR (store)

Spill way

DAM

4 The reservoir behind the dam stores some of the floodwater. Notice: it can only hold so much. That is its *capacity*.

River channel pathway OUTPUT

6 Flood plain

6 Parts of the floodplain are used as emergency stores of water for very high discharges.

Getting the timing right

South-western USA is an ARID region, and Colorado water is precious. So, the dam schemes do not only control floods. They also produce HYDROELECTRIC POWER (HEP), and supply 25 million people and millions of hectares of IRRIGATED farmland with water.

Each year, the water engineers face a crucial decision: *How much water to release from the reservoirs during the winter.* They do this to have plenty of storage space when the floodwaters arrive from April onwards. If they release too much and the snowpack melt is small, they cannot meet the peak summer demands from cities and agriculture. Because of the limited capacity of the river channel below a

dam (look again at Source C), it takes weeks to lower the level of a huge reservoir. So they plan ahead. What happens if they do not release enough water? The 1983 story on pages 70–1 tells you.

The Glen Canyon Dam. Notice how Lake Powell fills the deep gorge behind the dam. The buildings at the base house the HEP station.

6.3 THE COLORADO FLOODS (1983)

Pages 68–9 showed how the mighty Colorado River has been 'tamed'. It is now a controlled cascade of water (Source A). The US Bureau of Reclamation is the government agency whose engineers decide the way water flows through the system. Their job is to make sure that water is available to cities, power stations, and industries throughout the year. How then, could one of the most expensive river control systems in the world break down in 1983, causing widespread flooding?

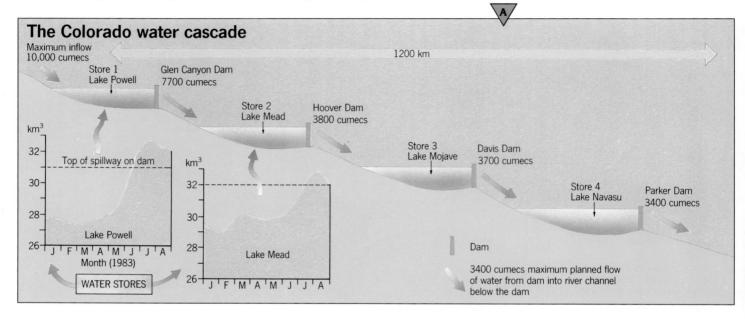

The Colorado water cascade

How the system is controlled

At the beginning of each month during the winter, the water engineers receive a forecast from the National Weather Service. This gives the run-off that is likely from the melting snowpack during April–July in the mountains which feed the river. The engineers need this because they want to know how much room to leave in the reservoirs. They can then work out how much water they need to let out during the winter. Source C shows the forecasts for January to July 1983.

1 **a)** Use Source A to describe the Colorado water cascade. Include the names of the water stores, dams, and the maximum flow of water in your description.
b) In 1983, during which months did Lakes Powell and Mead begin to fill rapidly, and then to overflow?
c) Why did this happen later at Lake Mead?
d) Which dam can release water most quickly?
2 Use the photograph (Source B) to describe the environment in the area of the Hoover Dam.

What went wrong?

At the beginning of January 1983, the snowpack was about normal. The graph in Source C shows how much room there was left in the set of reservoirs. For example, in January there were about 8.7 cubic kilometres (km³). The table in Source C shows the National Weather Service forecasts. At the beginning of January 1983, the engineers were told the April–July snowmelt would give a run-off of 9.6 km³. Now compare the run-off forecasts and the available reservoir storage with the run-off line for an average year. You can see that until April, the engineers felt no danger: the run-off from snowmelt seemed likely to be about normal, and there was plenty of space in the reservoirs. Remember, the run-off can be rather higher than the storage room because some water continues on down the river, or is diverted to aqueducts and canals.

Hoover Dam on the Colorado

70

Work in pairs and study Source C carefully.

3 **a)** Describe the change in storage room in the reservoirs between January and July 1983.
   b) By how much each month was the forecasters' expected run-off figure different from the average?

4 **a)** When did the engineers realise the danger that they might not have enough storage space in the reservoirs?
   b) Describe how the situation changed from the beginning of April to the end of June.

5 How does Source D help to explain the amazing rise in the April–June run-off forecasts?

6 Why does it take time to make extra room in the reservoirs? (Look at the maximum outflow from each reservoir on Source A.)

C River Colorado: balance between runoff forecasts and reservoir space available in 1983

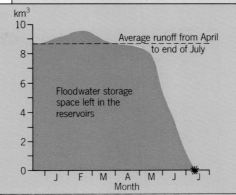

The forecasters changed their estimates of how much floodwater run-off from snowmelt and rainfall would occur during the period from 1 April to 31 July 1983. This is what they told the water engineers to expect.

On 1 January they said: 9.6 km^3
On 1 March they said: 8.5 km^3
On 1 April they said: 9.9 km^3
On 1 June they said: 11.2 km^3
On 15 June they said: 13.7 km^3
On 1 July they said: 17.5 km^3

D Diary of the main weather events in the Rocky Mountains, 1983

▷ *Jan/Feb:* Snowfalls and temperatures about normal.

▷ *March:* Several falls of snow keep the total snowpack about normal.

▷ *April:* First half is cool, and snowmelt is delayed.

▷ *May:* Storms sweep across the mountains, with unusually low temperatures giving heavy late snowfalls.

▷ *June:* From the last weekend in May, and through the first half of June, a sudden heatwave causes very rapid snowmelt.

▷ *June 25–28:* Thunderstorms bring heavy rains to some mountain areas.

E A river reborn

The Parker Strip, an almost solid stretch of resorts and restaurants between Parker Dam and Parker, was all but closed last year, during the man-caused flood on the river.

The Bureau of Reclamation miscalculated the amount of runoff from the melting snowpack in the river's Rocky Mountain watershed and delayed making large water releases from Lake Mead and Lake Powell until June 1983.

The releases, when they were started, were massive and caused widespread, heavy damage to resorts and marinas along the river. The floods cost local businessmen millions of dollars, both in damage and loss of revenue.

Critics claim that the Bureau of Reclamation tried to keep the reservoirs as full as possible to accommodate the Central Arizona Project, failing to realize that there was not enough room in the reservoirs to hold the sudden rise of water because of melting snow.

As a result, the bureau was forced to make a heavy water release throughout the rest of the year, even when the danger of flooding was over, to prevent a repeat of the flooding this year.

A river is supposed to be wet

As bad as it is that homes and businesses along the Colorado River in Arizona are flooded, it's a little difficult to sympathize with people who build in a river bottom, then complain when the water runs exactly where it is supposed to flow.

The property owners are complaining because the bureau did not make a smaller release earlier. Unfortunately, nature conspired against such a precaution. The runoff into the Colorado surged suddenly when snowpacks in the Rockies were melted by an onset of hot weather, accompanied by heavy rains.

F Changes on the Colorado floodplain south of Parker Dam

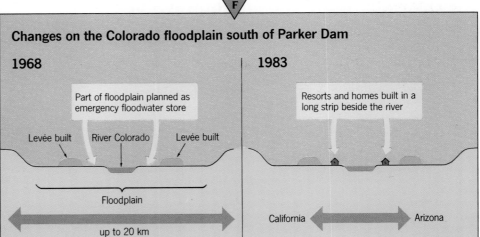

7 Study Source F and read the newspaper articles in Source E.
   a) Describe the land use on the Colorado floodplain in 1968 and 1983.
   b) Why was part of the floodplain planned as an emergency floodwater store?
   c) Suggest why the planners were ignored and building had taken place on the floodplain by 1983.

8 Group discussion:
   a) Use Sources E and F to decide who was to blame for the floods and for the damage they caused.
   b) Why do you think the water engineers did not release more water earlier?
   c) How could future flooding and damage be prevented? (There are several possible answers.)

6.4 WATER BELOW THE SURFACE

The GROUNDWATER STORE is just as important as the surface water stores. The volume of water stored varies according to the balance of inputs and outputs shown in the FLOW DIAGRAM (Source A). This balance is called the WATER BUDGET.

Using the groundwater store

The groundwater store is a reservoir. We need two basic understandings about it:

- If we use the store, we cannot take out more than is put in, or it will gradually decrease.
- Human activities can easily upset the balance of the groundwater store.

1   Describe the movement of water from its *input* at the surface to its *output* by transpiration from plants. Use Source A.
2   To check your understanding,

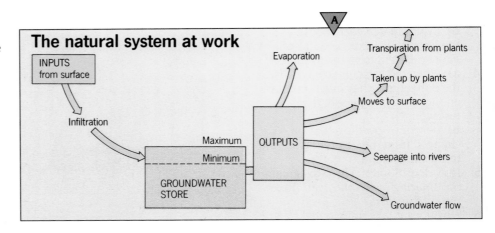

The natural system at work

change one of the inputs or outputs at a time, and explain to a partner what may happen to the groundwater store.

Study Source B.

3   Explain the following terms:
    a) WATER TABLE;
    b) AQUIFER;
    c) IMPERMEABLE rock.
4   Why does the level of the water table move up and down?

5   Wells 1 and 2 are used to supply water.
    a) What would happen to the water level in Well 1 during a long dry spell?
    b) Explain why Well 2 would be a better source of water at all times.
6   In small groups discuss:
    In what environments will the groundwater be an important source of water for people?

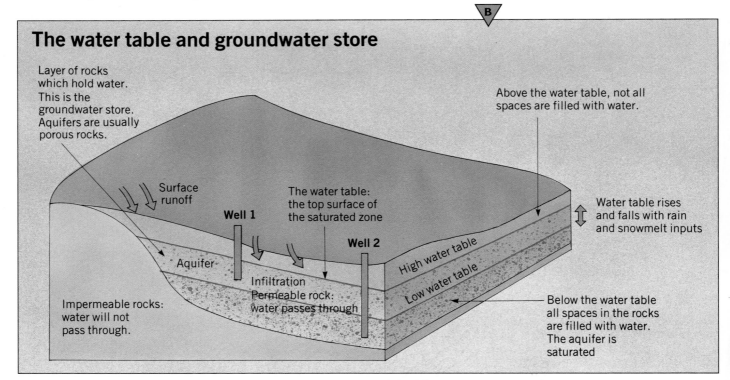

The water table and groundwater store

The two case studies on page 73 show changes in DRAINAGE BASINS as a result of people using the basin and the groundwater store.

Balancing the budget: the Ocotillo Basin, California, USA

The little Ocotillo Basin (pp. 66–7) has yet another urgent problem. The groundwater store has been used as a source of water. Changes have occurred as shown in Source C.

7 Compare columns 1 and 2 in Source C.

a) What is happening to the groundwater store and the water table?

b) What is causing these changes to occur?

c) How is the groundwater used? (Source D.)

d) Why will this be difficult to reduce?

e) What is likely to happen in the future?

Ocotillo township well and water tank

C

Changes in the Ocotillo basin		
	1 *The natural basin (1925) cubic metres per year*	**2** *The basin used by people (1985) cubic metres per year*
Input. Infiltration of rainwater each year	3,200	3,200
Outputs per year pumped from wells	0	1,470
Evaporation	800	400
Groundwater flow out of the basin	2,400	2,300
Total outputs	3,200	4,200
Total water store	79,700	78,000
Fall in level of water-table 1925–1985	–	3 metres

D

Users of water outputs (wells) (cubic metres per year)	
1 People of Ocotillo township	240
2 US Gypsum Company makes plasterboard at a factory 12 km outside the Ocotillo Basin.	800
3 McDougall Water Company – a local company which exports water to Mexico in tankers.	430
Total	1,470

Ups and downs: the Harquahala Valley, Arizona, USA

E

In 1935 the Harquahala basin (Source E) was in its natural state. The water table (WT) followed the surface of the land, and was nearest to the surface along the main wash (channel) bed. Wells were sunk where the WT was nearest to the surface. Around the wells the WT has been lowered (Y). Below the irrigated land the WT has been raised (X).

Working in pairs, study Source E.

8 a) Describe the environment of the Harquahala Valley.

b) What is the groundwater used for in this area?

c) What has happened to the level of the water table at X and Y?

d) Explain these changes using systems terms (*inputs/stores/outputs*) in both cases at X and Y.

e) What is likely to happen in the future at X and Y?

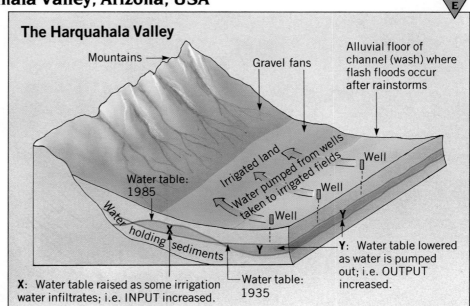

The Harquahala Valley

Mountains

Gravel fans

Alluvial floor of channel (wash) where flash floods occur after rainstorms

Irrigated land

Water pumped from wells taken to irrigated fields

Well

Well

Well

Water table: 1985

Water holding sediments

X

Y

Y

Water table: 1935

X: Water table raised as some irrigation water infiltrates; i.e. INPUT increased.

Y: Water table lowered as water is pumped out; i.e. OUTPUT increased.

9 For each of these two case studies, describe briefly which of the two understandings given on page 72 they illustrate.

10 In a small group, discuss how we can keep the groundwater *store* topped up.

A simple supply of water?

Dry lands can be 'brought to life' by adding irrigation water (look at Source A). In arid and semi-arid areas people store the precious rainwater in wetter months to use on crops in drier months or in even drier places (see pp. 52–3). It sounds simple: add a supply of water and crops can be grown.

Irrigation problems in Australia

Alex Gibson farms in the dry state of Victoria, Australia. He hoped irrigation was simple, but as Source C shows, crops on 65 of his 1,000 hectares have suddenly failed. He is not alone: in Victoria state 100,000 hectares have suffered. Across the drier areas of the world, more land is being lost each year by poor irrigation methods than is being added by expensive new irrigation schemes. What is going wrong?

Irrigating fields with water from Lake Albert, Victoria

A build-up of salt

Deserts are naturally salty places. Alex Gibson knew this. He also knew that plants need certain salts, but can tolerate only so much. What he did not realise was just how much salt would build up in the soil as a result of irrigation.

Follow Source B and find out what can happen. Watch particularly what happens to the water table and to the salts in the soil.

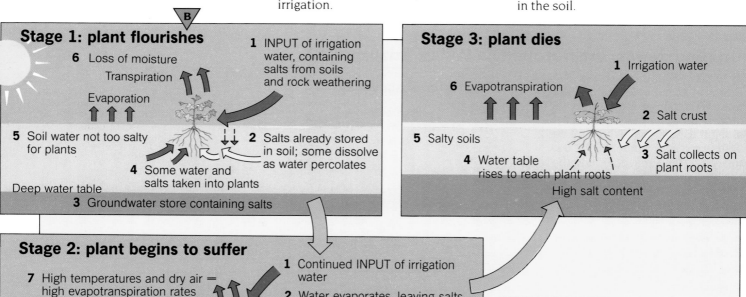

Stage 1: plant flourishes
6 Loss of moisture
Transpiration
Evaporation
5 Soil water not too salty for plants
4 Some water and salts taken into plants
1 INPUT of irrigation water, containing salts from soils and rock weathering
2 Salts already stored in soil; some dissolve as water percolates
Deep water table
3 Groundwater store containing salts

Stage 3: plant dies
6 Evapotranspiration
1 Irrigation water
2 Salt crust
5 Salty soils
4 Water table rises to reach plant roots
3 Salt collects on plant roots
High salt content

Stage 2: plant begins to suffer
7 High temperatures and dry air = high evapotranspiration rates
6 More salts stored in the soil and water becomes saltier
Salts rising
Water table rises
5 Some irrigation water reaches the groundwater store and so the water table rises
1 Continued INPUT of irrigation water
2 Water evaporates, leaving salts behind
3 Salt crust forms on ground surface
4 Salts dissolved in water are drawn up through the soil

1 In pairs, study Source B and describe what is happening to the water at Stage 1. Follow the numbers to help you.
2 What is causing stress to the plant at Stage 2?
3 What changes in the soil system at Stage 3 have caused the plant to die?

Alex Gibson in one of his fields ruined by salinisation

Finding an answer

The process which has ruined Alex Gibson's soil is called SALINISATION: the gradual build up of salts in the soil. Alex says, 'There's little to do but turn your back and leave.' But is he right? His basic problem is: How to stop the levels of salt in the soil from increasing? In systems terms, he has two alternatives (Source D).

In humid parts of the world the THROUGHPUT of water is large enough to dissolve and wash away surplus salts. In arid and semi-arid areas this does not happen, and this is why soils in drier regions are *naturally* salty: there is too little water and high evaporation rates. Farmers like Alex Gibson may make things worse by adding irrigation water containing salts. Their irrigation water may also cause salts to be released from the soil and groundwater stores. Poor drainage (on, for example, clays or LATERITES) means that although salts are flushed through the soil, salty waters do not move away.

D

Reducing salinisation: the alternatives

1 INPUT	STORE	OUTPUT 2
Reduce the salt input	Soil store	Increase the salt output

Change the water throughput

E

Improved drainage removes the salts

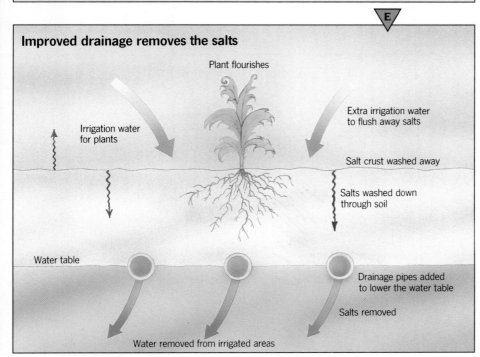

Plant flourishes

Irrigation water for plants

Extra irrigation water to flush away salts

Salt crust washed away

Salts washed down through soil

Water table

Drainage pipes added to lower the water table

Salts removed

Water removed from irrigated areas

Good drainage

4 Farmers are learning that the secret is in good drainage. Use the information in Source E to explain how salinisation can be reduced or prevented.

In groups, discuss the following:

5 The processes shown in Source E increase the output of salts from the soil store. Is it possible to reduce the inputs of salts? How? Is it practical?

6 In dry regions, why might farmers and governments be reluctant to increase the volumes of water used?

7 In schemes like that suggested in Source E, where will the salts go, and what might their effects be?

A salty problem

The River Murray has a CATCHMENT AREA of 1 million square kilometres, and is a major source of water for three Australian states (see Source A). Its natural discharge varies seasonally, but barrages and dams now regulate the flow. Large irrigation schemes use its water. Cities draw on the river for supplies.

Australians are now worried about the quality of the Murray water. Every year, 1.3 million tonnes of salt enter the river, dissolved from the natural stores and irrigated farming (see pages 74–5). This is the same as 350 ten-tonne trucks each tipping a full load into the river every day! The amount is increasing every year.

If water is to be used for domestic supplies, then the World Health Organisation recommends a maximum of 500 milligrams (mg) of dissolved salts per litre. Citrus trees and vines cannot grow with salt levels above 600 mg/litre.

1 What was the maximum salt level in the River Murray in 1980? (See Source B.)
2 Describe what happens to salinity levels as the river flows downstream. (Source B.)
3 Why are people concerned about water quality for the future? Which state should be most worried? (Sources A and B.)

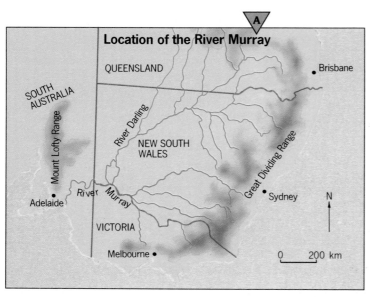

A

Location of the River Murray

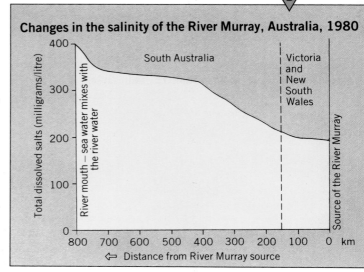

B

Changes in the salinity of the River Murray, Australia, 1980

Solving the problem

Semi-arid environments like the Murray Basin are naturally salty (pages 74–5). Irrigation can add to this salinity, bringing the water table nearer to the surface, as Alex Gibson has found out. A water table near the surface not only affects crops, but makes it easier for salts to reach the main river.

4 If Alex Gibson succeeds in getting rid of the salt on his land, why might this make matters worse in the River Murray?
5 Look carefully at Source C, and explain how water engineers are trying to keep down the salt levels in the River Murray.

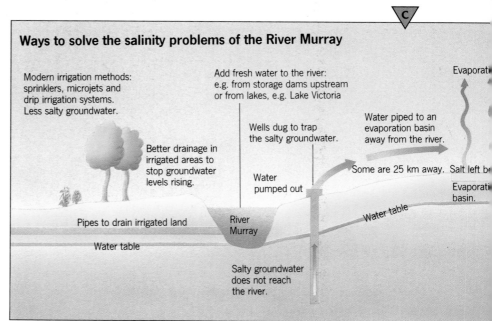

C

Ways to solve the salinity problems of the River Murray

Modern irrigation methods: sprinklers, microjets and drip irrigation systems. Less salty groundwater.

Add fresh water to the river: e.g. from storage dams upstream or from lakes, e.g. Lake Victoria

Evaporati

Wells dug to trap the salty groundwater.

Water piped to an evaporation basin away from the river.

Better drainage in irrigated areas to stop groundwater levels rising.

Some are 25 km away. Salt left be

Water pumped out

Evaporati basin.

Pipes to drain irrigated land

River Murray

Water table

Water table

Salty groundwater does not reach the river.

A water problem for Adelaide

Adelaide (population about 1,000,000) is the capital of South Australia: the driest state, in the driest continent on Earth. South Australia possesses only 2% of Australia's water resources, but has 12% of the land area and 9% of the population. Some water is piped from the Mt Lofty Ranges, but Adelaide relies increasingly on the River Murray (Source D).

Water consumption per person in Adelaide is four times the amount used in England and Wales. The average household in Adelaide uses over 500 litres a day. More than one-third of this is used on gardens. On present trends, water demands for people and industry will increase by 50% by the year 2000.

Working in pairs, study Sources D and E.

6 Using Source D, describe how Murray water is supplied to the people of Adelaide.

7 Draw graphs to show the data in Source E. Use your graphs to explain why Murray water is important to Adelaide.

8 In systems terms, Adelaide lies near the end of the Murray cascade Explain what this means, and what problems it may cause for the city. (Think of *quantity* and *quality* of water supply.)

The alternatives for Adelaide

Adelaide faces long-term water supply problems. Remember that a 50% increase is needed by the year 2000. There are two ways of meeting the increase in water demand:

● Find new sources of water.
● Save water by water conservation methods (up to 20% saving could be achieved).

In Source F, you can study the possible alternatives that the Adelaide Water Authority could use to increase the water supply to Adelaide.

9 Work in groups. You are a committee of the Adelaide Water Authority and you are planning the future water supply for Adelaide. Write a report on the possible alternatives. In your report include the following:
a) The advantages and disadvantages of each of the options available to you. (Think carefully about

the water quality from each source, and how the supply will vary over the year compared with the variations in demand over the year.)
b) How you plan to cut water consumption to make savings.

c) The options you favour in the next ten years.
d) How you will raise the money to pay for the new schemes.
e) Your recommendations for the long-term future.

Adelaide area

- Proposed water treatment works
- Reservoir catchment boundaries
- Built-up area

Water supply in Adelaide

Month	J	F	M	A	M	J	J	A	S	O	N	D
Water use (% of year's total)	14	13	11	7	6	4	4	4	5	8	11	13
Rainfall (% of year's total)	2	2	4	8	14	14	14	14	10	9	5	4
Mean temp. (°C)	25	24	20	15	14	12	11	12	15	16	20	22

Water supply alternatives in Adelaide

	Amount of water produced	Financial cost of production
1 Stop evaporation from the reservoirs in the Lofty Mountains	Low	Low
2 Use groundwater in the area	Medium	Low
3 Pipe extra water from the River Murray	High	Low
4 New reservoirs in the Lofty Mountains	Medium	Medium
5 Icebergs towed from Antarctica	Unlimited	Med/high
6 Remove the salt from seawater	Unlimited	Med/high
7 Reuse sewage effluent for gardens etc	High	Med/high
8 Bring in water by tanker	Medium	High
9 Collect runoff from the city	Medium	High
10 Collect and store more rain in tanks	Low	High
11 More efficient irrigation in the Murray Basin	Low	High

Sediment: a heavy load

Source A shows water pouring from the Sanmenxia Dam, on the Yellow River (Huang He) in China. Like the Colorado, the Murray and many other great rivers, the Yellow is now a managed system. A series of dams and reservoirs control the flow, to prevent floods, give water for towns and irrigation, and provide power. But look again at the photograph – the water is very muddy. When water moves, it uses some of its energy to carry sediment: this is the SUSPENDED LOAD of a river. All rivers carry loads, but the Yellow River has a very special problem: each year it carries enough sediment to build a wall one metre high by one metre wide, 27 times round the Earth!

Muddy waters of the Yellow River at the Sanmenxia Dam

Heavier than average

Work in pairs on these questions:

1 a) Using Source B, put the rivers in rank order (put the largest first) for catchment area, annual load and average sediment load.
   b) What do your lists tell you about the Yellow River?
2 How many times more sediment is being carried by the Yellow River than by:
   a) the Ganga?
   b) the Mekong?
   c) the Colorado?
3 How do the tributaries Yen and Ching of the Yellow River affect its sediment load (Source C)?
4 By how much can the sediment load of the Yellow River vary from the average figure?

The suspended sediment loads recorded in some major world rivers

River	Catchment area (sq km)	Annual sediment load (millions tonnes)	Average sediment load (kg/m³)
Yellow (China)	752,000	1,600	38.0
Ganga (India)	956,000	1,450	3.9
Amazon (Brazil)	5,776,000	400	0.1
Mississippi (USA)	3,222,000	345	0.6
Mekong (Vietnam)	795,000	190	0.5
Colorado (USA)	637,000	135	28.0

Deep gullies cut into the flat loess landscape in Chunhua County, Shaanxi Province ▶

And it gets worse!

① Some tributaries of the Yellow River may reach 1200 kg/m³, e.g. River Yen and River Ching.

② Maximum sediment load recorded in the Yellow River: 666 kg/m³

③ Average sediment load in the Yellow River: 38 kg/m³

Tributaries of the Yellow River have even higher concentrations. The cylinders show river water samples in which the muddy sediment has been allowed to settle.

Where does sediment come from?

The Yellow River passes through a large area which is covered by a fine, wind-deposited material called LOESS. This is easily ERODED by the river (Source D) and is carried away to form most of the Yellow River's sediment load.

5 Refer to the map in Source E.
a) Describe the course of the Yellow River.
b) What happens to the amount of sediment in the river as it passes through the loess region? ·
c) Why is the loess so important?

d) How has human activity caused the sediment load to increase?
6 How do you think the amount of sediment in the river will vary between winter and summer? Explain your answer.

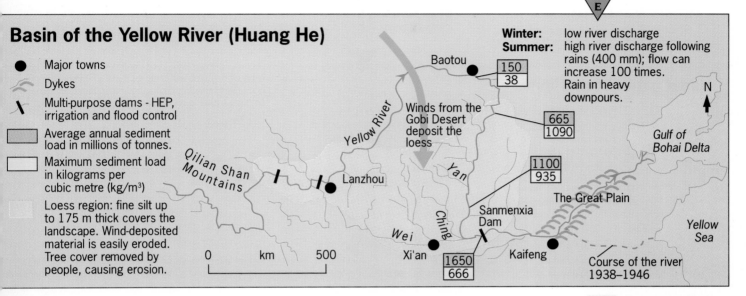

Basin of the Yellow River (Huang He)

● Major towns

〰 Dykes

\ Multi-purpose dams - HEP, irrigation and flood control

▬ Average annual sediment load in millions of tonnes.

▭ Maximum sediment load in kilograms per cubic metre (kg/m³)

Loess region: fine silt up to 175 m thick covers the landscape. Wind-deposited material is easily eroded. Tree cover removed by people, causing erosion.

Winter: low river discharge
Summer: high river discharge following rains (400 mm); flow can increase 100 times. Rain in heavy downpours.

Baotou
150 / 38

Winds from the Gobi Desert deposit the loess
665 / 1090

Gulf of Bohai Delta

Yellow River

Qilian Shan Mountains

Lanzhou

Yan

1100 / 935

The Great Plain

Sanmenxia Dam

Wei

Ching

Xi'an
1650 / 666

Kaifeng

Course of the river 1938–1946

Yellow Sea

N

0   km   500

Muddy problems and clear solutions

The purpose of dams is to create reservoirs, i.e. water stores. However, as the water is stopped by a dam, it loses its energy, drops its sediment load and steadily fills in the reservoir (Source F). We know that loess gives an easy supply of sediment to the Yellow River. This huge sediment load has caused the storage capacity of the reservoir behind the Sanmenxia Dam (Source A) to be reduced by 40% in only four years.

So when seasonal flood discharges come, the reservoir can hold less, and the engineers have to let more water flow downstream. Yet, the purpose of the dam is to reduce flooding in the fertile Great Plain (Source E) where millions of people live.

One answer

The water engineers choose times to open the bottom sluice gates through the dam. The water rushes out with great energy and flushes the sediment from the reservoir bed. This is what is happening in the photograph in Source A.

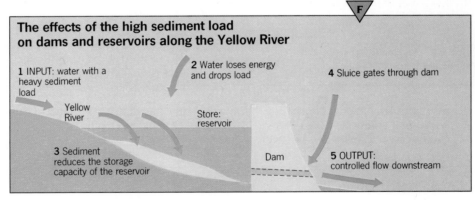

The effects of the high sediment load on dams and reservoirs along the Yellow River

1 INPUT: water with a heavy sediment load

Yellow River

2 Water loses energy and drops load

Store: reservoir

3 Sediment reduces the storage capacity of the reservoir

Dam

4 Sluice gates through dam

5 OUTPUT: controlled flow downstream

7 a) Use Source F to explain why the high sediment load poses problems for Chinese water engineers.
b) How do they overcome this problem?

8 Another answer is to stop the sediment getting into the river in the first place. Use Source G to draw a labelled sketch to explain what has been done in the easily eroded loess region.

Terraced hillsides and tree-planting in a loess region (Shaanxi Province)

6 WHAT HAPPENS DOWNSTREAM?

Managing the Yellow River

1 Use Source A to:
a) describe what happened to the sediment load when the river was working naturally, before the dams were built,
b) explain why the water deposited its load across the floodplain,
c) explain why control schemes were built upstream (pages 78–9).

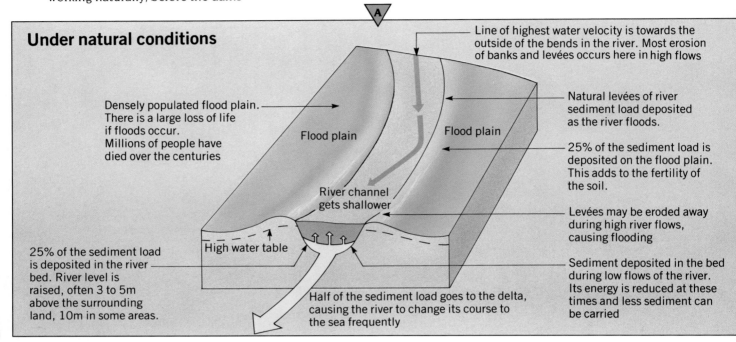

Under natural conditions

Line of highest water velocity is towards the outside of the bends in the river. Most erosion of banks and levées occurs here in high flows

Densely populated flood plain. There is a large loss of life if floods occur. Millions of people have died over the centuries

Flood plain

Flood plain

Natural levées of river sediment load deposited as the river floods.

25% of the sediment load is deposited on the flood plain. This adds to the fertility of the soil.

River channel gets shallower

Levées may be eroded away during high river flows, causing flooding

25% of the sediment load is deposited in the river bed. River level is raised, often 3 to 5m above the surrounding land, 10m in some areas.

High water table

Sediment deposited in the bed during low flows of the river. Its energy is reduced at these times and less sediment can be carried

Half of the sediment load goes to the delta, causing the river to change its course to the sea frequently

2 **a)** Use Source B to explain what additional solutions have been tried along the lower Yellow River.
b) How has the flow of water in the river channel been altered?
c) What have been the effects of these alterations on the channel shape and the suspended load?

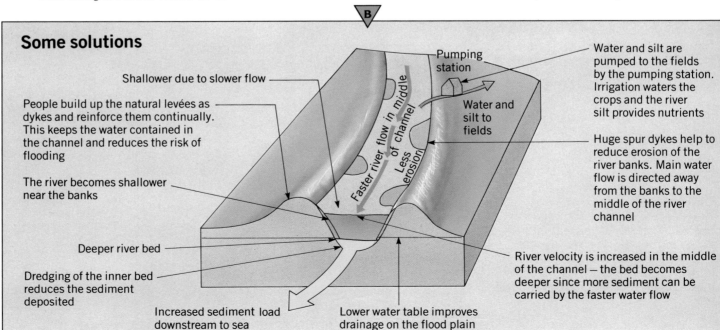

Some solutions

Shallower due to slower flow

People build up the natural levées as dykes and reinforce them continually. This keeps the water contained in the channel and reduces the risk of flooding

The river becomes shallower near the banks

Deeper river bed

Dredging of the inner bed reduces the sediment deposited

Increased sediment load downstream to sea

Pumping station

Faster river flow in middle of channel

Less erosion

Water and silt to fields

Lower water table improves drainage on the flood plain

Water and silt are pumped to the fields by the pumping station. Irrigation waters the crops and the river silt provides nutrients

Huge spur dykes help to reduce erosion of the river banks. Main water flow is directed away from the banks to the middle of the river channel

River velocity is increased in the middle of the channel — the bed becomes deeper since more sediment can be carried by the faster water flow

DESERTIFICATION

Niger: cattle being herded over the sand dunes to green pasture

7.1 WHAT IS DESERTIFICATION?

You may have helped to raise money for hungry and homeless people in Africa or Asia. You may have been part of the huge Live Aid and Sports Aid charity efforts organised by Bob Geldof and others. One of the main reasons millions of people need aid is that the land they live on is suffering from what is called DESERTIFICATION. Desertification produces desert environments where they did not exist before (see Source A). So, we need to understand what it is, what causes it, and whether it can be prevented.

Desertification defined

Professor Kassas of Cairo University says:

> Desertification is a process by which land that was once productive becomes non-productive. When I say 'once productive', I mean this is not the natural desert, the climatic desert where rainfall is so low that no productivity can be there. But we are talking of areas where rainfall is 300–500 mm a year. This is enough to produce something.

Left: Jean-Marie is holding millet and sorghum from 1986 and 1987

Gradually more and more forest was cleared, until each clearing met the next

In my father's time

'In my father's time we never had a bad year,' Jean-Marie remembers. 'Millet filled all the granaries and was piled up outside the compound under the straw shelters.

'When we were boys the SAVANNA (woodland) was all around us. It was too thick to penetrate or cultivate. The wild animals were too many to count. There were antelope, elephants, buffaloes.

Gradually more and more of the trees were cleared around the compounds, until each clearing met the next and created the great oneness you see now. Today the hills are bare. The only animals we see are hares. Fig trees will not grow any more. The last kapok tree fell down twenty years ago.

'When I was young, the land was fertile. You could farm the same piece of land for five years, ten years, with no fertiliser, before resting it.

'There was enough space for you to leave it for ten or twenty years before you came back to it again. Today we have to farm the same fields year after year. A piece of land that used to fill two granaries would not even fill one now: last harvest it would not even fill half a granary.

'The soil has been carried away. When I was young, you could dig a hole as deep as your body before you reached hard rock. Now in many of my fields you reach the rock if you just dig as deep as my hand.

'When I was a boy we used to have tremendous rains. It would start in the morning, and rain until the evening, and still be raining long into the night. We used to grow cotton, rice, sweet potatoes. But now it is too dry for any of these.

'Year by year the rain got less. Today when the rain starts, it continues for twenty or thirty minutes, and then stops. Sometimes we see it rain behind the mountain, but it doesn't rain here. Every year we worry whether the rain will fall or won't fall. Every year we say. "Last year we had more rain than this".'

Burkina Faso, West Africa
Read Source B.
1 What does Jean-Marie Sawadogo say his home area was like when he was a boy?
2 How has the environment changed since then?
3 The type of farming Jean-Marie tells us about is called SHIFTING CULTIVATION. Describe how this used to work when he was young.
4 Give two reasons why the soil is less fertile and produces less today
5 Make two lists comparing the WEATHER, soil, crops grown and natural vegetation. List 1: when Jean-Marie was a boy; list 2: today.
6 With a partner, read the definition in Source A.
   a) Decide what is the most important fact that the definition tells us.
   b) How do the lists you have made for question 5 illustrate the definition of desertification?

82

South of the Sahara

One area of the world seriously affected by desertification is the Sahel. The Sahel is a belt runing west–east across Africa, to the south of the Sahara Desert (Source C). It includes Jean-Marie's homeland of Burkina Faso.

7 Name the countries of the Sahel numbered 1–10 on Source C. (Use an atlas.)
a) Between what latitudes does the Sahel lie?
b) What is the west–east distance across the Sahel? From an atlas, compare this disance with that from London to Moscow. Which is greater? By how much?
c) What is the approximate area of the Sahel? (Remember: Area = length × width.)

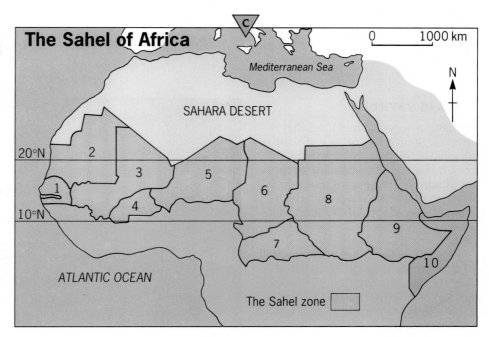

The Sahel of Africa

Mediterranean Sea

SAHARA DESERT

20°N

10°N

ATLANTIC OCEAN

The Sahel zone

0   1000 km

N

The world scale

As Source D shows, desertification is a huge problem. Each year, 6 million hectares of farmland turn to sand. At least one family in three in the world is now affected by desertification.

Use Source D and an atlas.
8 For each continent, name a country.

with severe desertification.
9 How much of Africa is:
a) desert?
b) becoming severely desertified?
10 Which continent is suffering most from
a) moderate desertification?
b) desertification? Explain your

choice.
11 Does desertification occur only in the poorer parts of the world?
12 a) Between which latitudes is severe desertification found?
b) How is the pattern of moderate desertification different from (a)?
13 Is desertification a global problem?

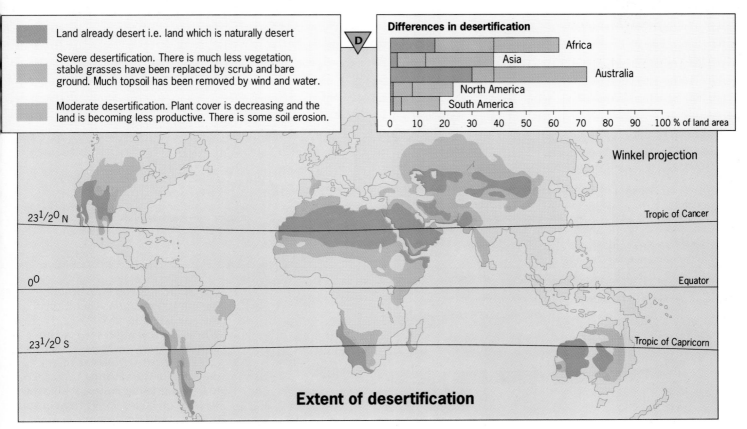

Land already desert i.e. land which is naturally desert

Severe desertification. There is much less vegetation, stable grasses have been replaced by scrub and bare ground. Much topsoil has been removed by wind and water.

Moderate desertification. Plant cover is decreasing and the land is becoming less productive. There is some soil erosion.

Differences in desertification

Africa
Asia
Australia
North America
South America

0 10 20 30 40 50 60 70 80 90 100 % of land area

Winkel projection

23½°N — Tropic of Cancer

0° — Equator

23½°S — Tropic of Capricorn

Extent of desertification

THE SAHEL: SAVANNA AND CULTIVATION

What is savanna?

The natural vegetation of the Sahel is savanna (Source A). This is a mixture of tall grasses, bushes and scattered trees. It is adapted to stand up to the hot months of the year without rain, and then to use the water from the irregular heavy storms of the short wet season.

In the south of the Sahel, where rainfall is higher, there are more trees in the savanna. Further north, as the dry season becomes longer and the rainfall scarcer, the savanna has more grass and fewer trees.

The savanna soils are good at storing the wet season rains, despite the great heat of the dry season. Note how the plants cover at least half of the ground surface.

A

Savanna vegetation with grazing animals

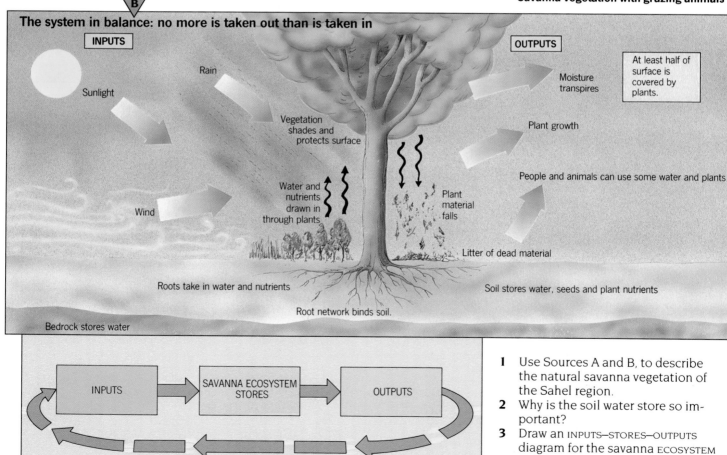

B

The system in balance: no more is taken out than is taken in

INPUTS

OUTPUTS

At least half of surface is covered by plants.

Sunlight

Rain

Moisture transpires

Plant growth

Vegetation shades and protects surface

Water and nutrients drawn in through plants

Plant material falls

People and animals can use some water and plants

Wind

Litter of dead material

Roots take in water and nutrients

Soil stores water, seeds and plant nutrients

Root network binds soil.

Bedrock stores water

INPUTS → SAVANNA ECOSYSTEM STORES → OUTPUTS

1 Use Sources A and B, to describe the natural savanna vegetation of the Sahel region.
2 Why is the soil water store so important?
3 Draw an INPUTS–STORES–OUTPUTS diagram for the savanna ECOSYSTEM in balance, using Source B. Use the sources on pages 88–91 to help add details about the savanna CLIMATE.

Do people cause desertification?

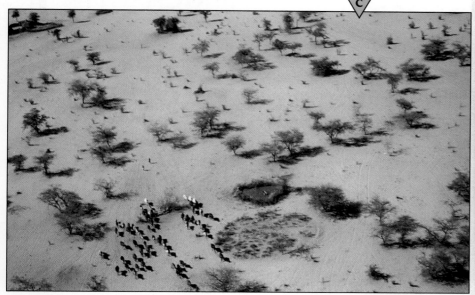

Desertified savanna

Read Source D.
4 Why did the shifting cultivators have to return more often to farm the same plot of land?
5 Describe the vegetation changes which occurred. (Use Sources A and C to help you.)
6 List the reasons for the vegetation changes.
7 What happened to the soil?

The natural system breaks down
Follow the arrows through the flow chart (Source E) and you will begin to understand what is happening.

Without massive aid from richer countries, people and animals die. This means fewer people and animals, but, even then, the savanna grassland may never return.

Creeping desert in the Yatenga region

In the past there was enough land near to Jean-Marie Sawadogo's home for the shifting cultivators to rest the soil for at least ten years. The vegetation grew back, the soil fertility and water store built up. But as the population increased, the farmers were forced back on to the same plots of land more often. With less rest, the soil became less fertile. It held less water and there was less vegetation. More people meant more cattle and sheep. They ate off all the grass leaving wider and wider bare patches. Goats chewed the young trees before they could mature.

Once the surface was bare, wind and rain could carry away more soil. Smaller soil particles wedged themselves between larger particles and the surface dried out to form an IMPERMEABLE crust. Even in wet years less water seeped into the soil.

Grasses died first, then a year or two later, the bushes withered and died. Trees with their deeper roots hung on till the last, but finally they died as the water table dropped, the soil store was no longer refilled by the rains each year. The trees dead branches were stripped and used for fuel (See page 86). As trees became fewer in number even their roots were torn out. What was once savanna woodland is now a bare crust: a desertified land, useless to people or animals.

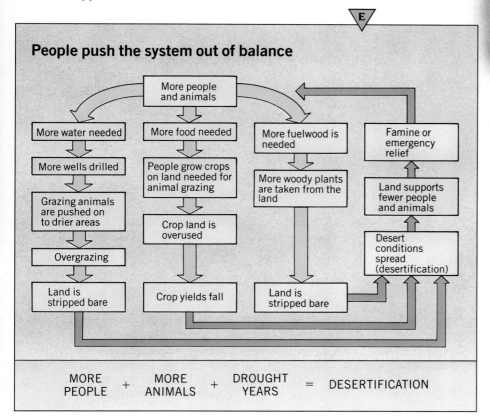

People push the system out of balance

MORE PEOPLE + MORE ANIMALS + DROUGHT YEARS = DESERTIFICATION

8 Look again at the photograph on page 81. Use Source E to explain what is happening.
9 After several dry weeks, a storm releases 40 mm of rain in two hours on two types of surface:
    ● a natural savanna where 65% of the ground surface is covered by plants.
    ● a desertified area where only 25% of the surface is covered by plants.
    a) Describe what will happen in each area as the rain falls.
    b) List the main differences between the effects of the rain on each surface.
    c) Give reasons for the differences in (a) and (b).
10 What could happen in the future years in the Yatenga region?

Burkina Faso: the search for wood

In Source A Henriette (Jean-Marie's wife) and other Kalsaka women are gathering firewood. They are in a valley away from the village. As more and more trees are cut, the women must travel further from the village.

On this day they had set out at 7.50 a.m. and returned home at 11.30 a.m., with 23 kg packs of wood on their heads. The women do this trip three times every week. Their day had only just begun. They had water to fetch and the crops to tend. This was essential work; wood is the only fuel they have for cooking, heating, and light at night. The Kalsaka women are not alone – nine out of ten Africans use wood as their main source of fuel.

1 Describe the vegetation shown in Source A.
2 Why is firewood so important?
3 Why must the women walk so far from the village to find firewood?

Gathering firewood: Henriette says wood is 'more precious than gold'

Vendor taking wood for sale at a market, Senegal

The fuelwood crisis in Africa

N

Tropic of Cancer
20°N

10°N

Equator

10°S

20°S

Tropic of Capricorn

Firewood shortage or future shortage likely

0   1000 km

Countries with a firewood shortage

4 Use an atlas and Source B:
   a) Name the countries which have a wood shortage.
   b) Where in Africa are most of these countries found? (Use the lines of latitude to help you.)
   c) Why do you think there is not a firewood crisis in most of the countries near the Equator, or in the area north of the Tropic of Cancer?

Firewood for the cities
Source C shows a wood merchant heading for market in Senegal. Poor families in cities may pay up to 30% of their incomes on firewood.

5 The Kalsaka women can collect firewood from the surrounding countryside.
   a) How do city dwellers obtain their firewood? (Source C.)
   b) What is likely to happen in the future as supplies become scarcer and there are more people?

6 Group discussion:
   a) What are the reasons for the increasing firewood crisis?
   b) How does the demand for firewood affect desertification?

What happens when the wood is all burnt?

Source D shows a traditional farming SYSTEM in the Sahel, for a typical village like Kalsaka.

7 **a)** Describe the system in balance.
   b) How is the soil FERTILITY maintained?
8 **a)** What are the sources of fuel once the trees have gone?
   b) What effect does using these new sources have on the soil and the nutrient CYCLE?
9 **a)** How do decreasing wood supplies affect the people's health?
   b) Suggest what could happen to the quality of the crops and cattle in the future.

Plans to solve the crisis

Scientists estimate that tree planting in the Sahel is 50 times slower than is needed to replace the wood being used. Various ways have been tried to solve this firewood crisis. The solutions fall into three main groups:
- Increase the supply, e.g. by more government tree-planting schemes.
- Make better use of what wood there is, e.g. by encouraging village women to use more efficient cooking stoves.
- Reduce the demand for wood by using other materials, e.g. oil-burning stoves.

Many of these schemes have failed – sometimes because they did not involve the local people in running the project; sometimes because the project ignored traditional ways of life; sometimes because methods were too expensive.

10 In a small group, discuss the advantages and disadvantages of each of the three alternative ways of solving the firewood crisis.

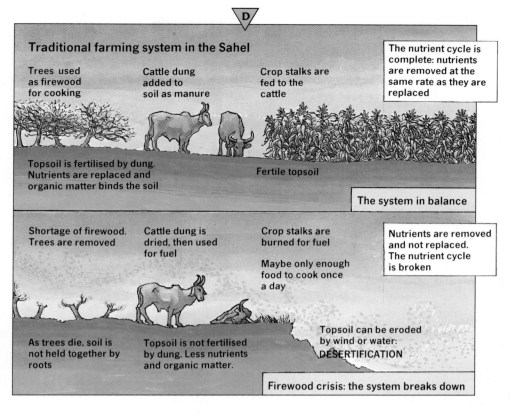

D

Traditional farming system in the Sahel

Trees used as firewood for cooking | Cattle dung added to soil as manure | Crop stalks are fed to the cattle

The nutrient cycle is complete: nutrients are removed at the same rate as they are replaced

Topsoil is fertilised by dung. Nutrients are replaced and organic matter binds the soil | Fertile topsoil

The system in balance

Shortage of firewood. Trees are removed | Cattle dung is dried, then used for fuel | Crop stalks are burned for fuel

Maybe only enough food to cook once a day

Nutrients are removed and not replaced. The nutrient cycle is broken

As trees die, soil is not held together by roots | Topsoil is not fertilised by dung. Less nutrients and organic matter. | Topsoil can be eroded by wind or water: DESERTIFICATION

Firewood crisis: the system breaks down

The Majjia Project

E

The Majjia Valley in Niger was once wooded, but had become densely populated farmland surrounded by bare slopes stripped of vegetation. Winds blow at up to 60 km/h, removing topsoil at the rate of 20 tonnes per hectare per year. In the rainy season, the wind slowed the rate of plant growth and buried seedlings under sand that was blown in.

The project began with the setting up of a tree nursery. In 1975, the young trees were planted in long double rows, each tree four metres apart and 100 m between the rows.

Local farmers planted and cared for the trees. It was important to keep animals away until the trees were strong. The windbreaks have resulted in an increase in crop yields of 20%, less topsoil is blown away, and sand is not blown across the fields.

Village women were able to start cutting the wood for fuel in 1984. With proper management of the cutting, the trees have regrown rapidly to give future supplies. Crop stalks are again used as animal fodder, and cattle dung is applied to the soil.

F

New trees provide windbreaks to reduce soil erosion in the Majjia Valley, Niger

The Majjia Valley Project, Niger
However, there are some success stories, such as the Majjia Valley Project (Sources E and F). The main aim of the project, funded by the charity CARE, is to stop desertification, but the extra firewood produced is a bonus. People from 30 villages in the valley have been working together to plant 300 km of windbreaks in the valley.

11 Use Sources E and F to draw an annotated diagram of the Majjia Project. An annotated diagram has notes showing the important points. Draw your diagram in a similar way to Source D and add details of the following:

a) the windbreaks and their effects,
b) the role of the local people,
c) the nutrient cycle within the environment.
12 **a)** Explain why crop yields have risen by 20%.
   b) What will be the advantages for the village women of having trees nearby for firewood?

7.4 THE SAHEL: PATTERN OF RAINFALL

Rainfall features of the Sahel

Source A shows a satellite photograph taken in September 1983. There is a lot of cloud in the south of the photograph near to the Equator, but only isolated thunder clouds over the Sahel. On these pages we will try to understand the causes of this, and the pattern of rainfall in the Sahel.

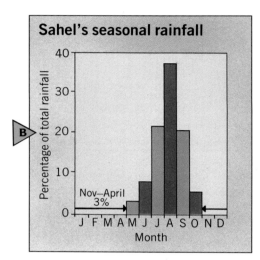

Sahel's seasonal rainfall

Nov–April 3%

A

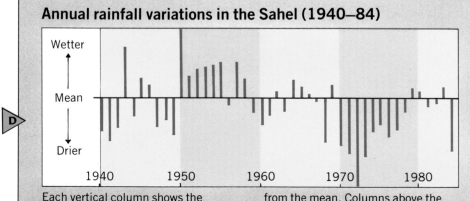

Satellite photograph of cloud over north Africa, 25 September 198.

Climate and rainfall data for Niamey, Niger 13°N, altitude 216 metres

Month:	J	F	M	A	M	J	J	A	S	O	N	D	Year
Average rainfall (mm)	0	0	5	8	33	81	132	188	94	13	0	0	554
Number of rainy days	0	0	1	1	4	6	9	12	7	1	0	0	41
Average daily maximum temperature (°C)	34	37	41	42	41	38	34	32	34	38	38	34	

C

1 For the Sahel (Source B):
   a) Which is the wettest month?
   b) How long is the wet season?
   c) How long is the dry season?
2 Draw a climate graph for Niamey Niger from the data in Source C.
3 A large part of the rainfall in Niamey is lost by evaporation. Use Source C to suggest why.

Does climate cause desertification?

Scientists agree that series of dry years do occur. By 'dry' they mean years when rainfall is well below average. We call such dry spells DROUGHTS. In the semi-arid Sahel, even small variations in rainfall can affect how the ENVIRONMENTAL SYSTEM works.

The Sahel ecosystems have adapted to survive one or even two years of drought. In any ten-year period, three or four years are likely to be 'dry'. It is when these dry years come together that the water stores in the system (in the plants, the soil, and the rocks beneath) become empty. Then, the system begins to break down through lack of water. Source D shows how variable rainfall in the Sahel can be.

4 For each decade from 1940, count how many years have received:
   a) above-average rainfall,
   b) below-average rainfall,
   c) which have been the wettest and driest decades?
5 Jean-Marie says that there was more rain when he was young in the 1950s. Is he right?
6 Make a list of sets of three or more successive dry years, e.g. 1940–2.
7 How do the figures suggest that climate may have helped the spread of desertification since the 1960s?

Annual rainfall variations in the Sahel (1940–84)

Wetter

Mean

Drier

1940   1950   1960   1970   1980

D

Each vertical column shows the variation from the mean (average) rainfall in a particular year. The longer a column is, the greater the difference from the mean. Columns above the 'mean' line show 'wet' years; columns below the 'mean' line show 'dry' years.

Rainfall in Niger

Jean-Marie's cousin, Payiba, farms further north in the Sahel near to Niamey, the capital of Niger. Payiba has been told that the average rainfall in his district is 554 mm a year. What are his chances of receiving this much? The very minimum he needs for crop cultivation is 230 mm, and unless at least 400 mm falls, his crop yields will be very poor. Look at the bucket (Source E) to find out what life is like for Payiba.

Work in pairs:

8 a) How often is Payiba likely to suffer crop failure or poor yields?
b) Why is it not very useful for Payiba to be told the 'average' annual rainfall?

What are the chances?

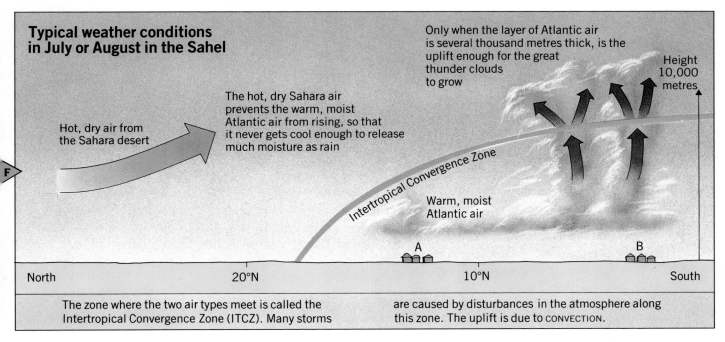

E

RAINFALL

A farmer can expect:

1150mm, 1 year in 10

700 mm, 3 years in 10

Average annual rainfall — 550 mm, 4 years in 10

400 mm, 6 years in 10

230 mm, the minimum for crops to survive

200 mm, 8 years in 10
At least 100 mm every year

c) What would be the most useful information about the rainfall for Payiba to know?
d) It is often said that in the semi-arid tropics, average rainfall figures are kept as high as they are by a few very wet years surrounded by a larger number of dry years. Do these figures for Niamey support this statement?

Typical weather conditions in July or August in the Sahel

Hot, dry air from the Sahara desert

The hot, dry Sahara air prevents the warm, moist Atlantic air from rising, so that it never gets cool enough to release much moisture as rain

Only when the layer of Atlantic air is several thousand metres thick, is the uplift enough for the great thunder clouds to grow

Height 10,000 metres

Intertropical Convergence Zone

Warm, moist Atlantic air

North   20°N   A   10°N   B   South

F

The zone where the two air types meet is called the Intertropical Convergence Zone (ITCZ). Many storms are caused by disturbances in the atmosphere along this zone. The uplift is due to CONVECTION.

Why does rainfall vary?

Remember that Jean-Marie said (page 82): 'Sometimes we see it rain behind the mountains, but it doesn't rain here.' Can we explain why this happens? In Source F, Jean-Marie's village, Kalsaka, is shown at A, and is suffering drought. The air is moist but no rain falls. Further to the south, village B is enjoying rainstorms. Why?

For rain to fall, two things must happen: first there must be a lot of moisture stored in the atmosphere; second, something must cause this moisture to be released from the store.

For seven months of the year the Sahel is covered by hot, dry air moving southwards from the Sahara Desert (the north-east Trade Winds). Only from May to September does warm, moist air from the Atlantic push northwards across the Sahel (the south-east Trade Winds), swinging to become south-west as they cross Africa.

We do not know exactly why, but in some years this moist air does not push so far north and does not stay so long. These are the 'dry' years. Source F shows why even when the moist air does arrive, rain may not fall. The mass of moist air must be thick enough for tall thunder clouds to develop, and for the heavy rains to fall.

Study Source F.
9 What is stopping thunder clouds growing over Kalsaka (village A)?
10 Why is it raining over village B?
11 In September, the ITCZ moves southwards past village B. What is the weather in October likely to be in both villages?
12 How does Source F help to explain:
a) the cloud pattern in Source A?
b) the rainfall pattern of the Sahel shown in Sources B and C?

7.5 SUDAN: TOO LITTLE, TOO MUCH

Drought and floods

Sudan's 23 million people are among the poorest in the world. The capital, Khartoum (population 3.5 million) is situated where the Blue and White Niles meet.

In June 1988, Sudan appealed to the United Nations for help in dealing with several years of drought. Then on 4 August, it started raining heavily. More than 200 mm of rain fell without a break in the next 13 hours. Over the next few days further rain brought the total to 320 mm. Most of the houses in Khartoum are made of mud brick, which the flood waters easily demolished (Source A). Up to 10,000 homes have been destroyed. Everything was awash for 48 hours.

Use Source B to answer the following:
1. Which is normally the wettest month in Khartoum?
2. Compare the downpour in August 1988 with:
   a) the average monthly rainfall for August,
   b) the mean annual rainfall for Khartoum.

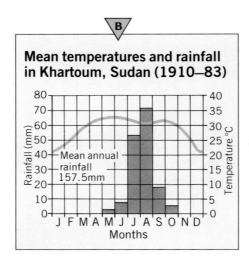

Mean temperatures and rainfall in Khartoum, Sudan (1910–83)

Mean annual rainfall 157.5mm

Months

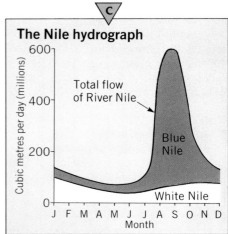

The Nile hydrograph

Total flow of River Nile

Blue Nile

White Nile

Month

3. Why were so many homes damaged by the floods which followed the rain?
4. Study the River Nile HYDROGRAPH (Source C). It shows the amount of water from the Blue and White Niles where they meet at Khartoum.
   a) Which river contributes the most DISCHARGE to the total flow?
   b) ● When does the level of the River Nile start to rise rapidly?
   ● When is the river's maximum discharge?

c) How does the Nile hydrograph help to explain why the river flooded so quickly at Khartoum during August 1988?
5. **a)** What is the probability (or chance) of drought in Khartoum? (Source D.)
   b) How does Khartoum compare with the rest of Sudan in terms of the probability of drought?
6. Why was it likely that the people of Khartoum would be short of water again by October 1988?

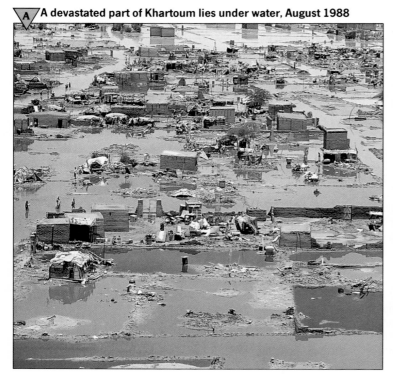

A A devastated part of Khartoum lies under water, August 1988

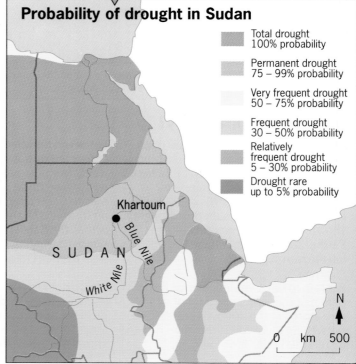

Probability of drought in Sudan

Total drought 100% probability

Permanent drought 75 – 99% probability

Very frequent drought 50 – 75% probability

Frequent drought 30 – 50% probability

Relatively frequent drought 5 – 30% probability

Drought rare up to 5% probability

Khartoum

SUDAN

Blue Nile

White Nile

N

0 km 500

Variation in rainfall

The four settlements in Central Sudan (Source E) all lie about the same latitude in the dry savanna region. All have mean annual rainfall totals between 390 and 450 mm. Most rain falls between July and September. These four settlements all seem to have similar rainfall features. But do they?

Rainfall is just enough to grow crops, particularly millet, around oases and wells. Also, there are many groups of nomadic herders, with cattle, sheep, goats and camels. This means that there is much pressure on the land, so *any* variation in rainfall can be very serious.

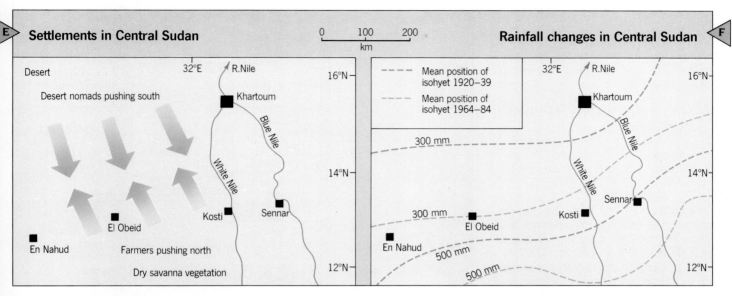

E Settlements in Central Sudan

F Rainfall changes in Central Sudan

0   100   200
km

Desert
Desert nomads pushing south
32°E R.Nile
16°N
Khartoum
Blue Nile
White Nile
14°N
Kosti
Sennar
El Obeid
En Nahud Farmers pushing north
Dry savanna vegetation
12°N

- - - Mean position of isohyet 1920–39
- - - Mean position of isohyet 1964–84

32°E R.Nile
16°N
Khartoum
Blue Nile
White Nile
14°N
Sennar
Kosti
300 mm
300 mm
El Obeid
En Nahud
500 mm
500 mm
12°N

7 Why do the movements of nomads and cultivators shown in Source E make desertification more likely in Central Sudan?

8 How far from each other are the four settlements (Source E)?

9 **a)** What has happened to the position of the 300 mm and 500 mm isohyets (contour lines of equal rainfall) between 1920–39 and 1964–84? (Source F.)
   b) What does this tell us about rainfall trends of the settlements?

c) How will the rainfall changes add to desertification problems in Central Sudan?

10 **a)** What is the mean annual rainfall for each settlement in Source G?
   b) For each settlement, give the year when the rainfall totals are:
   ● the furthest above the mean,
   ● the furthest below the mean.
   c) What do your answers show about the occurrence of rainfall in Central Sudan? For example, are the wettest and driest years the

same for all four settlements?

11 Will desertification problems vary from year to year? Explain your answers.

12 In small groups, discuss the following:
   a) How will the variability of rain (both in time and place) make planning and decision-making about the environment and settlements difficult and risky in the Sudan?
   b) Do people, climate (or both) cause desertification?

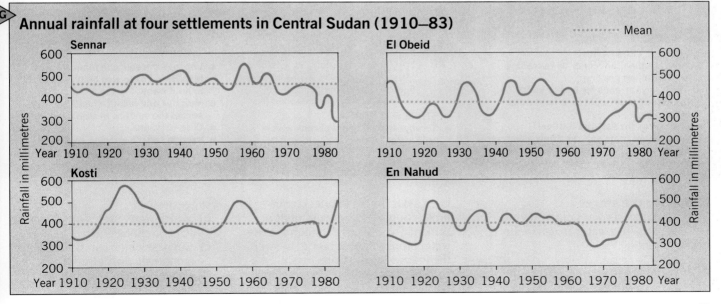

G Annual rainfall at four settlements in Central Sudan (1910–83)

· · · · · · · · Mean

Sennar

Kosti

El Obeid

En Nahud

Rainfall in millimetres

Water stores

We have learned that increasing numbers of people and animals are one cause of desertification (Source E, pages 84–5). We know, too, that climate is important (pages 88–9). The flow chart (Source A) shows the effects of a series of dry years.

1 What is the first effect of less water being stored?
2 Why does this cause greater soil EROSION?
3 Give two examples of FEEDBACK at work.

One of the main results of the changes shown in Source A is that the size of some of the water stores has changed (e.g. there is now less vegetation, less soil). In a region where water is so precious, it is vital that every drop is saved and used. A key problem is to build up the water stores once more.

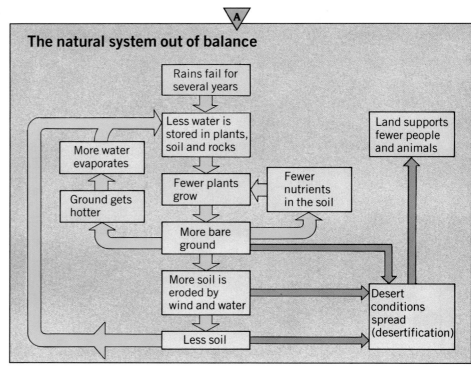

A

The natural system out of balance

Rains fail for several years → Less water is stored in plants, soil and rocks → Fewer plants grow → More bare ground → More soil is eroded by wind and water → Less soil

More water evaporates
Ground gets hotter
Fewer nutrients in the soil
Land supports fewer people and animals
Desert conditions spread (desertification)

B

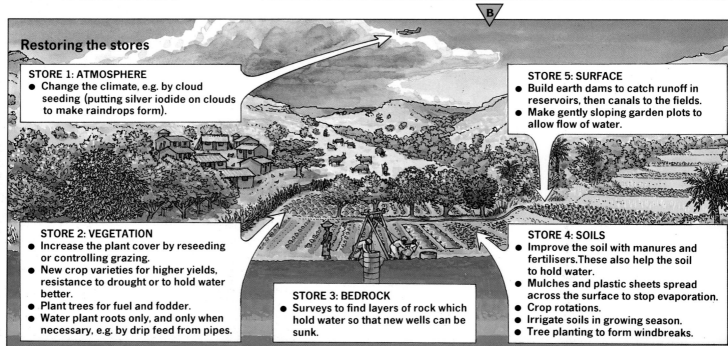

Restoring the stores

STORE 1: ATMOSPHERE
● Change the climate, e.g. by cloud seeding (putting silver iodide on clouds to make raindrops form).

STORE 5: SURFACE
● Build earth dams to catch runoff in reservoirs, then canals to the fields.
● Make gently sloping garden plots to allow flow of water.

STORE 2: VEGETATION
● Increase the plant cover by reseeding or controlling grazing.
● New crop varieties for higher yields, resistance to drought or to hold water better.
● Plant trees for fuel and fodder.
● Water plant roots only, and only when necessary, e.g. by drip feed from pipes.

STORE 3: BEDROCK
● Surveys to find layers of rock which hold water so that new wells can be sunk.

STORE 4: SOILS
● Improve the soil with manures and fertilisers.These also help the soil to hold water.
● Mulches and plastic sheets spread across the surface to stop evaporation.
● Crop rotations.
● Irrigate soils in growing season.
● Tree planting to form windbreaks.

Restoring the stores

Source B suggests ways of improving the use of the five water stores in the environment.

Work in pairs.
4 You are water engineers who have been asked to make brief recommendations to the government of Burkina Faso on how to improve the water stores. In your report, answer the following questions:
a) Which water stores can be most easily changed by the solutions suggested?
b) Which water stores are the most difficult to change? Why?
c) Suggest which solutions would be most realistic for Burkina Faso, which has little money and few resources.

The soil store

One problem is that the precious rain usually falls in sudden, heavy storms. So, much of the water runs away and is wasted. The problem is how to reduce this wastage and allow more water to seep into the soil store, where plants and farmers can use it.

Finding the answer

The villagers saw the soil being carried away and the land dying. They realised something had to be done. An old traditional trick was to clear stones from their fields and pile them around the boundaries. They had noticed that the stones slowed down the water running off the land. But it built up at low spots and gushed through, carving gullies through the fields below.

The problem in Yatenga was first tackled in 1979. Oxfam thought the answer to erosion was trees, planted inside semicircles of stones which would focus water onto the roots. But people complained they hadn't enough water to drink for themselves in the dry season. They made it plain that growing food was their top priority. So Oxfam worked with farmers to save the soil and also increase food output. They found that by building the stone lines more solidly and along the contours of the land, they dammed the rainfall back 4–8 metres. This gave it time to soak in, even where the soil had sealed itself with a crust.

C

Women carrying stones from their fields

E

Stage 1

On the flat land near Kalsaka, farmers from neighbouring villages gather for a lesson in line making. 60 year old Salam Sawadogo who has lost 4 of his 7 hectares to erosion, volunteers to play the part of a farmer returned from abroad to find his land barren. The soil is soaked with a watering can to represent the first rains of the year. Salam hoes up the surface. The soil beneath is bone dry. The water has overflowed round the stone walls instead of soaking into the soil. Salam cannot sow his seed.

Learning the lesson

F

Stage 2

A local Oxfam trainer Robert Sawadogo shows Salam how to make the new lines, with rising 'wings' at each end so the water will not overflow. It 'rains' again. But this time the water stays in place, and soaks slowly into the soil. The soil is wet where Salam hoes and he can sow his crops. Salam vowed to start building lines on his fields the very next day.

The 'magic stones' trick

Jean-Marie and his villagers have tried several ways, as Source D shows.

5 What was the farmers' traditional method and why did it fail?

6 Why did the villagers dislike the first Oxfam method?

7 Describe what the women in Source C are doing.

8 How does the present scheme work to improve the amount of water stored in the soil? (Draw a labelled sketch to help you.)

9 Use Source E to describe what happened when they first built the lines of stones.

10 Why did the scheme work better when they modified the lines as in Source F?

11 The scheme aims to use every drop of rain to increase the water store in the soil. Draw a flow chart similar to Source A, to show how this will have benefits throughout the system. Start with a box labelled 'Rain falls'.

A

Key to the satellite image colours:

Brown: Timbuktu and other settlements

Blue: Floodplain and water surfaces of the River Niger

Light green colours: Sand and sand dunes

Dark green: Vegetation (savanna)

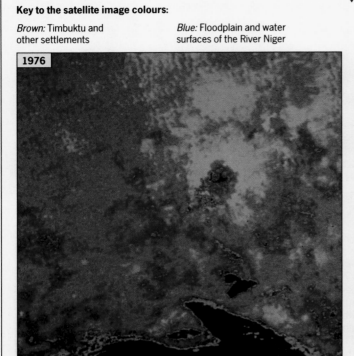

1976

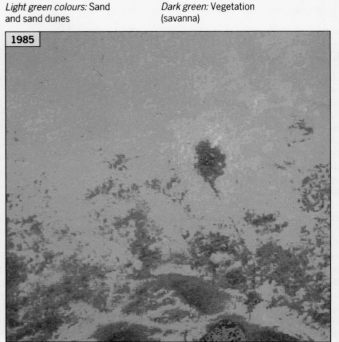

1985

In this Unit so far we have seen that both people *and* climatic factors can help to cause desertification – the explanation is not simple or the same for all areas. Source A shows two satellite images of the area around Timbuktu, Mali taken in February 1976 and 1985. This area is in the northern part of the Sahel on the fringe of the Sahara Desert, where the climate is semi-arid. The satellite images show how a series of drought years can cause desertification.

1 **a)** Study Source B. What is the soil type around Timbuktu?
   b) What does this tell you about the climate here?
2 Look closely at the two satellite images. Place a piece of tracing paper over the 1976 image. Draw the frame and then draw a line marking the junction between desert and non-desert. Now place the tracing over the 1985 image and attempt to draw the boundary. (You may find that a single continuous line is not possible.)
3 **a)** In the area that changed between 1976 and 1985, was the change total (i.e. in a solid zone), or a series of blocks or patches?
   b) Why do you think this was the case?
   c) Which soil type has changed the most? Suggest why.
4 In 1976, stream channels and lakes were found between Timbuktu and the River Niger. What has happened to them in the 1985 image?
5 Lakes and rivers tell us that the water table is at or above the land's surface. What has happened to the water table at Timbuktu between 1976 and 1985?
6 What is the evidence that there has been a series of drought years in this area?
7 What might happen if the rains came back?
8 In contrast to Burkina Faso, the area around Timbuktu is not cultivated. Suggest reasons why all these changes have taken place in spite of this.

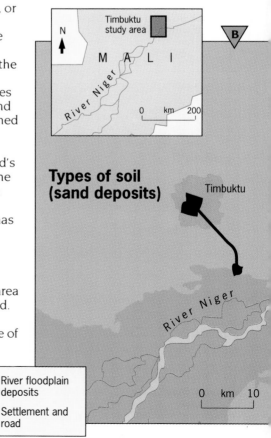

B

Timbuktu study area

MALI

River Niger

0 km 200

Types of soil (sand deposits)

Timbuktu

River Niger

| | Wind deposits, mobile in 1976 | | River floodplain deposits |
| | Wind deposits, stable in 1976 | | Settlement and road |

0 km 10

ENVIRONMENTS UNDER THREAT

UPLANDS AND WETLANDS

**The Scottish flow country: Badanloch Bog,
with Ben Griammor in the background**

8.1 BRITAIN'S LAST WILDERNESS

The Scottish flow country

Look at the environment in the photograph on page 95. It is wet, boggy, exposed and difficult to walk across. However, scientists regard this as 'One of Britain's most prized natural assets'. Wealthy celebrities looking for profitable investments are involved in a battle about it. Read on to find out why.

New Scientist, 8 January 1987

The 'flow country' of Caithness and Sutherland is in the northern Highlands of Scotland. These open, treeless moorlands stretch across 400,000 hectares. They are the largest single area of BLANKET PEAT left in the northern hemisphere.

In the whole world there are only about 10 million hectares of blanket peat ECOSYSTEMS. The Scottish flow country is such a rare environment that in 1986 a team of international scientists rated it as 'one of the world's outstanding ecosystems, equivalent to the Serengeti savannas of Africa or the Brazilian rainforest'. Yet, since 1980, more than 50 hectares a week have been lost to AFFORESTATION schemes.

A

0 10km

Tongue
Thurso
Wick
N
•Kinbrace

Peatland
Protected land
Forestry land

▲ **Forestry land is increasing faster than nature reserves and other protected sites in Scotland's blanket bogs.**

1 Cut a piece of tracing paper slightly bigger than the map, Source A. On it draw a grid of 5-kilometre squares. (Note the scale of the map.) Use this grid to work out *approximately* the area of:
   a) peatland;
   b) forest;
   c) protected land.

2 At present, 2600 hectares are lost to tree-planting each year. If this goes on, how much peatland will be left in 10 years?

3 Peat ecosystems contain an extra store in the decomposition cycle: the peat store. Draw a diagram like Source B, but add the peat store in the correct place.

What is peat?

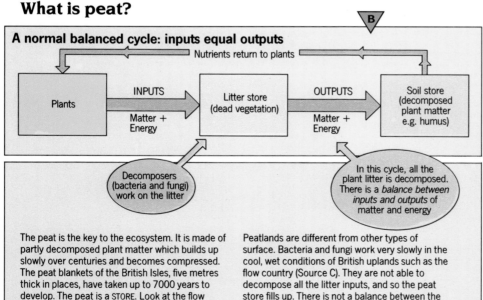

B

A normal balanced cycle: inputs equal outputs

Nutrients return to plants

Plants → INPUTS (Matter + Energy) → Litter store (dead vegetation) → OUTPUTS (Matter + Energy) → Soil store (decomposed plant matter e.g. humus)

Decomposers (bacteria and fungi) work on the litter

In this cycle, all the plant litter is decomposed. There is a *balance between inputs and outputs* of matter and energy

The peat is the key to the ecosystem. It is made of partly decomposed plant matter which builds up slowly over centuries and becomes compressed. The peat blankets of the British Isles, five metres thick in places, have taken up to 7000 years to develop. The peat is a STORE. Look at the flow diagram to see how the decomposition CYCLE works for most ecosystems. (Refer back to pages 6–7 for more information on this.)

Peatlands are different from other types of surface. Bacteria and fungi work very slowly in the cool, wet conditions of British uplands such as the flow country (Source C). They are not able to decompose all the litter inputs, and so the peat store fills up. There is not a balance between the INPUTS and OUTPUTS of matter in this ecosystem

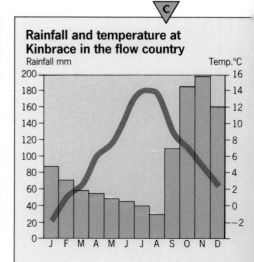

C

Rainfall and temperature at Kinbrace in the flow country

Rainfall mm   Temp.°C

J F M A M J J A S O N D

A very special ecosystem

The severe environmental conditions mean that there are not many species of plants, birds and animals in the flow country. Those which do well have had to adapt – they have become very *specialised* and very *sensitive to change*. They rely on high water levels and waterlogged conditions all year round, especially the sphagnum mosses.

Study Source D and answer these questions.

4 Why is peat short of the MINERAL NUTRIENTS needed by plants?

5 **a)** Which plants have adapted especially well to overcome this problem?
b) Where do they get their nutrients from?

6 **a)** Describe the main features of the blanket peat ecosystem.
b) Why is it so sensitive to change?

7 Foresters and farmers try to improve the drainage and lower the WATER TABLE. If they succeed, what is likely to happen to the blanket peat ecosystem?

8 Study Source E. In March 1988 the Chancellor, Nigel Lawson, took away the tax relief which people planting trees had previously been allowed. However, they are still given grants and free advice. In groups, discuss whether you think the government have done enough to conserve the flow country.

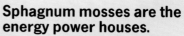

Sphagnum mosses are the energy power houses.
The compact peat blanket lets few mineral nutrients pass up from the soil below. So, the sphagnum mosses (left) have become good at drawing the nutrients they need from the rain water. They give much of the litter supply to the peat.

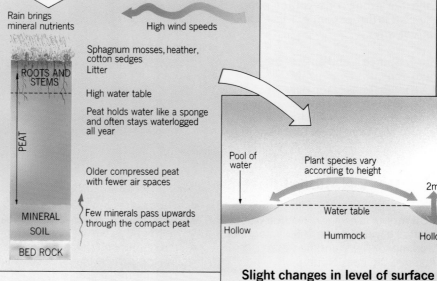

Rain brings mineral nutrients

High wind speeds

ROOTS AND STEMS

PEAT

Sphagnum mosses, heather, cotton sedges
Litter

High water table

Peat holds water like a sponge and often stays waterlogged all year

Older compressed peat with fewer air spaces

MINERAL SOIL

Few minerals pass upwards through the compact peat

BED ROCK

Pool of water

Plant species vary according to height

2m

Water table

Hollow

Hummock

Hollow

Slight changes in level of surface and water mean different species

Each plant species thrives in very special conditions, e.g. there are several species of sphagnum moss – some like it wet and some like it very wet.

Whose side are you on?

Conservationists argue that:
• This is a *rare* environment, with a worldwide reputation.
• It is so *sensitive* that any changes will damage it: sphagnum mosses especially must have high water levels.
• The HABITAT is home for *rare birds* such as the merlin, hen harrier, arctic skua, golden plover.
• The 'flow country' is *too wet* and exposed to grow trees profitably.
• It is the last place in Britain where people can experience the true *wilderness*.
• The PLANTATIONS are huge blocks of *single species* – foreign species such as Sitka spruce.
• More money and jobs would come to the Scottish people from a policy which *balances conservation and tourism* than from forestry.

A tree plantation across the flow country

Some landowners argue that:
• They get little income from the land, but would profit from softwood plantations.
• They can plant land themselves or sell at a profit to private forestry companies.
• Individuals and private companies are encouraged to plant trees, by the Government e.g. they are given £250 per hectare and free advice on planting and management.
• The plantations bring money and jobs into a high unemployment area.
• If Britain is able to produce more timber, we will need to import less and our balance of payments will be better.

8.2 WHAT IS HAPPENING TO OUR UPLANDS?

Peat moorlands used to cover large areas of upland in England and Wales, as well as in Scotland. The peat is not only under threat from afforestation. For more than 150 years people have been destroying the peatlands. What little remains is mostly found in Britain's NATIONAL PARKS. Even here, where there are strong conservation policies, the peat is disappearing. These pages look at why.

Study Source A and answer these questions.

1 **a)** What has taken over most of the peatland?
   b) Approximately what percentage of the original peatland was left in 1980?

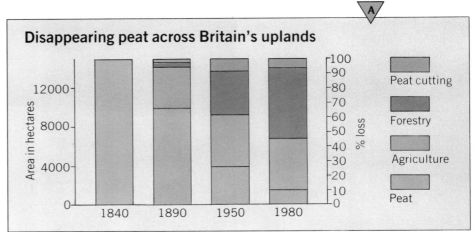

Disappearing peat across Britain's uplands

Legend: Peat cutting, Forestry, Agriculture, Peat

2 Why are conservationists so concerned? (Refer back to pages 96–7 to help you answer.)

The Peak National Park

A major threat to the remaining upland peat moors is EROSION. Source C shows what is happening. In 1980, scientists working for the Planning Board (who manage the Peak National Park) reported:

- There were 3,250 hectares of moorland stripped of vegetation, exposing bare peat and soil.

- This bare area was increasing.
- Bare areas showed little sign of new vegetation growing.
- Sheet and gully erosion were lowering the surface by as much as four centimetres a year.

3 Draw a sketch of Source B and label the three layers (see Source C).

What laid the surface bare?

'The critical event in the peat erosion of the past 200 years was the destruction of the sphagnum carpet on top of the peat.' (1980 report to the Peak National Park Planning Board)

4 Use Source C to explain what caused the sensitive sphagnum mosses to die. (Unit 13, pages 164–6, tells you more about acid rain.)

Section through blanket peat. The underlying soil layer contains LEACHED iron.

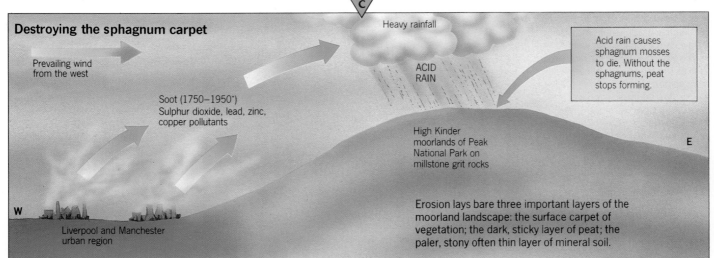

Destroying the sphagnum carpet

Prevailing wind from the west

Soot (1750–1950*) Sulphur dioxide, lead, zinc, copper pollutants

Heavy rainfall

ACID RAIN

Acid rain causes sphagnum mosses to die. Without the sphagnums, peat stops forming.

High Kinder moorlands of Peak National Park on millstone grit rocks

Liverpool and Manchester urban region

Erosion lays bare three important layers of the moorland landscape: the surface carpet of vegetation; the dark, sticky layer of peat; the paler, stony often thin layer of mineral soil.

*The Clean Air Acts of the 1950s stopped the output of soot from the chimneys

Height, slope and the weather

5 **a)** Use the scattergraph (Source D) to name the parishes with the highest and lowest proportions of peat eroded.
b) Are these parishes the highest and lowest in altitude?

6 Which of these statements is nearest to the pattern shown on the graph?
a) The higher the parish, the greater the erosion.
b) As altitude increases, erosion seems to increase, but not in every case.
c) There is little connection between altitude and erosion.

7 **a)** Use the table in Source E to draw a scattergraph that relates percentage of peat eroded to steepness of slope.
b) Write a sentence to sum up the relationship shown on your graph.

8 Sum up the relationships between the three variables you have studied.

D

The relationship between altitude and peat erosion

Scattergraph: % of area over 470m in altitude (y-axis, 0–70) versus % of peat eroded (x-axis, 0–25)

Points plotted: 9, 6, 10, 2, 8, 12, 13, 7, 1, 5, 3, 4, 11

Parish

1	Bradfield	8	Holmfirth
2	Charlesworth	9	Hope Woodlands
3	Colne Valley	10	Langsett
4	Derwent	11	Meltham
5	Dunford	12	Saddleworth
6	Edale	13	Tintwistle
7	Hayfield		

E

Percentage of area which is steeply sloping

Bradfield	11
Charlesworth	17
Colne Valley	20
Derwent	20
Dunford	3
Edale	41
Hayfield	27
Holmfirth	22
Hope Woodlands	23
Langsett	4
Meltham	20
Saddleworth	29
Tintwistle	33

Does climate affect erosion?

The scientists found that rainfall intensity, number of days with frost, number of days with snow cover, and wind strength are the four most important climatic factors. Putting all four together, the climatic impact on plants and peat increases sharply with altitude. Stronger impact leads to more likelihood of erosion.

9 **a)** Use the information in Source F to describe how CLIMATE changes with altitude.
b) Suggest why the high moorlands are most likely to suffer erosion.

Planning for the future

People visiting the moorlands are also causing erosion (pages 106–10 in Unit 9 consider this in more detail). Farmers are grazing more sheep on the moors too. As sheep's feet are so small, they put even more pressure on the ground than humans do!

10 Work with a partner. Imagine you are the scientists who have been asked to report to the Peak National Park Planning Board. Write a report covering the following areas:
● the character of the moorlands – consider relief, vegetation, soils;
● the nature of the problem, and why it is important;
● the causes of erosion;
● suggestions for slowing down the erosion.

F

Climate data for different altitudes in the Peak National Park

● **Annual rainfall**

Altitude (m)	Rainfall (mm)
305	1250
450	1600
600	1800

At 350 m intense storms of more than 25 mm occur at least five times a year. At 605 m there are at least ten such storms.

● **Mean monthly temperature**

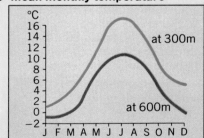

Graph of °C (−2 to 16) by month (J F M A M J J A S O N D), showing curves at 300m and at 600m

● **Wind strength**

The average wind speed is twice as great at 600 m as at 300 m.

● **Growing season**

Buxton (370 m)	220 days
Kinder Moors (610 m)	160 days

● **Dry weather**

Dry weather can cause erosion too. In the hot summers of 1976 and 1984 the heather and peat dried out. Serious fires stripped large areas. Peat itself burns well when dry; it has been used as a fuel in Scotland and Ireland for centuries.

● **Snow cover**

Altitude (m)	200	300	400	500	600
Days a year	25	33	44	59	78

Florida, USA

If you are lucky enough to go to Florida, the three places you are most likely to visit are Disneyworld, the NASA Space Center and the Everglades National Park. These three places provide amazingly different experiences. The one *natural* environment is, of course, the National Park, which is one of the world's great wetland ecosystems. It was set up in 1947 and covers 46,600 sq.km. The area is so precious that it has been named an International BIOSPHERE RESERVE and a World Heritage site. But the Everglades are under threat, and *the whole ecosystem may die from a lack of water*.

To help you understand how the ecosystem could die, use the information on these pages (Sources A–I) to complete these activities:

1 Describe the way the natural SYSTEM works and list the main features of the Everglades ecosystem. You should consider such things as climate, slope, soil, vegetation.
2 Make a list of the main changes caused by humans. Say how these changes affect how the ecosystem works.
3 Less than one-half of the Everglades are protected by the National Park. Why do the National Park Rangers feel that the main threats to the Park ecosystem come from the outside?

A

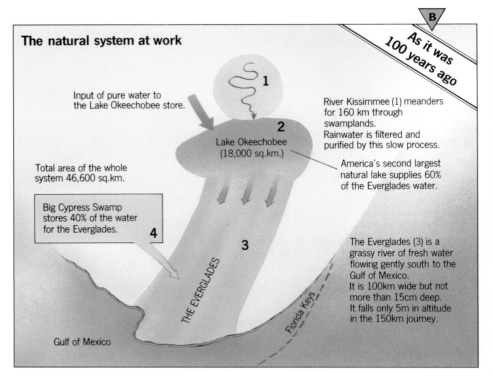

The natural system at work

B *As it was 100 years ago*

Input of pure water to the Lake Okeechobee store.

1

2 Lake Okeechobee (18,000 sq.km.)

Total area of the whole system 46,600 sq.km.

Big Cypress Swamp stores 40% of the water for the Everglades.

4

3

THE EVERGLADES

Florida Keys

Gulf of Mexico

River Kissimmee (1) meanders for 160 km through swamplands. Rainwater is filtered and purified by this slow process.

America's second largest natural lake supplies 60% of the Everglades water.

The Everglades (3) is a grassy river of fresh water flowing gently south to the Gulf of Mexico. It is 100km wide but not more than 15cm deep. It falls only 5m in altitude in the 150km journey.

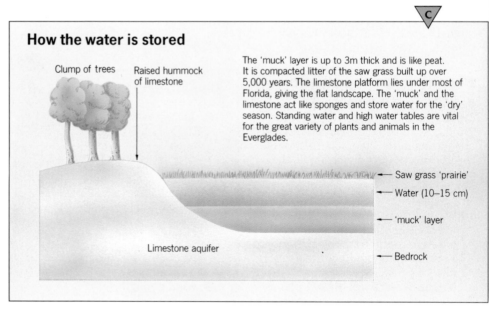

C

How the water is stored

Clump of trees

Raised hummock of limestone

Limestone aquifer

The 'muck' layer is up to 3m thick and is like peat. It is compacted litter of the saw grass built up over 5,000 years. The limestone platform lies under most of Florida, giving the flat landscape. The 'muck' and the limestone act like sponges and store water for the 'dry' season. Standing water and high water tables are vital for the great variety of plants and animals in the Everglades.

← Saw grass 'prairie'
← Water (10–15 cm)
← 'muck' layer
← Bedrock

◄ **The Everglades rely on a constant** *throughflow* **of fresh pure water.**

Climate data for Miami (26°N, 80°W)

D

	J	F	M	A	M	J	J	A	S	O	N	D	Total or average
Rainfall (mm)	55	50	53	91	155	229	176	171	222	208	69	42	1519
Mean temperature (°C)	19	20	22	24	26	27	28	28	28	25	22	20	24
Relative humidity (%)	74	73	70	69	71	72	72	72	75	75	71	74	72

The Everglades today

The same amount of water enters the system, but there are more users to be satisfied.

The National Park Everglades struggle for water

Follow the arrows and notes and you will see how things have changed

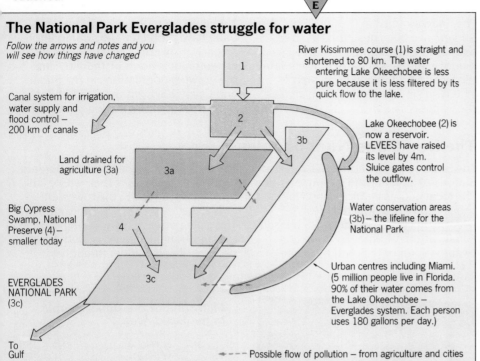

River Kissimmee course (1) is straight and shortened to 80 km. The water entering Lake Okeechobee is less pure because it is less filtered by its quick flow to the lake.

Canal system for irrigation, water supply and flood control – 200 km of canals

Land drained for agriculture (3a)

Big Cypress Swamp, National Preserve (4) – smaller today

EVERGLADES NATIONAL PARK (3c)

To Gulf

Lake Okeechobee (2) is now a reservoir. LEVEES have raised its level by 4m. Sluice gates control the outflow.

Water conservation areas (3b) – the lifeline for the National Park

Urban centres including Miami. (5 million people live in Florida. 90% of their water comes from the Lake Okeechobee – Everglades system. Each person uses 180 gallons per day.)

- - - - Possible flow of pollution – from agriculture and cities

Straightened course of R. Kissimmee and its old winding course

Lake Okeechobee sluice gates and levée

Housing subdivision in Fort Lauderdale, Florida

4 Source J lists the measures that the Florida State Governor proposed in 1983 to preserve the Everglades. Working in pairs, design and make an illustrated leaflet appealing for money for the project. The leaflet should be aimed at the general public and should tell people:
a) Why it is important to preserve the Everglades.
b) How this can be done.
c) Why money is urgently needed.

Draining land for agriculture also affects protected Everglades

Drained agricultural land. Chemicals added

Protected natural Everglades

4 Drying out

3 Water table falls

1 Lower water table needed to grow crops. Surface level falls as the land dries out

2 Water seeps to drained land because water level is lower

The vegetation and the 'muck' of the protected Everglades dry out as the water table falls. This causes problems for the water-loving plants and animals, e.g. alligators. It also increases the fire hazard. Fires have always been important – they burn old vegetation and give ash as plant food. When the surface was wet, the fires were not severe. Today, with the dry surface, the 'muck' burns as well and the great heat destroys everything.

SAVE OUR EVERGLADES

In 1983 the Florida state governor launched a campaign to:
● Buy land and set buffer zones around the edge of the Everglades keeping development farther away.
● Restore the natural water flows.
● Return the River Kissimmee to its natural meandering flow, so that it can do its job of water purification again. (Cost at least $50 million.)
● Rebuild the main east–west highway (called 'Alligator Alley') to improve the north–south water flow and help animal movements ($2.5 million is being spent on passages under the road for the 30 or so remaining Florida panthers).

Sudd swamps in the wet season

The Sudd swamps in the southern Sudan have been described as the world's largest swamps. The word 'Sudd' is Arabic for 'barrier'. The swamp (Sources A and B) covers an area of 11,000 sq.km. This is the same area as the whole of Jamaica.

The Sudd's remoteness and inaccessibility have protected the swamp until recently. However, the increasing need for water for IRRIGATION, industry, and the growing populations in the Sudan and Egypt, have put the Sudd under serious threat from the Jonglei Canal.

The Dinka and Nuer peoples

The Sudd swamp is home to large populations of animals and swamp plants. The local peoples – Dinka and Nuer tribes – have developed a lifestyle which is in close harmony with the seasonal pattern of water levels in the swamp (Sources C, D and E).

The Dinka people are nomadic herders. Cattle are the basis of their whole culture. Crops or jobs in the towns are only to get money to buy more cattle. The Nuer people live by fishing. Now the traditional lifestyles of both these peoples are also under threat.

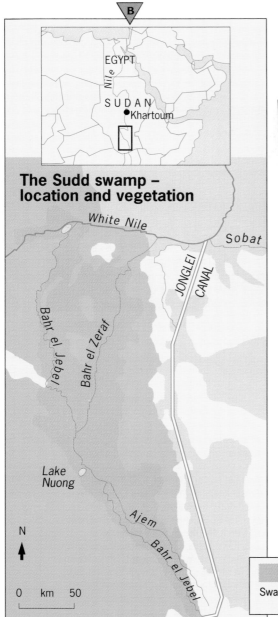

The Sudd swamp – location and vegetation

Swamp | River-flooded grassland | Rain-flooded grassland | Lake

> **A man without cows is a man without a future, for ownership proves membership of a cattle camp, wives, children, personal pride, and personal immortality. To be without them is to be defenceless.**

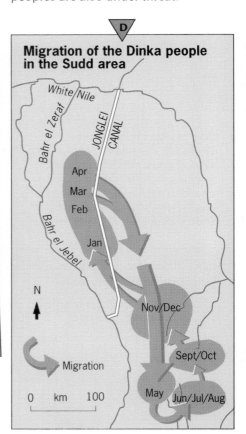

Migration of the Dinka people in the Sudd area

Migration

1. Use Sources A, B and E to describe the natural ecosystem of the Sudd swamps.
2. Explain why the Jonglei Canal is being built.
3. Describe the traditional lifestyle and migration patterns of the Dinka people. Use Sources C, D and E.

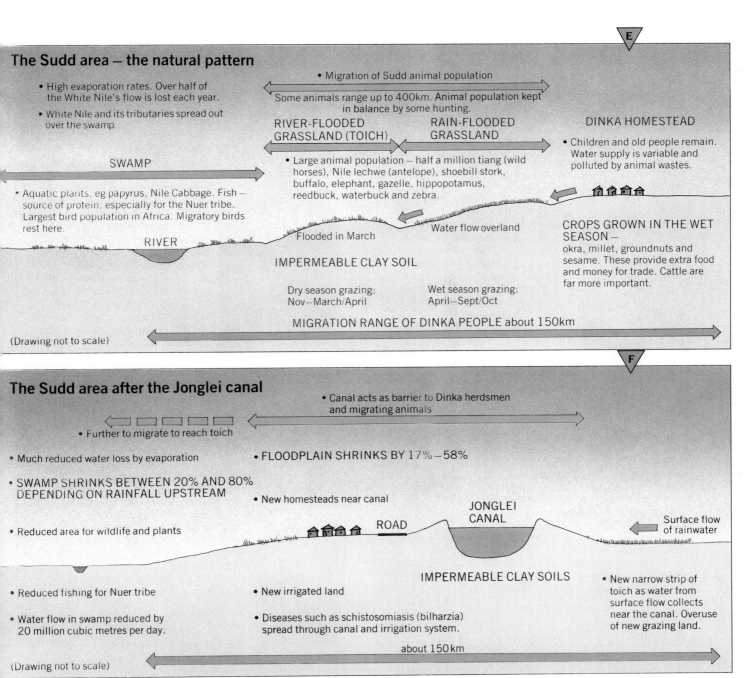

The Sudd area — the natural pattern

E

- Migration of Sudd animal population

Some animals range up to 400km. Animal population kept in balance by some hunting.

- High evaporation rates. Over half of the White Nile's flow is lost each year.
- White Nile and its tributaries spread out over the swamp.

RIVER-FLOODED GRASSLAND (TOICH) RAIN-FLOODED GRASSLAND DINKA HOMESTEAD

SWAMP

- Children and old people remain. Water supply is variable and polluted by animal wastes.

- Large animal population — half a million tiang (wild horses), Nile lechwe (antelope), shoebill stork, buffalo, elephant, gazelle, hippopotamus, reedbuck, waterbuck and zebra.

- Aquatic plants, eg papyrus, Nile Cabbage. Fish — source of protein, especially for the Nuer tribe. Largest bird population in Africa. Migratory birds rest here.

RIVER

Flooded in March   Water flow overland

CROPS GROWN IN THE WET SEASON — okra, millet, groundnuts and sesame. These provide extra food and money for trade. Cattle are far more important.

IMPERMEABLE CLAY SOIL

Dry season grazing: Nov–March/April   Wet season grazing: April–Sept/Oct

MIGRATION RANGE OF DINKA PEOPLE about 150km

(Drawing not to scale)

F

The Sudd area after the Jonglei canal

- Canal acts as barrier to Dinka herdsmen and migrating animals

- Further to migrate to reach toich

- Much reduced water loss by evaporation

- • FLOODPLAIN SHRINKS BY 17%–58%

- SWAMP SHRINKS BETWEEN 20% AND 80% DEPENDING ON RAINFALL UPSTREAM

- New homesteads near canal

JONGLEI CANAL

Surface flow of rainwater

- Reduced area for wildlife and plants

ROAD

IMPERMEABLE CLAY SOILS

- New narrow strip of toich as water from surface flow collects near the canal. Overuse of new grazing land.

- Reduced fishing for Nuer tribe

- New irrigated land

- Water flow in swamp reduced by 20 million cubic metres per day.

- Diseases such as schistosomiasis (bilharzia) spread through canal and irrigation system.

about 150km

(Drawing not to scale)

The Jonglei Canal

G

The White Nile and its tributaries flood and spread out to create the swamps. Large amounts of water are lost by evaporation in the hot, dry climate. The proposed Jonglei Canal aims to divert the water from the Sudd into the north of the Sudan and Egypt. The two governments will share the cost of the scheme and the extra 4.75 billion cubic metres of water gained each year. The canal was started in 1978 but was held up by war and engineering difficulties. The scheme is expected to be completed by the early 1990s.

Excavation work in progress on the Jonglei Canal

4 Describe the changes in the Sudd area after the canal has been completed. Use Sources F and G. Think in terms of the effects on vegetation distribution and animal life.

5 How is the Dinka lifestyle threatened?

6 How is the lifestyle of the Nuer people threatened?

103

THE EFFECTS OF THE JONGLEI CANAL SCHEME

Sudanese government official

The new canal and road will bring many benefits to Sudan as well as the much-needed extra water for us and Egypt.

Communications between the north and south of the country will be improved by the road, and navigation by the canal. Grain and livestock will be traded. Grain will help the people in DROUGHT years. There will be better health and veterinary services.

The new irrigated farmland will bring much-needed jobs and food for the country. The Dinka people will be encouraged to settle and grow crops. This will give them a better life as there will be cleaner water, education and health services.

Dinka herdsman

The canal and road will change our lifestyle completely. The canal cuts across the area where we graze our herds. We will have to cross the canal twice a year if we are to find pasture to survive the dry season.

The grassland areas will be much smaller. The quality of our herds will decline. The road will encourage our young men to move to the cities. The government wants us to settle down and grow crops. That is women's work.

What will happen to the wild animals and fish? These provide us with meat for our diet in bad years.

Conservationist

The Sudd swamp is a prime habitat for birds and large herbivores. It supports large numbers of the endangered shoe-bill stork, and the largest number of water birds anywhere in Africa. There are nearly half a million liang and most of the remaining Nile lechwe, as well as many other large animals. All these animals and the wetland plants will be threatened as the swamp shrinks.

Migrating animals like the liang must cross the canal twice a year in seach of pasture: first in December/January when

the females are pregnant, secondly in March/April with the small calves. Many animals may drown in the confusion. As they congregate to cross, they will be more easily attacked by predators and tribal hunters. The natural balance will be upset.

The disease schistosomiasis spreads by water snails. These cannot survive the dry season at present, but the canal and new irrigation channels will cause the snails to spread. Both people and cattle will be affected.

I'm not sure that the impermeable clay soils in the area are suitable for crops.

Work in small groups.
1 Use all the information on this page, and the previous two, to carry out a cost–benefit analysis of the Jonglei Canal scheme. Make a large copy of the table opposite. Add notes in the appropriate boxes. You may not be able to fill in both costs and benefits for all parts of the list.
2 Do you think that the scheme should be completed? Use your cost–benefit analysis to support your point of view.
3 Suggest what might be done in the region to protect the interests of local people.

	Cost	Benefit
Water supply		
Animal and plant life		
Communications – increased accessibility of the region		
Health and disease for people and cattle		
Education		
Lifestyle of the Dinka and Nuer people		
Employment in agriculture and industry		

Above and below: Hard work and fun in the Peak District

9.1 FOOTPRINTS ON THE LAND

In the Three Peaks area

> ❝ The worst footpath EROSION I have seen anywhere in the country. ❞

This was what a scientist told the Yorkshire Dales National Park Committee. He was talking about the Three Peaks area: where you find the famous mountains of Ingleborough (723 m altitude), Whernside (735 m) and Pen-y-ghent (694 m). Footpath erosion in this area is described in the newspaper article (Source A).

The National Park Committee had three choices:
- Doing nothing, and letting the footpaths become mudbaths.
- Keeping people off the hills and allowing the paths to recover on their own.
- Carrying out restoration work.

A

Ramblers put the boot in

Most paths across the wild, upland Three Peaks Area have been trampled into a boggy morass, with an average width of 11.4 m – twice the width of a 'B' class road. In one place the path has been eroded to an incredible 150 m wide.

The situation is worst along the route of the Three Peaks Challenge Walk. This 40 km challenge attracts 15,000 walkers each year, and is also the route for an annual fell-running race (400 competitors) and a cyclo-cross event (200 racers). Each year about 150,000 people climb Ingleborough; 50,000 climb Whernside and 50,000 climb Pen-y-ghent.

1 Read Source A. In the Three Peaks area, what is the problem and what is causing it?
2 Describe what the photograph in Source A shows you.

3 With a partner, discuss the advantages and disadvantages (and *for whom*) of each of the three alternatives facing the National Park Committee.

At the southern end of the Pennine Way

B

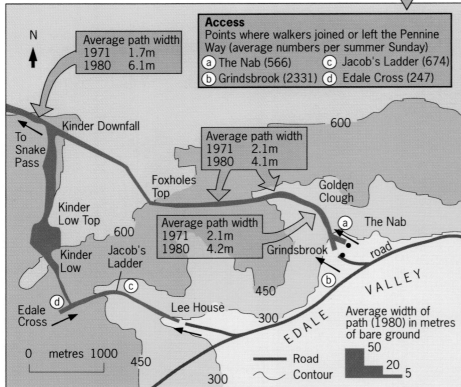

N

Average path width	
1971	1.7m
1980	6.1m

Access
Points where walkers joined or left the Pennine Way (average numbers per summer Sunday)
- ⓐ The Nab (566)
- ⓒ Jacob's Ladder (674)
- ⓑ Grindsbrook (2331)
- ⓓ Edale Cross (247)

To Snake Pass

Kinder Downfall

600

Average path width	
1971	2.1m
1980	4.1m

Foxholes Top

Golden Clough

Kinder Low Top

600

Average path width	
1971	2.1m
1980	4.2m

ⓐ The Nab

Kinder Low

Jacob's Ladder

Grindsbrook

road

ⓑ

ⓒ

450

VALLEY

ⓓ

Edale Cross

Lee House

300

EDALE

Average width of path (1980) in metres of bare ground

50

20

5

0 metres 1000

450

300

Road
Contour

The problem is widespread. The Pennine Way is Britain's most famous long-distance footpath. It runs for about 400 km between Derbyshire and Northumberland. The map (Source B) shows the most heavily used section, where it begins above Edale Valley in the Peak National Park. For the climb to Kinder Downfall, there are two routes and four access points (**a–d** on the map).

Study Source B.
4 How many walkers use this part of the Way on a typical summer Sunday? (Most people do not go past Kinder Downfall.)
5 Which sections of the path are likely to have the most walkers?
6 Are the widest sections of the path where there are most walkers? If not, what factors other than numbers of people might affect the footpaths?
7 What was happening to the Pennine Way between 1971 and 1980?

Some solutions

A rescue bid is under way

Simon Rose is in charge of a five year project costing £750,000 to save the Three Peaks moorland. He says: "The major thing which struck me was the speed at which the erosion was taking place. I could not believe that the gully I was standing in had been cut in only five years."

Footpath diversion to control erosion

Guardian, 15 August 1986

8 In pairs, discuss why Simon Rose (Source C) and the National Park Committee decided to restore the footpaths. Write a paragraph giving the main reasons.

9 Look at the photographs on page 105. They were taken in the Peak National Park in Derbyshire. What are the people in the photographs doing?

10 a) Source E shows one scheme to combat erosion on the Three Peaks Walk. Describe the scheme and say how it will help.
b) Whom will this scheme help?

11 What could the Peak National Park Committee do to control footpath erosion at the southern end of the Pennine Way? Use all the information on these pages to write a short report giving your suggestions.

12 The cross-sections in Source F show a four-stage model of the changes as the impact of feet increases. The stages progress from *light impact* to *extreme impact*. Describe what is happening at each stage.

A helicopter to the rescue

A Chinook helicopter from RAF Odiham, near Basingstoke, yesterday helped to combat erosion on the Three Peaks Walk in Yorkshire.

It lifted four skips containing 30 tons of granite hardcore five miles to a site 400 metres up Ingleborough in the Dales National Park.

Park staff and volunteers will fashion a 100-metre experimental length of path and drainage channels as part of a £20,000 pilot scheme to find ways of conserving peat moorland which comes under 120,000 pairs of boots annually.

At first, the stone path will show up strongly as a line up the fell. But it is thought that, in time, weathering and use will make it blend more into the hillside.

Guardian, 15 August 1986

What to look for

More walkers usually mean more erosion ● Vegetation is damaged, then disappears ● Bare areas are spread ● Soils are compacted ● Water, wind and frost erosion increase ● The model on Source F will be useful if you are doing fieldwork about footpath erosion.

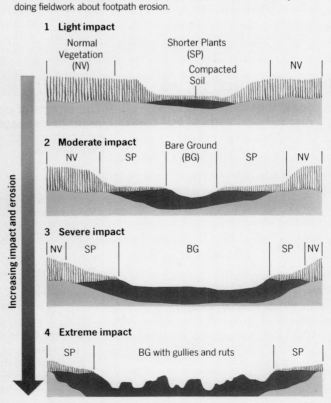

Increasing impact and erosion

1 Light impact
Normal Vegetation (NV) — Shorter Plants (SP) — Compacted Soil — NV

2 Moderate impact
NV — SP — Bare Ground (BG) — SP — NV

3 Severe impact
NV — SP — BG — SP — NV

4 Extreme impact
SP — BG with gullies and ruts — SP

Feet, hooves and wheels

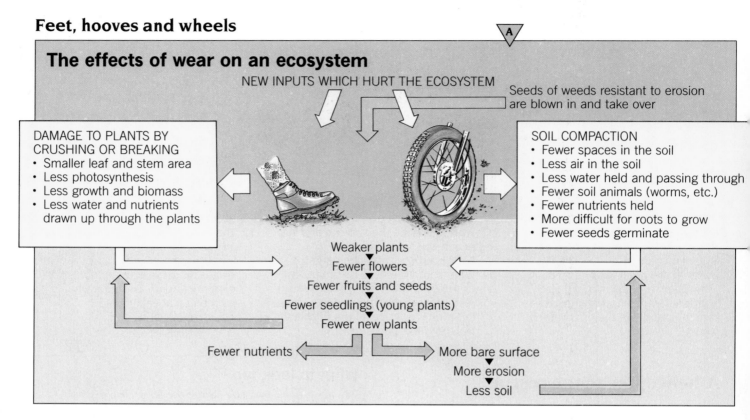

The effects of wear on an ecosystem

NEW INPUTS WHICH HURT THE ECOSYSTEM

Seeds of weeds resistant to erosion are blown in and take over

DAMAGE TO PLANTS BY CRUSHING OR BREAKING
- Smaller leaf and stem area
- Less photosynthesis
- Less growth and biomass
- Less water and nutrients drawn up through the plants

SOIL COMPACTION
- Fewer spaces in the soil
- Less air in the soil
- Less water held and passing through
- Fewer soil animals (worms, etc.)
- Fewer nutrients held
- More difficult for roots to grow
- Fewer seeds germinate

Weaker plants
Fewer flowers
Fewer fruits and seeds
Fewer seedlings (young plants)
Fewer new plants

Fewer nutrients — More bare surface
More erosion
Less soil

1 Look at the diagram (Source A) showing how the actions of feet, hooves and wheels can destroy an ECOSYSTEM. What causes an area of bare ground to spread? Note the effects on vegetation and the soil.

2 In pairs, talk about how this CYCLE of erosion could be reduced and yet people still be able to enjoy the environment. Jot down some ideas.

How resistance varies

3 Look at the table of statistics (Source B) and work out how many more times sedge reed meadows are resistant to being walked on than flower meadows.

4 Source D shows the impact of walkers on the flower meadows of Mount Rainier in the USA. There seems to be a THRESHOLD of numbers of walkers the meadows can bear before the vegetation begins to suffer badly. This threshold number is known as the CARRYING CAPACITY. What is the carrying capacity of this meadow ecosystem?

5 How could the rangers (wardens) of Mount Rainier National Park use this information to lay out a network of footpaths?

6 Work in a group. Scientists have found that in general:

The effects of people walking on mountain ecosystems

Main type of plant	How many people can walk across it in a week before the plant cover is halved.
Flower meadows	25
Cushion mosses and grasses	50
Heathland	100
Wet meadows	200
Mountain prairie grasses	400
Sedge reed meadows	750

● Wet environments are affected more easily, but recover more quickly than dry environments.
● Ecosystems with more species are more resistant.

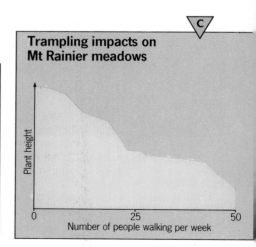

Trampling impacts on Mt Rainier meadows

Plant height

Number of people walking per week

● Healthy ecosystems are stronger than those under stress.
Suggest reasons why each of these findings is true. Use what you know about ecosystems and the information in Source A to help you.

Trail bikes and dune buggies

7 Use Source D and the diagram in Source A to describe what the ORVs are doing to the desert surface and the vegetation.

8 Use the photographs (Sources E and F) to describe the effects of ORVs on different types of desert surface.

D▷

In the Californian desert

Pit area, Salton Sea, USA

The large vehicles in the photograph are camper vans and mobile homes. Look more closely and you will see smaller vehicles – trail bikes and dune buggies. These are just a few of the many thousands of vehicles scattered across the beautiful Californian desert on a typical weekend. The big vehicles drive along the main dirt tracks and then park. The smaller vehicles are specially built and equipped to go just about anywhere. They are all-terrain vehicles (ATVs) or off-road vehicles (ORVs). ORVs have one thing in common – special tyres designed to grip on soft sand, mud and rocky slopes. When driven by powerful engines they can tear the desert surfaces apart.

Left: Sand and fine-grained silty muds are resistant to tyres, whereas stony crusts are easily torn up.

Above: A pit area on fine silts open for racing. All vegetation has gone, but erosion is limited.

What can be done?

9 In pairs, discuss the following three options for limiting the damage to deserts from ORVs:

A Ban ORVs from the desert. (However, consider that they are very popular and there are few fences around these huge areas.)

B Keep the numbers down by allowing only a certain number of permits.

C Discover which surfaces can withstand the impacts and mark out zones where ORVs can go.

a) What problems are there with options B and C?

b) Can you suggest other options?

c) What might happen if nothing was done?

10 Study Source G. What has been the Californian answer to the problem?

Skiing may be good for you, but it doesn't do much for the mountains.

This was the title of a magazine article. What does it mean? Why should sport and having fun have disastrous effects on the environment?

Problems in the Alps

1 Study Sources A, B and C to help you understand what is happening in the Alps. Are the floods and the Les Arcs ski resort connected? Write a brief answer which *describes* and *explains* what has happened.

2 The photograph in Source C shows the three things about natural environments that are popular for skiing:
   ● Slopes are steep.
   ● Natural vegetation is usually CO-NIFEROUS FOREST.
   ● There are heavy snowfalls which may melt quickly.
   Draw an outline sketch of the photograph in Source A. Label in one colour all the features which may cause rapid runoff of water. In another colour label the features of the environment which may be affected by this runoff. Show what might happen. Use all the information on this page to help you.

Diary of a problem

1969 The brand new ski resort of Les Arcs in the French Alps is opened, despite the opposition of many local people. Trees are felled and the ski slopes opened up.

1973 Landslides sweep into the River Ravoire below the resort. Floods and mudflows pour down the valley, gouging out the stream bed and eroding the banks.

1977 The French government orders that the drainage into the River Ravoire is to be reduced. Expensive barrages and defences are built to fix the bed and banks of the river.

1981 On 31 March and 14 April major flooding sweeps down the River Ravoire valley. Landslides of rock, trees and mud hurtle down the slopes and into the river, carrying 300,000 cubic metres of debris. Chalets, roads and a railway line are destroyed.

A mud slide at an Alpine ski resort

Disaster in the Alps

ON 20 July 1987, avalanches of mud swept down mountainsides around the villages of Tartano, Sondrio and Bergamo in northern Italy, near the Swiss border. Twenty people were killed, and buildings, roads, bridges and power lines uprooted. At the same time, swollen rivers and landslides blocked many roads in southern Switzerland. In three weeks more than 60 people died. 7000 were made homeless, and 50 towns, villages and holiday centres wrecked.

Several days of freak torrential rain precipitated these disasters – but that is only part of the answer. Landslides are common in the Alps but human activities make the slopes even more vulnerable.

Over the past two decades, the tourist industry in the Alps has boomed. Stunning scenery and excellent skiing attract tourists all year round, often bringing economic benefits to areas of high unemployment. But hundreds of square kilometres of forestry have been destroyed to make way for ski pistes, cable cars, holiday buildings and roads.

Mounting evidence suggests that the woods help to protect mountainsides from snow avalanches, mudslides and falling rocks. DEFORESTATION is now directly linked to such disasters.

The reason is simple. A good, strong forest holds snow on the branches of its trees as well as the ground between the trees. This patchy snow cover helps to prevent large masses of snow accumulating at weak points where avalanches could be triggered. But where the ground is treeless, the snow cover allows any weakness – say, surface water runs, or particularly weak geological formations – to develop into an avalanche of mud or snow. Dense tree cover also helps to cushion runaway rocks rolling down a steep slope, which alone killed about 25 people in Switzerland last year. The trees also help to lessen the impact of rain, as their roots absorb water and bind the soil together into a mat. Without the tree roots, the soil is freed, allowing slippage.

Much more water passes down mountainsides that have lost their natural tree cover, carrying fine soil material with it.

A scientist says, 'Any destruction by machinery or fertilisers will destroy the carpet of plants. Even if it looks poor, a few thousand years could have gone into it ... you can't restore it in a few years.'

Where the slopes have been cleared above the tree line (the altitude above which trees cannot grow), the vegetation has not regenerated. Seeding of grass below the tree line to restore some of the vegetation initially gives good results, but usually only for a season or two. Eventually the soil becomes exposed, and liable to erosion. Pistes also cut into surface water channels, often changing the underlying geology and causing erosion. Skiers who think themselves blameless might consider how their skis slice through young trees and the low mountain shrubs.

The destruction caused by flash floods

Looking for causes

Ski area in Les Arcs

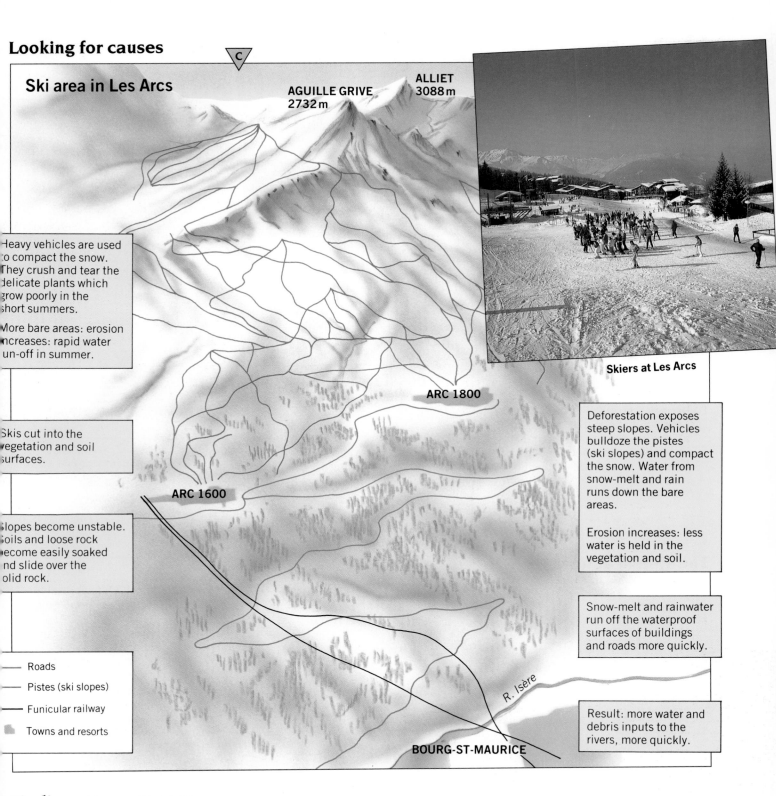

AGUILLE GRIVE 2732 m

ALLIET 3088 m

ARC 1800

ARC 1600

BOURG-ST-MAURICE

R. Isère

Heavy vehicles are used to compact the snow. They crush and tear the delicate plants which grow poorly in the short summers.

More bare areas: erosion increases: rapid water run-off in summer.

Skis cut into the vegetation and soil surfaces.

Slopes become unstable. Soils and loose rock become easily soaked and slide over the solid rock.

Deforestation exposes steep slopes. Vehicles bulldoze the pistes (ski slopes) and compact the snow. Water from snow-melt and rain runs down the bare areas.

Erosion increases: less water is held in the vegetation and soil.

Snow-melt and rainwater run off the waterproof surfaces of buildings and roads more quickly.

Result: more water and debris inputs to the rivers, more quickly.

Skiers at Les Arcs

— Roads
— Pistes (ski slopes)
— Funicular railway
▪ Towns and resorts

Finding some answers

Work in pairs or a small group.
3 Look at the information in Source C carefully.
  a) Make a list of the changes to the environment caused by the development of a ski resort.
  b) Select three reasons why there is more bare surface.

  c) Draw a large labelled diagram to show what happens to the water as the area of bare surface increases.
4 Prepare a brief report on
  a) why a ski resort has been built;
  b) what problems the environment faces;
  c) who has caused these problems;

and
  d) ways in which the resort environment could be changed to reduce runoff, erosion and the danger of flooding.

111

9.4 PLAYING ABOUT WITH BEACHES

Sea and sand

SUN + SEA + SAND = HOLIDAYS FOR MILLIONS OF PEOPLE.
Have you ever wondered where all the sand on a beach comes from or what it is made of?

You can find the answers if you think of a beach as a part of the coastal ENVIRONMENTAL SYSTEM (look at the diagram in Source B).

A beach is a very special environment because it changes constantly due to:
● daily tidal movements;
● monthly rhythms in the height and strength of tides;
● seasonal variations in the strength and frequency of storms.

I   Use Sources A and B to explain what would happen to the beach if
a) the INPUTS became smaller and the OUTPUTS remained the same.
b) the *inputs* steadily exceeded *outputs*.

The beach faces strong onshore waves and winds.

The coastal environmental system

INPUTS	STORE	OUTPUTS

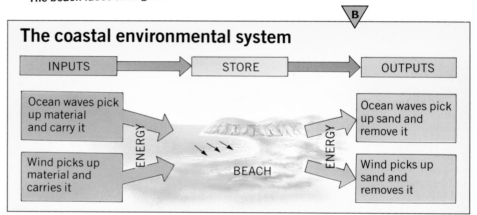

Ocean waves pick up material and carry it

Wind picks up material and carries it

ENERGY

BEACH

ENERGY

Ocean waves pick up sand and remove it

Wind picks up sand and removes it

The system at work

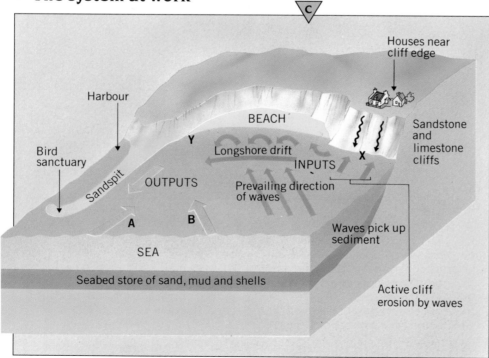

Houses near cliff edge

Harbour

BEACH

Y

Longshore drift

INPUTS

Bird sanctuary

Sandspit

OUTPUTS

Prevailing direction of waves

Sandstone and limestone cliffs

X

A   B

SEA

Waves pick up sediment

Seabed store of sand, mud and shells

Active cliff erosion by waves

3   Look at Source C. What materials do you think the beach will be made of?
4   This beach has been roughly the same for hundreds of years. What does this tell you about the nature of the inputs and outputs along this stretch of the coast?
5   What would be the effects on the beach of strong winds blowing from
a) direction A, and
b) direction B?
6   Imagine that the local council wants to build a sea wall along the foot of the cliffs at X and a GROYNE jutting out into the sea at Y.
a) Why might they want to do this?
b) What would be the effects on this coastline of building either or both?
Consider that the council is interested in developing the area's tourist industry.

Barrier islands

Look at the diagram, Source D. It shows how the islands are true barriers. They protect the coast, but are covered when there are great storms. The holiday-home builders have realised this and have tried to reduce the risk of flooding. The US National Parks Service (which owns and manages a number of the islands) has also carried out its own schemes.

7 Use the diagrams in Sources E and F and the photographs in Source G to explain what is the main purpose of the protection schemes.
8 List the main differences between natural and protected islands.
9 What methods have been used by people for protection?
10 What changes have been made to the way the beach SYSTEM works? Use systems language to explain your answer if you can. Think in terms of inputs (material and energy) → STORE → outputs.
11 Are the protected islands as good barriers as natural islands? Explain your answer.

D

Where not to build a holiday home

One of the worlds's greatest lines of beaches and offshore islands runs for 4000 km along the east coast of the USA around Florida and the northern rim of the Gulf of Mexico.

These 295 offshore islands may seem great places for thousands of holiday homes but, as the photograph shows, it is not always such a good idea. The people who built the causeways, roads, houses and boat docks ignored one thing: the islands have their own important job to do in the natural system.

Storm damage on Fire Island ▶

The natural barrier at work

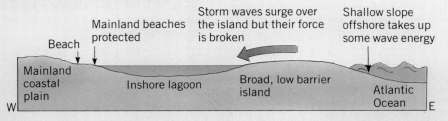

Mainland beaches protected

Storm waves surge over the island but their force is broken

Shallow slope offshore takes up some wave energy

Beach

Mainland coastal plain — Inshore lagoon — Broad, low barrier island — Atlantic Ocean

W — E

E

The natural barrier

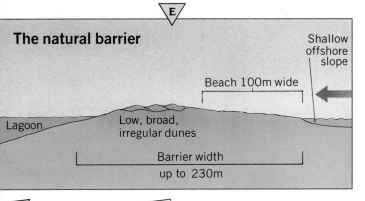

Shallow offshore slope

Beach 100m wide

Lagoon

Low, broad, irregular dunes

Barrier width up to 230m

F

The protected barrier

Trees and grasses planted

Mesh fencing to collect wind-blown sand

Holiday homes

Full force of storm waves hits steepened barrier

Road

Taller dunes

Lagoon

Beach 30m wide

Steeper offshore slope

Barrier width up to 130m

G

Efforts at protecting barrier islands by building or adding to dunes, and planting grass and shrubs, result eventually in beaches that are narrower than these on unprotected islands. Two islands in North Carolina are examples.
Left: Carebanks Island, which is in its natural state.
Right: Hatteras Island, scene of much protection work since the 1930s.

113

9.5 CORALS ARE SENSITIVE CREATURES

The coral reef

Coral reefs are beautiful underwater ecosystems. They are often found along attractive coasts being developed for tourism – and the coral reefs themselves are one of the biggest attractions. In economically developing areas such as the Caribbean Islands, visitors to the coral reefs bring much-needed money. But coral reef ecosystems are very sensitive and fragile and cannot stand many changes in conditions.

St Croix Island surrounded by a coral reef (Virgin Islands, Caribbean)

A

What is coral?

A coral reef is a massive limestone structure built by tiny animals called *coral polyps*. These polyps feed on minute organisms in the sea around them, and deposit sharp, stony skeletons which slowly build up the reef. The polyps need warm, clear shallow water at nearly constant temperatures. They cannot stand too much sediment in the water because it shuts out the sunlight and can smother the polyps.

B

How the parts depend on each other

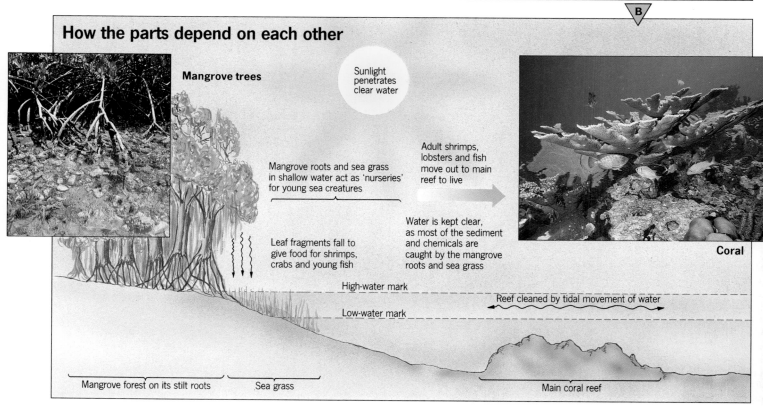

Mangrove trees

Sunlight penetrates clear water

Mangrove roots and sea grass in shallow water act as 'nurseries' for young sea creatures

Adult shrimps, lobsters and fish move out to main reef to live

Leaf fragments fall to give food for shrimps, crabs and young fish

Water is kept clear, as most of the sediment and chemicals are caught by the mangrove roots and sea grass

Coral

High-water mark

Low-water mark

Reef cleaned by tidal movement of water

Mangrove forest on its stilt roots   Sea grass

Main coral reef

1 In the Caribbean many coral reefs grow around land fringed with mangrove forests. Look at Source B and describe how the mangroves and sea grass influence life in the coral reef.

2 In many parts of the Caribbean the mangroves are being removed, often for tourist developments. What may happen to the coral reef ecosystem as a result?

The threats to a coral reef

3 Look at the diagram, Source D. List the inputs to the coral reef ecosystem caused by tourism.

4 List the changed outputs from the reef caused by tourism.

5 a) What would happen to the coral polyps (Source A) if the water became more cloudy?

b) What might make the water become more cloudy?

6 Imagine that there are more threats to the reef:

● Modern agriculture at A causes chemical fertilisers to enter the lagoon.

● Deforestation at B causes more sediment to be washed into the lagoon.

● A power station at C pours warmer water into the lagoon. How might these changes affect the coral reef? Think about the conditions coral needs.

Adapted from *New Scientist*, November 1981

▷ C

Caribbean coral reefs under threat

Silt, oil, tourists, even bombing; coral reefs that took thousands of years to grow can be destroyed in weeks. Reefs in one country may be damaged by people or pollution from distant lands. To preserve them is a challenge to the whole word.

Many things can threaten the balance of a coral reef ecosystem. In the one month of July 1980, more than 1000 live bombs were dropped on the small island of Viegues in the Caribbean by the US Navy. The island, which is fringed by coral reefs, has been a target area since the 1930s.

On any day 100 tankers of all sizes may be carrying oil in the Caribbean region. In a year, the equivalent of 75 million barrels of oil may be spilled there – accidentally or in cleaning work by tankers.

Tourists from all over the world put pressure on the Caribbean coral ecosystem.

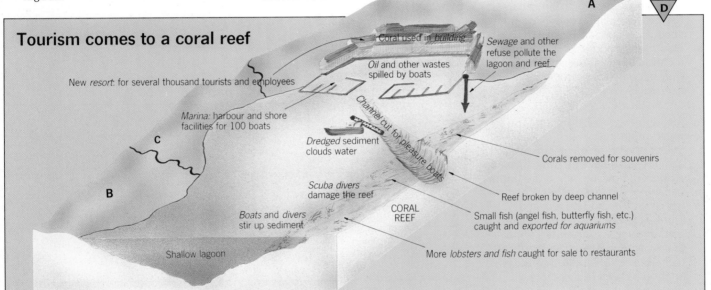

Tourism comes to a coral reef

A ▽ D

New *resort*: for several thousand tourists and employees

Coral used in *building*

Oil and other wastes spilled by boats

Sewage and other refuse pollute the lagoon and reef

Marina: harbour and shore facilities for 100 boats

C

Dredged sediment clouds water

Channel cut for pleasure boats

Scuba divers damage the reef

Corals removed for souvenirs

Reef broken by deep channel

B

Boats and *divers* stir up sediment

CORAL REEF

Small fish (angel fish, butterfly fish, etc.) caught and *exported for aquariums*

Shallow lagoon

More *lobsters and fish* caught for sale to restaurants

Preserving the coral reefs

▽ E

Saving the Great Barrier Reef

on and Valerie Taylor are underwater photographers. For years they have lmed on the world's largest coral reef: Australia's Great Barrier Reef, which overs an area as large as England and Scotland. Valerie said, 'I'm ashamed to admit that we treated the reef the same way as everyone else did. We speared more fish than we could possibly use or sell. The object was to land as many fish of different species as possible. . . . Then one day Ron and I simply had enough. We were struck by a sense of total waste.'

This is just one example of the many visitors who take more from the reef than it can produce. In 1979 Australia set up the Great Barrier Reef Marine Park to protect the reef – but even so the threat remains.

7 In a group discuss the argument that *'Conservation should take priority over tourism'*. Refer to Sources C and E. Decide whether you agree or disagree and give reasons to support your position. Refer back to any or all of the spreads in Unit 9 and use all the information and understandings you think are relevant.

115

9 IMPACTS OF RECREATION

Any type of outdoor leisure has some environmental impact. As examples in this Unit have shown, different activities make different impacts. Equally important, different environments can stand different amounts of recreation activity – some are sensitive and fragile, while some are resilient and strong. The level of leisure activity an environment can take is called its recreational carrying capacity. There are three aspects to this capacity:

- How many people can use a location before it is full: the PHYSICAL CAPACITY;
- How much use a location can take before the environment is damaged: the ECOLOGICAL CAPACITY;
- How many people can be using a location at the same time before they become less satisfied: the PERCEPTUAL CAPACITY.

In small groups, work on one of the following assignments.

1 Select one of the environments and activities used in this Unit. Give examples of how and when the limits of each of the three aspects of carrying capacity could be reached. Think of the best ways to present your answer, e.g. mounted photographs with written statements attached; a set of labelled cartoons; annotated sketches or block diagrams.

2 Choose an outdoor leisure activity, e.g. picnicking; motor-cycle scrambling; sailing. Find out as much as you can about the activity: its needs, locations, who takes part. You could contact local clubs, the Tourist Board and or the local council for help. If possible, visit a location where your activity takes place. Look carefully at the environment and what is happening. Notes, maps, sketches, photos, chats with people, are all useful.

a) List the space and resources needed, and what environments are best suited.
b) What impacts does the activity have on the environment?
c) Suggest what signs you would look for, showing that carrying

Action and effects of the four alternatives

CAPACITY ASPECT	ALTERNATIVE A	
	Action	*Effects*
Physical		
Ecological		
Perceptual		

Action: What you would do, e.g. Alternative A – 'Nothing'
Effects: What is likely to happen as a result of your action.

capacity has been reached: physical, ecological, perceptual.
d) Propose a simple way for measuring environmental impact.
e) When the carrying capacity of a location or environment has been reached, you have four alternatives:

A Do nothing.
B Improve the carrying capacity of the location – *concentrate* the activity.
C Open up a new location – *disperse* the activity.
D Control use by issuing permits, pricing, membership, etc.

Assess the four alternatives for your chosen leisure activity by completing this table for each alternative. (Draw the table to take up one page for each alternative.)

3 Select a local urban park, Country Park or Water Park. Adapt Assignment 2 above, to study the carrying capacity and environmental impact of recreation for your chosen park.

10.1 THE ATMOSPHERE AND OUR LIVES

The atmosphere as a system

The atmosphere, and what goes on in it, is vital to all ECOSYSTEMS and to the quality of our lives, every minute of every day. Remember: the atmosphere is the air above and around you.

Work with a partner.
1 Discuss the ways in which the atmosphere has affected your lives in the past 24 hours.
2 The photographs on page 117 show some of the ways that the atmosphere affects all living things. The titles for six photographs are given

below. Match up the titles with the correct photograph. Give a reason for your choice in each case: Playing; Working; Moving; Adapting; Surviving; Living. Compare your answers with others.

Why can we call Source A a SYSTEM? With your partner, use the diagram of the atmosphere system to:
3 List the INPUTS to the atmospheric system; what is STORED; and what comes out (OUTPUTS).

4 Draw a diagram of a CYCLE which includes the atmosphere. (For an example, see pages 4–7.)
5 Decide which of the components can be affected by human activity. In what ways are they affected?
6 Each of you find an example of feedback in the way the atmosphere works, and explain it to the other.

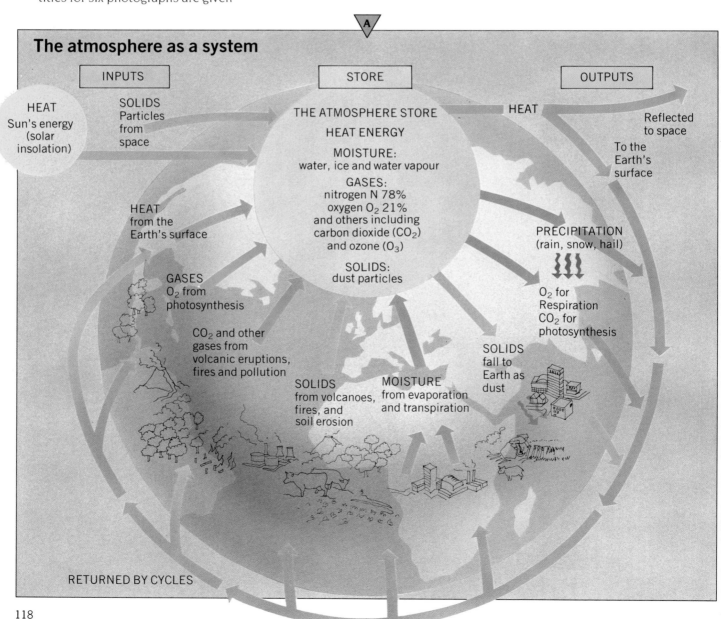

The atmosphere as a system

| INPUTS | STORE | OUTPUTS |

HEAT Sun's energy (solar insolation)

SOLIDS Particles from space

THE ATMOSPHERE STORE
HEAT ENERGY
MOISTURE: water, ice and water vapour
GASES: nitrogen N 78% oxygen O_2 21% and others including carbon dioxide (CO_2) and ozone (O_3)
SOLIDS: dust particles

HEAT
Reflected to space
To the Earth's surface

HEAT from the Earth's surface

GASES O_2 from photosynthesis

CO_2 and other gases from volcanic eruptions, fires and pollution

SOLIDS from volcanoes, fires, and soil erosion

MOISTURE from evaporation and transpiration

SOLIDS fall to Earth as dust

PRECIPITATION (rain, snow, hail)

O_2 for Respiration CO_2 for photosynthesis

RETURNED BY CYCLES

Weather, climate and air masses

WEATHER is what we see of the atmosphere at work day by day. It is a series of short-term events, as in a 'weather forecast'. When these events are averaged out over many years, we call this CLIMATE. The weather we experience depends upon the type of air which surrounds us and on the temperature (heat energy), wind (movement energy), moisture (humidity) stored in it.

The outstanding feature is the amazing variety of weather and climate conditions across the world. Why is this? The material below shows that the answer lies in AIR MASSES. An air mass is a large volume of atmosphere with similar characteristics of temperature and moisture.

Air masses around the world

Notice that we name an air mass after its source region. 'Tropical' and 'maritime' tell us that it gets its properties from tropical seas. Source C shows the main types of air mass found in the Earth's atmosphere.

If a region is covered all year round by just one air mass, its climate may be much the same all year, e.g. in Amazonia. Other regions show strong seasonal changes of climate because there is a change from one air mass to another, or because the surface is hot in one season and cold in another, e.g. in Central Asia.

A third group of regions are affected by several air masses. They are a battleground between air masses, and have very variable weather conditions, e.g. the British Isles.

Follow the diagram in Source B carefully, then answer these questions:

7 What do we mean by the *source region* of an air mass?
8 What affects the heat (temperature) and the moisture stored in the air mass?
9 Explain how an air mass can affect the weather of a place hundreds of kilometres from the source region.
10 What type of weather is this tropical maritime air mass likely to bring to Western Europe?

11 Use an atlas and an outline map of the world to mark and name the main source regions for each air mass type shown in Source C.
12 The climate graph (Source D) is an example of a region affected by *two* different air masses.
  a) Plot Calcutta onto your world map. Study the data carefully. Decide which months are affected by the two different air masses. Give reasons for your answer.
  b) Suggest the *types* of air masses affecting Calcutta.

B

pical maritime air on the move

⑤ The faster it moves, the less it will have changed by the time it arrives

④ Some of the air mass moves from the source region, taking its warmth and moisture with it

Atmosphere gets heat and moisture from the surface below by:
Radiation
Conduction
Evaporation

③ The huge volume of air stays over the ocean for a long time to become warm and moist

② The air gets its properties from the surface over which it spends time

① A large, warm ocean: the SOURCE REGION

THE AIR MASS

1000 km and more

C

Source regions of the world's main air masses

Name	Source region	Characteristics
Polar Maritime	Oceans near to Antarctica and the Arctic	Cool and moist
Polar Continental	Northern continental areas, Antarctica	Cold and dry in winter Hot and dry in summer
Arctic or Antarctic	Polar regions	Very cold and dry
Tropical Maritime	Oceans in the subtropics	Warm and moist
Tropical Continental	Tropical deserts, e.g. Sahara, Australia	Hot and very dry
Equatorial Maritime	Oceans near to the Equator	Warm and moist

D

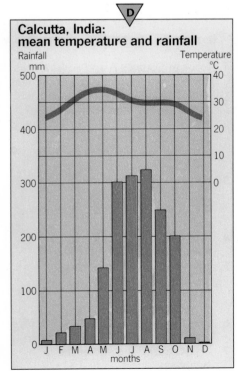

Calcutta, India: mean temperature and rainfall

119

The big heat of July 1987 in Greece

We expect the Mediterranean region to be hot in summer. The figures for Athens (Source A) show this. But July 1987 was quite different, as you can see in Source B.

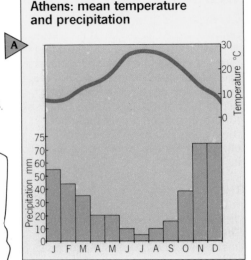

Athens: mean temperature and precipitation

A

B

Hundreds die in Greek heatwave

From Florica Kyriocopolous in Athens

A lethal week-long heatwave continued in Greece yesterday, claiming record deaths and keeping the country in a state of emergency.

More than 650 people have died in Athens and its vicinity since the blistering heat gripped the country on July 22. While the number of deaths directly attributable to the heat is not yet clear, officials have indicated that last week's death toll was nearly three times bigger than normal.

Greek newspapers yesterday put the total number of victims at between 650 and 900, most of them elderly people suffering from respiratory and heart problems.

Last Friday the Government declared a state of emergency to deal with the unprecedented crisis. All hospitals and military clinics have been put on alert and makeshift morgues have been set up in military hospitals to store the rising numbers of dead.

Hospitals in Athens, Piraeus, Salonika and other major cities are in a state of chaos. The state-run first aid centre, which has been receiving 6,000 calls for help a day, announced over the weekend that it could

only respond to emergency cases. Army helicopters and vehicles have also been mobilised.

The highest temperature in Attica yesterday was 41°C while in the islands and mainland coastline it hovered between 35°C and 38°C. Throughout the week, mainland temperatures have ranged from 39°C to 44°C.

Greater Athens, where nearly half the country's population lives, has suffered most. Repeated and prolonged cuts in water supply, apparently caused by a 30 per cent increase in consumption, have made life truly unbearable for most of its inhabitants.

A weekend exodus to the islands and coastline slightly improved water supplied yesterday but the water board continued to appeal for cuts in water use.

The heat has been attributed to high BAROMETRIC PRESSURES and the absence of the strong summer winds that normally blow between May and September.

The weather is due to improve slightly today as expected rain in the north-west will lower temperatures throughout Greece.

Athens, 26 July. A bus passenger fainted from the heat

Guardian, 27 July 1987

1 Look at Sources A and B. What was the highest temperature in the heatwave? How much was this above the expected mean temperature?

2 **a)** What effects did the heatwave have on the people?
b) Who suffered most from the effects of the heatwave?

3 **a)** Why did people escape to the seaside?
b) Do you think that everyone was able to do this?

4 What did the government and officials do to help?

5 **a)** What caused the heatwave?
b) What type of air mass gave these hot, dry conditions? (Use page 119 to help you.)

6 How do the two diagrams in Source C help to explain the heatwave?

7 What caused the end of the heatwave?

C

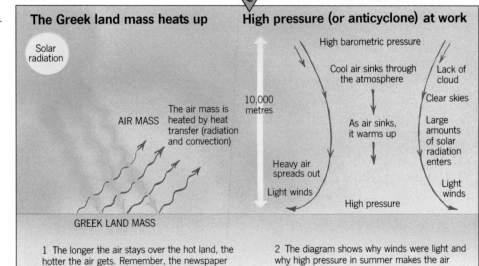

The Greek land mass heats up

Solar radiation

AIR MASS

The air mass is heated by heat transfer (radiation and convection)

10,000 metres

GREEK LAND MASS

1 The longer the air stays over the hot land, the hotter the air gets. Remember, the newspaper says there was little wind (air moving slowly).

High pressure (or anticyclone) at work

High barometric pressure

Cool air sinks through the atmosphere

Lack of cloud

Clear skies

As air sinks, it warms up

Large amounts of solar radiation enters

Heavy air spreads out

Light winds

High pressure

Light winds

2 The diagram shows why winds were light and why high pressure in summer makes the air even hotter.

The big chill of January 1987 in Britain

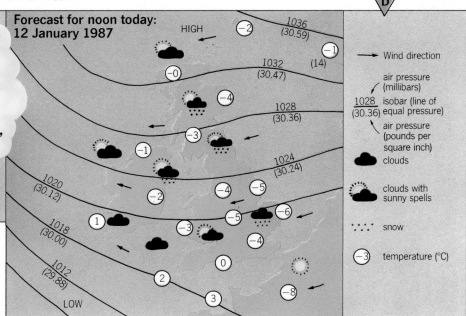

" The weather forecasters say that in areas from Kent to Scotland the cold weather is due to winds from Siberia. Temperatures today were −3.3°C, and it is expected that tonight temperatures in London will plunge to −5.6°C. This will be the lowest temperature since records started in 1961. This very cold air stream is likely to last for the rest of the week. "

Forecast for noon today: 12 January 1987

HIGH

LOW

→ Wind direction

air pressure (millibars)

1028 (30.36) isobar (line of equal pressure)

air pressure (pounds per square inch)

clouds

clouds with sunny spells

snow

−3 temperature (°C)

Mid-January 1987 was much colder than normal. The diagram (Source E) shows that the British Isles are one of the 'battleground' regions of the world where different air masses fight for control. This is the cause of our variable weather.

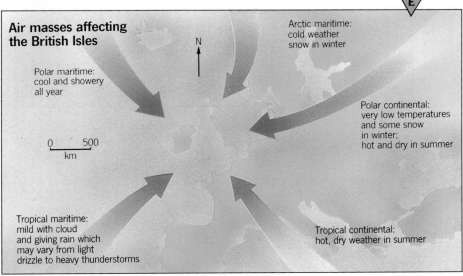

Air masses affecting the British Isles

N

Polar maritime: cool and showery all year

Arctic maritime: cold weather snow in winter

Polar continental: very low temperatures and some snow in winter; hot and dry in summer

Tropical maritime: mild with cloud and giving rain which may vary from light drizzle to heavy thunderstorms

Tropical continental: hot, dry weather in summer

0   500
km

8 Use Source D to describe the weather conditions over the British Isles on 12 January 1987. (You do not need to consider the AIR PRESSURE at this stage.)

9 Use Sources D and E to explain why January 1987 was so cold.

10 Why was the eastern part of the country the most affected?

11 How does such weather affect our lives? Give a few examples.

12 An 'AIRSTREAM' was mentioned in the news bulletin (Source D). An airstream is a moving mass of air. What air mass brought us this 'cold snap'?

How much colder was January 1987?

13 Source F shows data for Birmingham during the severe weather. Use Source F to draw graphs showing the temperatures in January 1987 compared to the average for the years 1984–7.

14 Write a letter to a friend in Calcutta, India, to explain what the weather was like in January 1987. Include how the temperatures compared with the mean for the years 1984–7.

15 Source F includes three types of temperature reading. Which temperature figures do you think are the most useful? Why?

F

Temperature data for Birmingham: 10–20 January 1987

Date	Max daily temperature	Mean 1984–7	Min daily temperature	Mean 1984–7	Mean daily temperature	Mean 1984–7
10	0.3	6.1	−0.6	1.5	−0.2	3.8
11	−4.5	4.2	−6.4	1.7	−5.4	3.0
12	−6.5	2.0	−8.8	−1.8	−7.6	0.1
13	−4.6	4.3	−11.2	−0.9	−7.9	1.7
14	−2.5	2.2	−6.0	−0.7	−4.3	0.8
15	0.0	1.8	−2.5	−0.2	−1.3	0.8
16	0.4	2.8	0.0	−1.2	0.2	0.8
17	−1.2	0.6	−7.2	−3.6	−4.2	−1.5
18	−1.6	3.6	−6.4	−2.0	−4.0	0.8
19	0.2	3.6	−3.4	0.0	−1.6	1.8
20	4.3	4.1	0.0	−0.5	2.2	1.8

Birmingham University

BLOWING HOT AND COLD

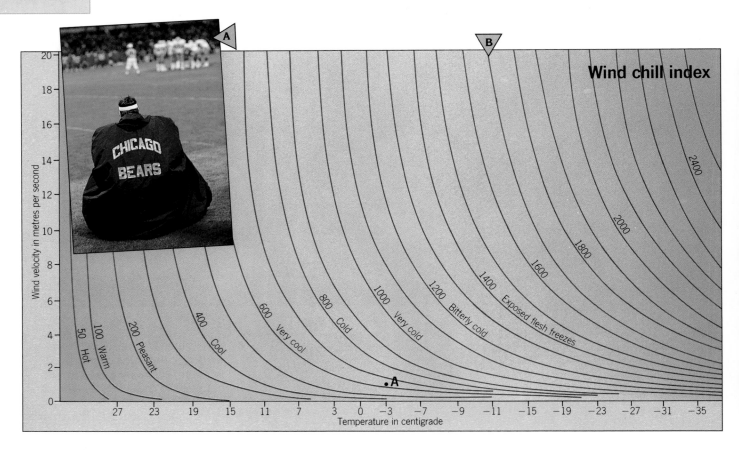

Wind chill index

Wind velocity in metres per second

50 Hot · 100 Warm · 200 Pleasant · 400 Cool · 600 Very cool · 800 Cold · 1000 Very cold · 1200 Bitterly cold · 1400 Exposed flesh freezes · 1600 · 1800 · 2000 · 2400

•A

Temperature in centigrade

The wind chill index

On 3 January 1988 a game of American football was played in Chicago. The actual temperature of the air was −9°C, but the temperature actually felt by the players and spectators was −29°C (Source A). This was because a strong wind was blowing. We call this effect the WIND CHILL FACTOR. It is one of the several ways wind affects the lives of all living things. (See also pp. 126–7.)

Measuring how cold it feels

As in the Chicago football game, high wind speeds clearly affect human comfort. A graph (Source B) allows us to work out how cold it will feel on any particular day. We need to know the *temperature* and the *wind speed*.

● For example, look at point **A** on the graph: with a temperature of −3°C and a wind speed of 1 metre per second, the wind chill index shows that it would feel very cool (index of 600).

1 For the Chicago football game the wind chill index was 1200 (bitterly cold). Use the graph (Source B) to find the wind speed during the football game. Remember that the actual temperature was −9°C.
2 Use data from your local paper or school weather station to find out the wind chill index for each day during the last week.
3 Read Source C. Look back at the weather map (Source D), page 121, and decide where the strongest winds were that day.

Wind is moving air. What causes it to move?

All the time there is a certain weight of air pressing down on you. This weight of the atmosphere is recorded as air pressure in units called millibars (mb). the pressure is shown on weather maps by lines of equal pressure, called ISOBARS. Look again at the map for 12 January 1987 (Source D on page 121). The lines, numbered 1012 up to 1036, are isobars, showing the air pressure. The higher the number, the higher the pressure. The average pressure at sea level is 1000 mb, but pressure varies in different places and at different times.

● The key point is this: *air pressure varies from place to place.* You can't feel the differences between air pressure in different places, but they are very important to the way the atmosphere works. We use instruments called barometers to measure the differences and changes in air pressure. Wind is the way the atmosphere works to even up the pressure between different parts of the world.

● The wind speed varies according to the difference in pressure between two places. *The greater the pressure difference, the stronger the wind will be.* The difference in pressure is called the PRESSURE GRADIENT. The isobars will be close together when there is a strong wind blowing. This is rather like a contour map of the land, where closely spaced contour lines mean steep slopes.

Swirling winds

Look at the satellite photograph (Source D) showing a low-pressure area over Britain on 16 October 1987. Meteorologists call low-pressure areas like this a MID-LATITUDE DEPRESSION.

You will see that the clouds are in huge swirls when seen from above. The clouds are being carried by the winds in a circular pattern. The winds blow into the low-pressure centre in the middle of the cloud mass, but they do not blow in a straight line. The rotation of the Earth causes the wind to curve as it blows *out of areas of high pressure and into areas of low pressure.*

4 Draw a sketch of Source D. On your sketch label the low-pressure centre and the cloud belts.
5 Are the winds circulating (swirling) in a clockwise or an anti-clockwise direction? Whichever you decide, this is a general rule for the northern hemisphere. Add the wind direction to your sketch of the mid-latitude depression. Remember to add a title.
6 The flow of air *outwards* from a high-pressure centre will be in the *opposite* direction. Draw a diagram to show the wind direction around a high-pressure centre or anticyclone like the one over Greece in July 1987 on page 120. Add a note about the wind strength and the amount of cloud.

Tornadoes

As well as wind chill, strong winds affect our lives in other ways. A TORNADO is a storm with an area of very low pressure in the centre. Air rushes in at very high speeds to fill in the low-pressure area. A zone of high-speed rotation results. The high wind speeds in the storm are a great hazard to humans and buildings. Source E shows the effects of a tornado on the city of Edmonton, Canada, in August 1987.

7 Describe the weather experienced during the Edmonton tornado.
8 Draw up a list of the effects of the tornado on people and their property.
9 How was the damage made worse by the tornado affecting a built-up area?
10 Compare the size of the low-pressure area causing the tornado

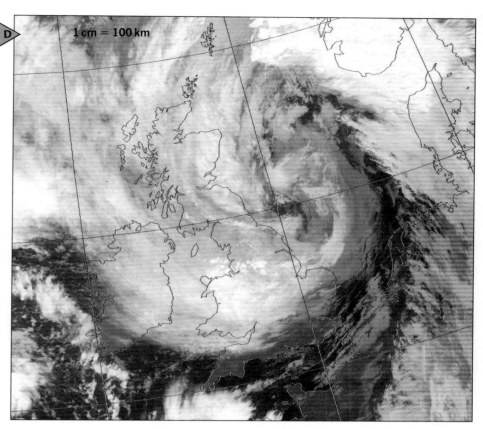

D   1 cm = 100 km

with the size of the mid-latitude depression shown in Source D. Use the buildings in the photograph of the tornado, Source E, and the scale of the satellite photograph to help you.

11 Group discussion:
   a) If you lived in an area affected by tornadoes, how would you adapt your life and your home to the possible hazard?
   b) How do you think that the effects of storms like tornadoes may vary between rich and poor parts of the world? Think in terms of warning systems, damage to property, help with recovery from the damage, etc.

E

Tornado kills 35 people in Canadian city

RESCUE workers were yesterday combing mountains of rubble to search for survivors of a series of violent tornadoes which struck Edmonton, Alberta, during Friday afternoon rush hour. At least 35 deaths have been reported and hospitals were packed with 350 wounded.

Cars and lorries were tossed about like toys as the cyclone, producing winds of up to 145 km/h, cut a wide trail of destruction. Fires were started by ruptured gas lines and fallen electrical cables. Phone lines were blocked by emergency calls.

Ken Nellis, a government weather forecaster, said that from the weather bureau office he could see five or six tornadoes forming west of the city. The storm was preceded by severe winds and hailstones the size of cricket balls. The temperature dropped from 30°C to below freezing in an hour.

The storm rips a deadly path through houses and factories

Adapted from *The Sunday Times*, 2 August 1987

10.4 RAINSTORM IN CENTRAL WALES

What causes precipitation?

Rain, snow, sleet, hail, dew and frost are all PRECIPITATION. They are the moisture outputs from the atmosphere. It is vital for us to understand what causes them in order to be able to forecast when they will occur.

On 18–19 June 1971, a rainstorm in the basin of the River Tywi gave over half of the month's total rainfall of 155 mm in just a few hours. Can we *explain* what caused this heavy downpour?

Location of the Upper Tywi catchment, Central Wales

☐ Field area boundary   ▨ Land over 450 metres

1 Use your atlas and Source A to describe the location of the part of the Tywi basin shown in the rectangle.
2 Using Source B (the rectangular area in Source A), describe the *pattern* of rainfall, e.g. did the same amount of rain fall everywhere? Where did it rain the most, least? etc.
3 Suggest who put the rain gauges there and why.

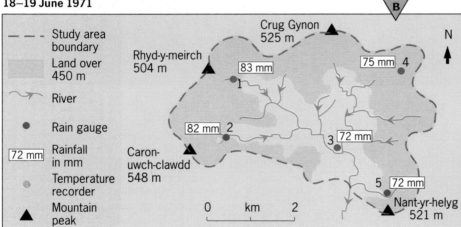

Rainfall in the upper Tywi catchment area during the summer storm of 18–19 June 1971

— — Study area boundary
▨ Land over 450 m
〜 River
● Rain gauge
[72 mm] Rainfall in mm
● Temperature recorder
▲ Mountain peak

Crug Gynon 525 m
Rhyd-y-meirch 504 m
[83 mm] 1
[75 mm] 4
[82 mm] 2
3 [72 mm]
Caron-uwch-clawdd 548 m
5 [72 mm]
Nant-yr-helyg 521 m
0 km 2
N

Weather Magazine

Rainfall intensity and temperatures during the storm

Rainfall intensity and temperature during the storm

Rainfall mm/h: 9 8 7 6 5 4 3 2 1 0
08 12 16 20 24 04 08
18 June   19 June
A   B

4 Source C is a diary of the storm, hour by hour. Put this into words. Notice that the rainfall figures are in mm/hour. This tells us how heavy the rain was at a particular time. This is called RAINFALL INTENSITY.
5 Read Source D. It explains how the storm happened. Suggest how precipitation, such as dew or frost, may form directly on the ground.

What causes moisture to be released from the atmosphere?

The atmosphere around you always contains some water. It is usually an invisible gas form called *water vapour* (see pp.4–5). Under certain conditions the water vapour may change state to form water droplets, by the process of *condensation*. Ice crystals may form if it is cold enough. For condensation to happen, the air must be cooled until it cannot hold the moisture any more. The temperature at which this happens is called the DEW POINT TEMPERATURE. This will vary with different air masses.

● The key understanding is that the *air must be cooled*.
You may have noticed at night that condensation occurs on windows. In the atmosphere, water can be released by contact with a cold surface, such as window glass or the ground. But usually, cooling occurs by the air

being forced to rise. As the air mass rises the atmospheric pressure becomes smaller and the air expands. In expanding, the air mass uses up heat energy. The result is that the air mass cools. METEOROLOGISTS call this type of cooling due to expansion ADIABATIC COOLING.

● The cooling must be enough to *bring the air to its dew point temperature.*
The moisture condenses to form tiny water droplets which we see as clouds. If temperatures are very low, tiny ice crystals may form. If rain, sleet, or snow are to fall from the cloud, the water droplets or ice crystals need to collide with each other, join together and become larger. This lets them fall through the cloud to earth. Source E shows the four ways of causing air to rise, cool, and release precipitation.

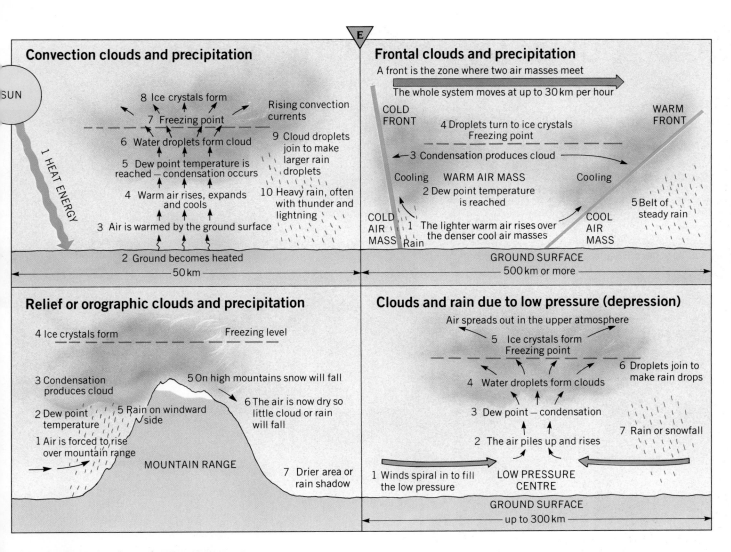

Convection clouds and precipitation

SUN

1 HEAT ENERGY

8 Ice crystals form

7 Freezing point

Rising convection currents

6 Water droplets form cloud

9 Cloud droplets join to make larger rain droplets

5 Dew point temperature is reached – condensation occurs

4 Warm air rises, expands and cools

10 Heavy rain, often with thunder and lightning

3 Air is warmed by the ground surface

2 Ground becomes heated

— 50 km —

Frontal clouds and precipitation

A front is the zone where two air masses meet

The whole system moves at up to 30 km per hour

COLD FRONT

WARM FRONT

4 Droplets turn to ice crystals
Freezing point

3 Condensation produces cloud

WARM AIR MASS

Cooling

Cooling

2 Dew point temperature is reached

COLD AIR MASS   Rain

1 The lighter warm air rises over the denser cool air masses

COOL AIR MASS

5 Belt of steady rain

GROUND SURFACE

— 500 km or more —

Relief or orographic clouds and precipitation

4 Ice crystals form   Freezing level

3 Condensation produces cloud

5 On high mountains snow will fall

6 The air is now dry so little cloud or rain will fall

2 Dew point temperature

5 Rain on windward side

1 Air is forced to rise over mountain range

MOUNTAIN RANGE

7 Drier area or rain shadow

Clouds and rain due to low pressure (depression)

Air spreads out in the upper atmosphere

5 Ice crystals form
Freezing point

6 Droplets join to make rain drops

4 Water droplets form clouds

3 Dew point – condensation

7 Rain or snowfall

2 The air piles up and rises

1 Winds spiral in to fill the low pressure

LOW PRESSURE CENTRE

GROUND SURFACE

— up to 300 km —

How can we explain the Tywi storm?

Source E shows the four ways of causing air to rise, cool, and release precipitation.

Source F is a weather (SYNOPTIC) CHART showing the air masses and FRONTS at noon on 18 June 1971. This frontal system was moving slowly eastwards as the arrow shows. Notice where the Tywi CATCHMENT is.

6 From Source E choose the diagram that shows the main cause of the Tywi storm.

7 Using your chosen diagram, and the weather chart (Source F), explain the pattern of rain shown by the graph (Source C).

8 The Tywi catchment area is very small (Source B), yet rainfall varied. The heaviest rainfall was on higher ground to the west. Look again at Source E and suggest which other cause of precipitation was at work. (Remember the direction of move-

ment of the frontal system.)

9 There are changes of temperature at points A and B in the Source C graph. These are due to changes of

air mass over the Tywi catchment. Explain what is happening by referring to Source F.

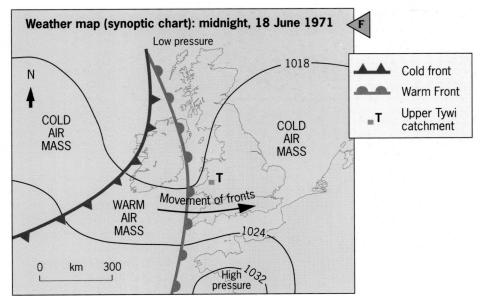

Weather map (synoptic chart): midnight, 18 June 1971

F

Low pressure

N

1018

COLD AIR MASS

COLD AIR MASS

T

Movement of fronts

WARM AIR MASS

1024

0   km   300

1032

High pressure

▲▲▲ Cold front

●●● Warm Front

T Upper Tywi catchment

Freak hurricane kills 13

The headline above appeared in the *Guardian* newspaper on the morning of 17 October 1987. In these pages we will try to understand the events which occurred during the night of 15–16 October 1987. An intense mid-latitude depression (see p. 123) nicknamed 'Mike' caused loss of lives and widespread damage as it passed over southern Britain.

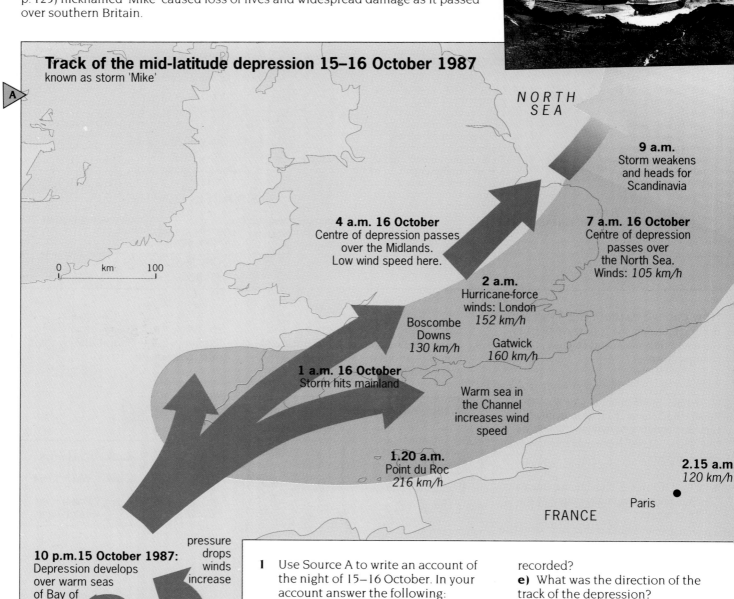

Track of the mid-latitude depression 15–16 October 1987
known as storm 'Mike'

A

NORTH SEA

9 a.m.
Storm weakens and heads for Scandinavia

4 a.m. 16 October
Centre of depression passes over the Midlands. Low wind speed here.

7 a.m. 16 October
Centre of depression passes over the North Sea. Winds: *105 km/h*

2 a.m.
Hurricane-force winds: London *152 km/h*

Boscombe Downs *130 km/h*

Gatwick *160 km/h*

0   km   100

1 a.m. 16 October
Storm hits mainland

Warm sea in the Channel increases wind speed

1.20 a.m.
Point du Roc *216 km/h*

2.15 a.m
120 km/h

Paris

FRANCE

10 p.m.15 October 1987:
Depression develops over warm seas of Bay of Biscay

pressure drops winds increase

pressure plunges to 957 mb

1   Use Source A to write an account of the night of 15–16 October. In your account answer the following:
  a) What was the order of events?
  b) Where was the origin of the storm?
  c) What was the size of the area affected by strong winds?
  d) Where were the strongest winds recorded?
  e) What was the direction of the track of the depression?

2   Work out the speed of the depression as it crossed southern Britain. Use the information given in Source A.

Effects of the hurricane, October 1987

Weather map (pressure pattern) 16 October 1987 0600 GMT

N

LOW

Shoeburyness

Reading

FRANCE

0 km 100

964 966 968 970 972 974 976 978 980 982 984 986 988 990

3 The photographs (Source B) show some of the effects of the storm. In small groups, discuss what might have happened if the storm had not occurred at night.

4 The diagrams in Sources C, D, E and F show the pressure and wind conditions recorded during storm 'Mike'. Use the map (Source C) and graph (Source D) to describe the pressure patterns.

5 When did the pressure centre pass over Reading University?

6 Use the pressure pattern in Source C to explain the wind speed pattern at 0600 hours recorded on the wind chart (Source F).

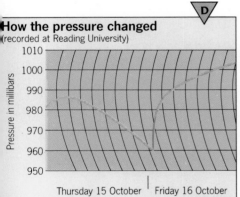

How the pressure changed
(recorded at Reading University)

Pressure in millibars

1010
1000
990
980
970
960
950

Thursday 15 October | Friday 16 October

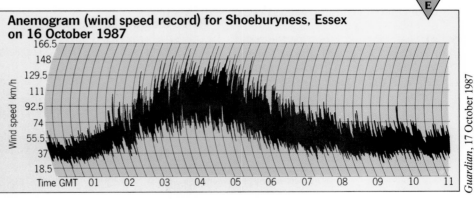

Anemogram (wind speed record) for Shoeburyness, Essex on 16 October 1987

Wind speed km/h

166.5
148
129.5
111
92.5
74
55.5
37
18.5

Time GMT 01 02 03 04 05 06 07 08 09 10 11

Guardian, 17 October 1987

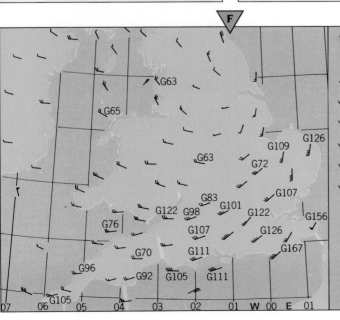

Wind chart
0600 GMT 16 October 1987

3 km/h   56km/h
8km/h   66 km/h
17km/h   74 km/h
29 km/h   82 km/h (strong gale)
37 km/h   92 km/h (storm)
45 km/h

A hurricane force wind is over 120 km/h

The maximum gusts of wind recorded at each weather station are given on the map, eg. G 72 means a gust of 72 km/h was recorded.

Wind arrow points into the wind

G63
G65
G63
G109 G126
G63 G72
G83 G101 G107
G122 G98 G122
G76 G156
G107 G126
G70 G111 G167
G96
G92 G105 G111
G105

07 06 05 04 03 02 01 W 00 E 01

7 a) Describe the direction of wind flow shown in Source F.
b) How can this be explained? (Refer to pp. 122–3.)

8 Use the ANEMOGRAM (Source E) to describe the nature of the wind. Was the wind constant in speed?

9 What was the maximum wind speed recorded and the maximum GUST SPEED recorded, in km/h, on Source F? Did these reach *hurricane force*?

Individual research work

In your research, you will find the information on pages 124–7 helpful. After storm 'Mike' had passed over southern Britain, many newspaper and TV programmes referred to the storm as a hurricane. Sources A–D show the structure of the mid-latitude depression 'Mike', and a typical hurricane.

1   Compare the plan view of 'Mike' (Source A) and a typical hurricane (Source B). In what ways are they similar, and in what ways are they different?
2   How does the vertical structure of 'Mike' (Source C) compare with the vertical structure of a hurricane (Source D)?
3   In what ways do the two storms obtain their energy?
4   How do the wind speeds of a hurricane compare with the wind speeds of 'Mike'?
5   **a)** Use Source C. Describe the pattern of rain belts with storm 'Mike'.
    b) Compare this with the pattern of rain with the hurricane in Sources B and D.

Temperature contrast between the two air masses provides the energy for the storm. On the night of 15 October 1987, a cold air mass of temperature 7°C was recorded in Essex. At the same time, 18°C was recorded in Kent in the warm air mass.

Plan of 'Mike' at 0300 GMT
Pressure pattern 16 October 1987

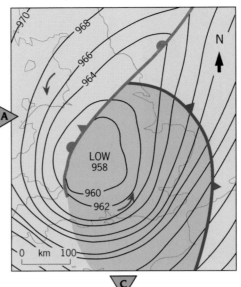

A

LOW
958
960
962

0   km   100

N

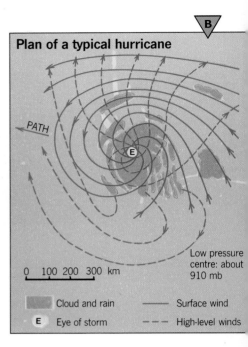

B

Plan of a typical hurricane

PATH

E

Low pressure centre: about 910 mb

0   100 200 300 km

▨ Cloud and rain   —— Surface wind
Ⓔ Eye of storm   ---- High-level winds

C

A mid-latitude depression

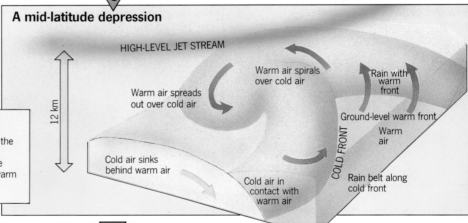

HIGH-LEVEL JET STREAM

12 km

Warm air spreads out over cold air

Warm air spirals over cold air

Rain with warm front

Ground-level warm front

Warm air

COLD FRONT

Cold air sinks behind warm air

Cold air in contact with warm air

Rain belt along cold front

D

The vertical structure of a hurricane

HIGH-LEVEL WINDS

Air spirals upwards in the form of a vortex

As air rises, condensation occurs, releasing heat to drive the storm

15 km

Heavy rain: up to 500mm in 24 h

RAIN

EYE OF STORM

RAIN

Surface winds rotate around the eye. Constant hurricane force over 120 km/h.

WARM OCEAN SURFACE
provides abundant heat and moisture to drive the storm

Library research

Use the school library or other books to find out the answers to these questions.

6   Which parts of the world are affected by hurricanes? Compare this with the area affected by mid-latitude depressions.
7   What are the local names given to hurricanes in different parts of the world?
8   Try to find a case study of a typical hurricane. Use this to compare the effects of hurricanes on people and property with the effects of storm 'Mike'.

LIVING ON THE LITHOSPHERE

Leninakan, USSR, after the 1988 earthquake

11.1 THE EARTH'S CRUST AT WORK

Moving layers

The Earth's crust is like a cracked egg-shell. Source A shows that the Earth is built of several layers. The rocky crust or LITHOSPHERE is the thin outer shell, 15–50 km thick. This shell is broken into a number of large pieces or PLATES, which slide slowly over the mantle (Source A). They move in different directions at 1–3 cm a year. So in 1 million years they could move 50 km. The driving forces are the mighty CONVECTION currents which churn through the upper mantle, dragging the crust plates with them.

Scientists have proved only recently that this is how the lithosphere works. They have called the process PLATE TECTONICS. It explains why continents, oceans, mountains, volcanoes and earthquakes are where they are and why some parts of the world are dangerous to live in.

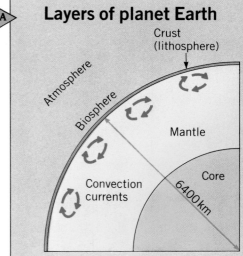

A

Layers of planet Earth

---	Plate margins moving apart
——	Plate margins moving together
→	Direction of movement
	Earthquake areas
••	Volcanic areas

B

Plates and continents

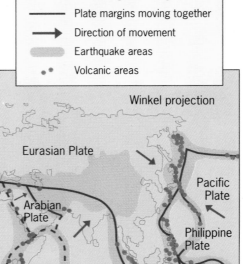

Winkel projection

North American Plate

Iceland

Eurasian Plate

Mount St Helens

San Andreas Fault

Pacific Plate

Arabian Plate

Caribbean Plate

African Plate

Philippine Plate

Pacific Plate

South American Plate

Nazca Plate

Indo-Australian Plate

Antarctic Plate

1 Use Source A to compare the thickness of the three layers which make up the Earth.
2 What are plates, and what makes them move?
3 Use Source B to compare the pattern of earthquakes, volcanic areas, mountains and plate boundaries. What do you notice?
4 Use the map (Source B) and an atlas to follow this example: an American geologist has worked out that in 50 million years' time, Australia could be crowded against China. If so, what might happen to the thousands of islands of Indonesia?
5 What might happen to the Mediterranean Sea in a few million years?

C

Three types of plate margin

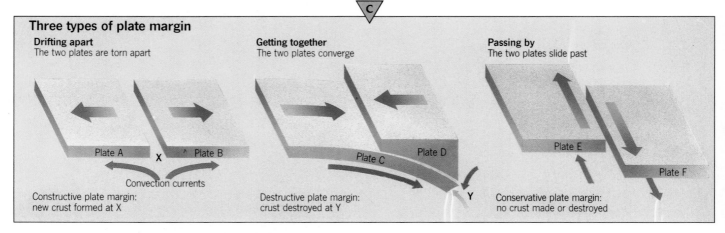

Drifting apart
The two plates are torn apart

Plate A   X   Plate B

Convection currents

Constructive plate margin: new crust formed at X

Getting together
The two plates converge

Plate C   Plate D

Y

Destructive plate margin: crust destroyed at Y

Passing by
The two plates slide past

Plate E

Plate F

Conservative plate margin: no crust made or destroyed

130

Drifting apart: Iceland

If you live in Iceland you can expect something like the scenes in Source D to happen at least once in your lifetime: exciting, dangerous and perhaps disastrous. Millions of tonnes of red-hot liquid material called MAGMA and hot ashes and fragments called *tephra* are exploding through FISSURES. These fissures show that the outer crust is weak here. So, the liquid magma can force its way upwards from the inner crust.

D

Left: Heimay eruption, Iceland, 1973

Right: Cleaning volcanic ash off house roofs after the Heimay eruption

6 The Atlantic Ocean has been widening for 200 million years (Sources E and F). Use an atlas to measure its width today (between, for example, New York and Lisbon).

7 With a partner, study Sources A–F and produce a wall display, including a set of labelled diagrams and sketch maps, to answer these questions:

   a) Why does Iceland have volcanoes?

   b) Why can we say that Iceland is breaking apart?

   c) Why can we say that a new Iceland is being constantly created?

   d) What do scientists believe may happen to the two parts of Iceland over the next one million years?

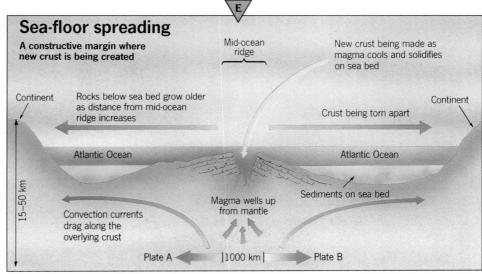

E

Sea-floor spreading

A constructive margin where new crust is being created

Mid-ocean ridge

New crust being made as magma cools and solidifies on sea bed

Continent

Rocks below sea bed grow older as distance from mid-ocean ridge increases

Continent

Crust being torn apart

Atlantic Ocean

Atlantic Ocean

15–50 km

Sediments on sea bed

Magma wells up from mantle

Convection currents drag along the overlying crust

Plate A |1000 km| Plate B

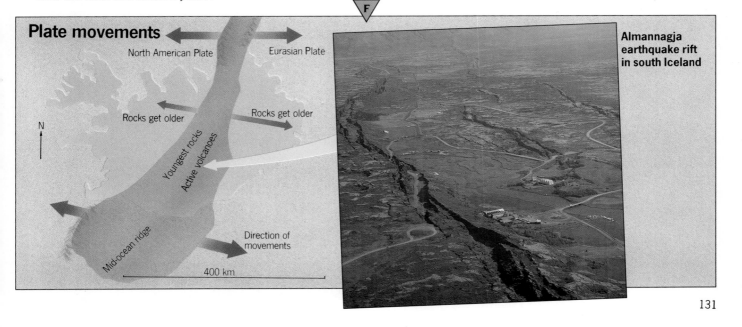

F

Plate movements

North American Plate

Eurasian Plate

Almannagja earthquake rift in south Iceland

N

Rocks get older

Rocks get older

Youngest rocks

Active volcanoes

Mid-ocean ridge

Direction of movements

400 km

131

The photographs in Source A show the impact on one spectator of the explosive eruption of the Mt St Helens volcano on 18 May 1980. Like other scientists, he knew that an eruption was likely – that is why he was there. The mountain had been giving signals for months, but no one had predicted the size and precise time of the eruption.

1 Describe the scenes shown in the photographs (Source A).
2 Follow the diary of the Mt St Helens eruption (Source B), and make a list of the different signs the mountain gave that an eruption was likely.

It's a knockout! The Mt St Helens eruption, 1980

A

B

The diary of an eruption — Mt St Helens, 1980

1980

20 March	3.47 pm. Earthquake measured at 4.0 on RICHTER SCALE. This ends a dormant period of 123 years for the volcano.
25 March	47 earthquakes of 3.0+ on the Richter scale. Their centres lay about 2 km below the north flank of the mountain. Such frequent tremors are known as an EARTHQUAKE SWARM. Geologists begin to study the volcano more closely.
26 March	'Hazard alerts' go out to the local population.
27 March	12.36 pm. *First emissions of steam and a new 70 metre crater* appear in the summit snows.
28 March	The steam and ash plume is 3 km high. Water level in Swift Reservoir, south of the mountain, is lowered by 8 metres. This is a precaution against floodwaters from snowmelt if an eruption occurs.
29 March	A second crater appears and from then the summit gradually collapses.
30 March	Many small eruptions of steam and ash.
3 April	The *first harmonic volcanic tremor*. These rhythmic vibrations last longer than earthquake tremors and are a sign that liquid magma is moving within the volcano. These occur frequently through April.

1980

12 April	A bulge on the north flank of the mountain, first seen on 1 April, reaches 2 km in diameter, and protrudes 100 metres. It lies directly over the earthquake swarm centre, and the source of harmonic tremors.
29 April	The new summit craters have joined up to become one big crater, 500 metres across and 200 metres deep.
30 April	A 30 km radius 'red zone' (or danger zone) is put round the mountain to keep out the thousands of sightseers.
7 May	After two weeks with little surface activity, the steam and ash eruptions begin again.
9 May	A geologist assures people in a local town that 'a series of small landslides' is 'probable'.
10 May	Several earthquakes of 4.0+ Richter and the north flank bulge is growing at 1.5 metres a day.
15–17 May	A series of earthquakes, and the bulge continues to grow.
18 May	8.32 am. An earthquake, 5.0 on the Richter scale, causes the north flank of the mountain to collapse in a landslide. This is followed by the lateral and vertical blasts which destroy the mountain.

What made Mt St Helens erupt?

The diagram in Source C explains how the eruption happened. Notice these points:

- The Juan de Fuca Plate (a fragment of the great Pacific Plate) slides under the north American Plate into the SUBDUCTION ZONE or BENIOFF ZONE (subduction means 'drawn under').
- Friction between the plates causes earthquakes centred deep within the crust.
- At greater depths the rocks melt to form liquid magma at a temperature of at least 1,000°C. Crustal rocks are destroyed – this is a destructive plate margin.

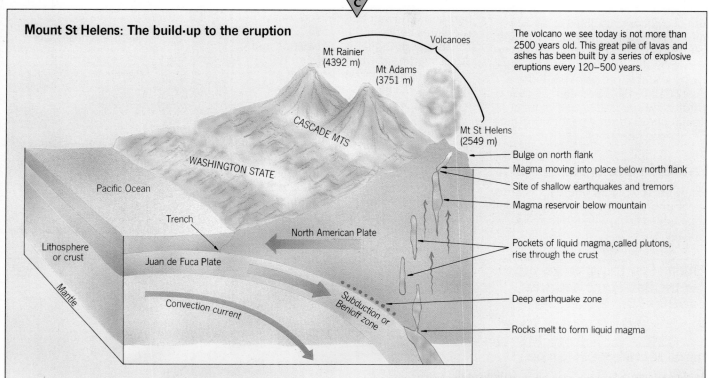

Mount St Helens: The build-up to the eruption

Volcanoes

Mt Rainier (4392 m)

Mt Adams (3751 m)

CASCADE MTS

WASHINGTON STATE

Mt St Helens (2549 m)

Pacific Ocean

Trench

North American Plate

Lithosphere or crust

Juan de Fuca Plate

Mantle

Convection current

Subduction or Benioff zone

Bulge on north flank

Magma moving into place below north flank

Site of shallow earthquakes and tremors

Magma reservoir below mountain

Pockets of liquid magma, called plutons, rise through the crust

Deep earthquake zone

Rocks melt to form liquid magma

The volcano we see today is not more than 2500 years old. This great pile of lavas and ashes has been built by a series of explosive eruptions every 120–500 years.

Using Source C, answer the following questions:

3 What do we mean by a 'subduction zone'? Where is it found? (see pages 130–1.)
4 Why do earthquakes occur in the subduction zone?
5 From where does Mt St Helens get its supply of magma?
6 Explain the bulge which grew on the north flank of the mountain in 1980.
7 Mt St Helens is one of a line of volcanoes which runs for 1,000 km from North California to Canada. Why is this line of volcanoes found where it is?
8 Use Source D to explain why Mt St Helens erupted laterally (sideways).
9 Explain why Mt St Helens, like many other active volcanoes, has long DORMANT periods followed by brief eruptive episodes. (Think of how the magma might occur.)
10 Why is it difficult to predict what will happen with volcanoes?

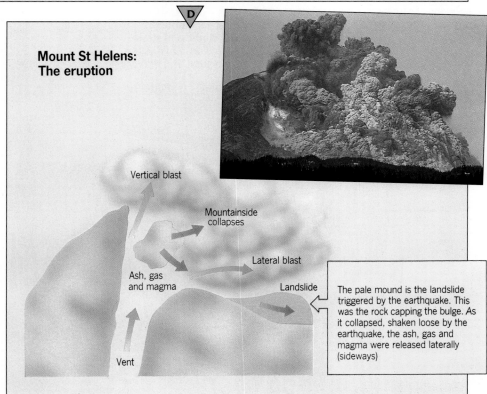

Mount St Helens: The eruption

Vertical blast

Mountainside collapses

Lateral blast

Ash, gas and magma

Landslide

Vent

The pale mound is the landslide triggered by the earthquake. This was the rock capping the bulge. As it collapsed, shaken loose by the earthquake, the ash, gas and magma were released laterally (sideways)

California: dream or nightmare?

'California' – the word carries the picture of a glamorous lifestyle, and 25 million people live in what Americans call 'The Golden State'. But how many of them realise they are living on one of the least stable pieces of the Earth's crust? California is fractured by thousands of FAULTS caused by two great crustal plates moving past each other in opposite directions.

Faults in the crust

Faults are the places where rocks *shear* (crack or break). This can happen when great forces are applied to the rock mass, twisting or sliding the rocks apart.

The great shear zone in California is the San Andreas Fault belt. The enormous pressures between the Pacific and North American Plates are twisting and stressing the rock masses there. The map in Source F shows the result of this stress: California is criss-crossed by fault networks.

1 Measure the length of the San Andreas Fault in California (Source A).
2 Look at Source B. Why are geologists more worried about section **a–b** on the San Andreas Fault than about section **b–c**?

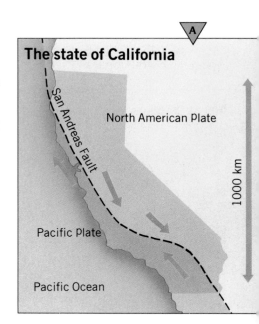

A

The state of California

North American Plate

San Andreas Fault

Pacific Plate

Pacific Ocean

1000 km

B

Map of earthquakes recorded in the San Francisco area 1968–79

In 1906, an earthquake, 8.3 on the Richter Scale, followed by fires, destroyed the city of San Francisco. The San Andreas fault moved violently, having been *locked* for many years

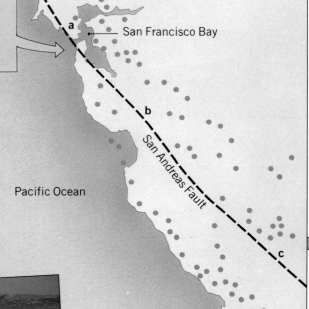

a — San Francisco Bay

b

San Andreas Fault

c

Pacific Ocean

The cause of major earthquakes

No big problem
Sections of faults where plates grind past by frequent short movements

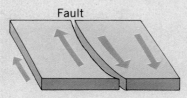

Fault

Plates grind past each other

This causes numerous small earthquakes

Big trouble
Sections of faults may lock or jam against each other. Movement stops, and strain energy builds up. Finally, the strain is too great and the rocks shear.

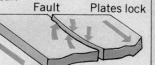

Fault   Plates lock

Result: major earthquake

C

3 Why could a major earthquake in California cause so much damage or loss of life? (Source C.)

San Francisco, a major city on the San Andreas Fault system. In October 1989 it was struck by an earthquake measuring 6.9 on the Richter scale.

Earthquakes

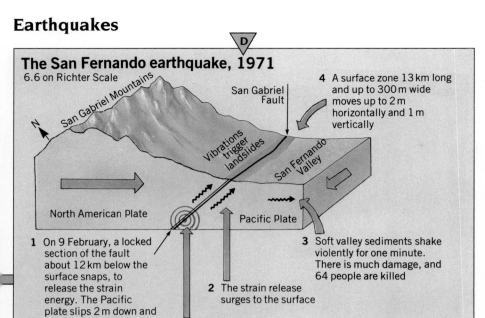

The San Fernando earthquake, 1971
6.6 on Richter Scale

4 A surface zone 13 km long and up to 300 m wide moves up to 2 m horizontally and 1 m vertically

San Gabriel Mountains

San Gabriel Fault

San Fernando Valley

Vibrations trigger landslides

North American Plate

Pacific Plate

1 On 9 February, a locked section of the fault about 12 km below the surface snaps, to release the strain energy. The Pacific plate slips 2 m down and to the left (NW)

2 The strain release surges to the surface

3 Soft valley sediments shake violently for one minute. There is much damage, and 64 people are killed

Earthquake focus

4 Study Source D.
a) What was the cause of the San Fernando earthquake in 1971?
b) What effects did the earthquake have in the valley?

5 Study Source E.
a) What are aftershocks?
b) Describe the pattern of after-shocks following the San Fernando earthquake.

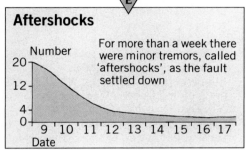

Aftershocks

Number

For more than a week there were minor tremors, called 'aftershocks', as the fault settled down

Date

6 a) Trace the major faults and earth-quakes from Source F. Shade in the areas along the faults where there have been no earthquakes in the last 200 years.
b) Where do you think US geol-ogists would be looking for future earthquakes to occur? Explain your answer.

7 a) What is a graben? (Source G.)
b) Why has a graben formed in Southern California and northern Mexico?
c) Suggest what this area might look like in 10 million years' time. Draw diagrams to help you.

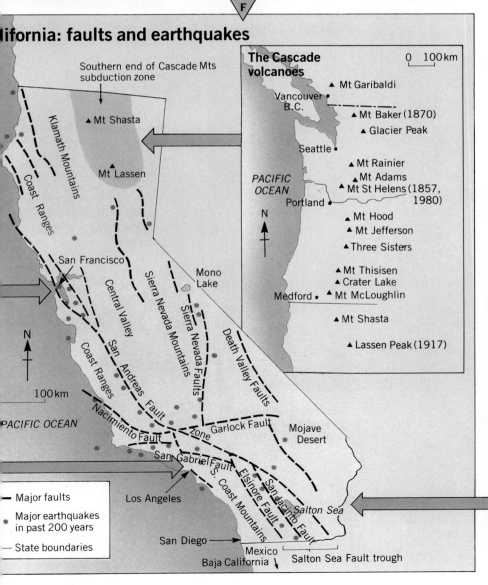

lifornia: faults and earthquakes

Southern end of Cascade Mts subduction zone

Klamath Mountains

Mt Shasta

Mt Lassen

Coast Ranges

San Francisco

Central Valley

Sierra Nevada Mountains

Sierra Nevada Faults

Death Valley Faults

Mono Lake

Coast Ranges

San Andreas Fault

Nacimiento Fault

Garlock Fault

Mojave Desert

San Gabriel Fault

Elsinore Fault

San Jacinto Fault

S. Coast Mountains

Los Angeles

Salton Sea

San Diego

Mexico
Baja California

Salton Sea Fault trough

100 km

PACIFIC OCEAN

— Major faults
• Major earthquakes in past 200 years
— State boundaries

The Cascade volcanoes

0   100 km

▲ Mt Garibaldi

Vancouver B.C.

▲ Mt Baker (1870)

▲ Glacier Peak

Seattle

▲ Mt Rainier
▲ Mt Adams
▲ Mt St Helens (1857, 1980)

PACIFIC OCEAN

Portland

▲ Mt Hood
▲ Mt Jefferson
▲ Three Sisters

▲ Mt Thisisen
▲ Crater Lake
Medford • ▲ Mt McLoughlin

▲ Mt Shasta

▲ Lassen Peak (1917)

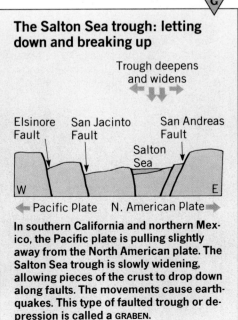

The Salton Sea trough: letting down and breaking up

Trough deepens and widens

Elsinore Fault   San Jacinto Fault   San Andreas Fault

Salton Sea

W   E

← Pacific Plate   N. American Plate →

In southern California and northern Mex-ico, the Pacific plate is pulling slightly away from the North American plate. The Salton Sea trough is slowly widening, allowing pieces of the crust to drop down along faults. The movements cause earth-quakes. This type of faulted trough or de-pression is called a GRABEN.

11.4 FIRM FOUNDATIONS

Asking the right questions

The road running across Mam Tor in Derbyshire (Source A) has clearly been destroyed. From what we have learnt about the Earth's crust, the damage may have been caused by tectonic processes. However, in this case other factors were responsible.

Anyone working in the construction industry must understand how the lithosphere system works. Whether you are building a shed in your garden, an office tower in Dallas, the Great Wall of China or a dam in Pakistan, you need to know about materials: how strong they are, how they behave, what you can and cannot do with them. You must know:

● the materials you are going to use to build your structures, e.g. wood, steel, cement.
● the soils, rocks and landscape on which you are going to build.

The information on these pages illustrates just how important soils, rocks and landscapes are. The photograph in Source A shows what can happen if we

A collapsed section of the A625 across Mam Tor

get it wrong. The layers of rock on Mam Tor were not strong, especially when soaked with water. The road placed an extra load on the slope, and heavy vehicles caused increasing vibrations. These new INPUTS made the hillside unstable, and several landslips occurred. The engineers rebuilt the road several times, but after another slope failure in 1978 they gave up; the road is unlikely to be re-opened.

1 Explain what caused the problems at Mam Tor. (Source A.)

Asking questions about soils

In many areas, the hard bedrock is covered by a skin of soil and partly weathered rock called the REGOLITH. This may be 30 metres thick, so structures are built on it rather than on the 'solid' rock. One characteristic which affects how a soil behaves is its *texture*: size and shape of soil particles, and hence the spaces between them (Source B).

2 With a partner, discuss how the size and shape of soil particles might affect SOIL COHESION. (How well the soil holds together.)
3 What happens to the spaces in the soil:
   a) when it rains heavily?
   b) after a long dry spell?

The next question we need to consider is: 'How does water in the soil affect its cohesion and strength?' But there is no single, simple answer to this.

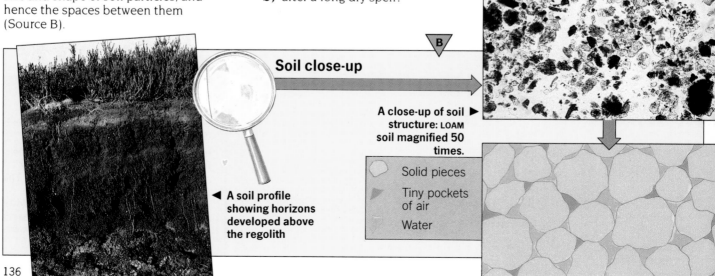

Soil close-up

◄ A soil profile showing horizons developed above the regolith

A close-up of soil ► structure: LOAM soil magnified 50 times.

Solid pieces
Tiny pockets of air
Water

The importance of water

The three pictures in Source C show the same material: sand.

4 What is making the difference in the way the sand behaves?

5 Why can you not build sandcastles with sand which is either too wet or too dry?

6 a) Rank the three pictures in order of their strength of materials.

b) If you wished to build a road across sandy soils, which conditions of sand would give the best foundations, and why?

We can make some general statements:
- Too little water and sandy soil behaves as a solid.
- Some water and sandy soils behaves as a plastic.
- Too much water and sandy soil behaves as a liquid.

Sandy soils seem to have greatest cohesion and strength when they are in the plastic state. However, *not all soil types behave the same way.*

The importance of water

Dry sand   Damp sand   Very wet sand

Where should I build?

7 Work with a partner. You are civil engineers, and a builder has asked you which type of soil is best to build houses on. Using the information in Source D, prepare a brief report which ranks the soils in order of preference. Give reasons for your ranking. (A question to consider: Would your ranking and reasons be the same in all climates?)

What civil engineers want to know about soils

	Texture Large pieces (Coarse grained) → Tiny pieces (Fine grained)			
	Gravel	Sand	Silt	Clay
How strong is it?	strong	strong	weak	weak
Does frost affect it?	little	little	greatly	greatly
Does water pass through it? (permeability)	very well	well	poorly	very poorly
Does it compress if weights are put on it? (when soil is wet)	very little	not much	some	a lot
Does it erode? (when soil is wet)	very variable	quite easily	very easily	rather slowly

Key questions for a builder

- What am I going to build?
- How strong are the soils and rocks?
- Am I going to change the shape of the land?
- Is the land stable, and will my structure (road, dam, house, offices) make it unstable?

The shape of the land

How much of your journey to school from home is absolutely flat? In most parts of the British Isles your answer may be 'not much'. Choose any three photographs in this book and estimate how much of the landscape is flat. Again, your answer is likely to be 'not much'.

The truth is that most land has at least *some* gradient, and most landscapes are made up of sets of slopes. This is important to understand, because TOPOGRAPHY (the shape of the land) has a great influence on whether an area of land is stable and what structures it can bear. Fortunately, in systems terms, most slopes remain in a state of balance for much of the time.

The slope in Source A seems to be stable. Much of it is covered with vegetation, and changes in it are likely to be slow. *But the slope is dynamic*, as materials and energy do pass through and down the slope.

Group discussion:
1 In systems terms, the slope is the store in a *cascade* of energy and materials, on and below the surface. List the materials being stored in, and passed through it.
2 List the inputs to the slope.
3 List the OUTPUTS from the slope.
4 What changes could cause the slope to become unstable and unbalanced? (Think of existing inputs and outputs, and new ones which might be introduced).

Buachille Etive Beag, Glencoe, Scotland

Changing shape

The cross-section in Source B is similar to the slope in Source A. The cross-section in Source C shows the changes to part of the slope caused by a road being built across the slope.

Work in small groups:
5 Describe the changes to the slope when the road is built:
   a) above the road,
   b) below the road.
6 Why are rockfalls likely to occur at x?
7 Why is there a possibility of landslides at Y?
8 **a)** Why has the building of the road made this slope less stable?
   b) Assume that the road *has* to be built. Brainstorm ideas about ways of stopping the slope becoming unstable.

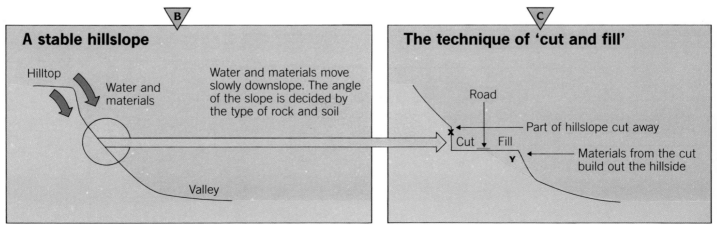

B A stable hillslope

Hilltop

Water and materials

Water and materials move slowly downslope. The angle of the slope is decided by the type of rock and soil

Valley

C The technique of 'cut and fill'

Road

x

Cut ↓ Fill

Part of hillslope cut away

Y

Materials from the cut build out the hillside

San Diego, southern California

The San Diego metropolitan area has a population of 1.5 million, and the numbers double every 20 years. It is part of America's 'sun belt'. The beautiful climate, plus a booming economy, attract people. The enormous demand for houses, office space, shopping plazas, industrial premises has encouraged the sprawl of low-density suburbs across the hilly topography. Building companies use huge earth-moving equipment to reshape the land. Sources D and E show that the builders and engineers have two main types of slope to deal with.

The slopes of this granite hill are very steep but the houses are safe because the rock is strong. The bare ground on the left has been levelled and a house will be built on the solid rock.

The hill on the left is how the landscape starts. Notice the trail-bike tracks eroding the hillside. The hill on the right is being cut into a series of levels or benches on which the houses will be built. This is 'cut and fill' (cut in one place to fill in another, and produce a flat area to build on).

9 In San Diego rain falls in a few storms each winter. The rest of the year is dry and sunny. When are the slopes in Source F most likely to be unstable, and so, landslides to occur? (See pages 136–7.)

10 CHAPARRAL is the natural vegetation. This gives a dense cover of bushes and SCRUB, with a network of roots.

a) How does this help to make the slopes stable?
b) What effect will building developments have, and which slopes will most easily become unstable?

11 San Diego is in the earthquake zone of southern California. How will this tend to make slopes less stable, especially when structures have been placed on the slopes? (Look again at pages 134–7.)

12 You have the plans for a 'dream home'. The builders tell you it will cost 50% more to build on the granite hills (Source D) than on the softer rocks (Source E), but say it will be worth it. Why do they give this advice?

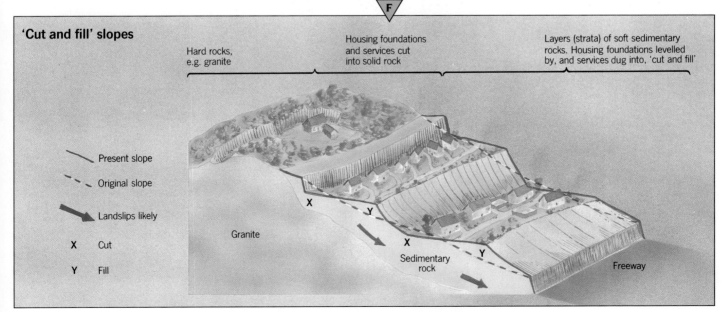

'Cut and fill' slopes

Hard rocks, e.g. granite

Housing foundations and services cut into solid rock

Layers (strata) of soft sedimentary rocks. Housing foundations levelled by, and services dug into, 'cut and fill'

— Present slope
--- Original slope
→ Landslips likely
X Cut
Y Fill

Granite

Sedimentary rock

Freeway

What a creep!

As you look at many slopes, it is hard to believe that anything is happening. Yet on almost all slopes, the regolith (soil and weathered material covering the bedrock) does move. There may be evidence of slope movement if you look closely.

1   Study Source A. List four pieces of evidence that this slope may be moving.

On a stable slope, the fragments may move only a few millimetres down the slope each year. Gravity, water, freezing and thawing, loosening by plant roots and animals, all help this downward drift. This slow, long-term movement is called SOIL CREEP.

How steep the slope is depends on the *angle of rest* of the materials, i.e. the gradient which suits the materials best. The fragments move downslope in a slow cascade (Source B). The slope is in *dynamic equilibrium*: always changing, but staying in a state of balance.

2   With a partner discuss:
a) why excavations and buildings can easily disturb the dynamic equilibrium (balance) of a slope SYSTEM,
b) what human activity *adds* to the slope and what it takes away.

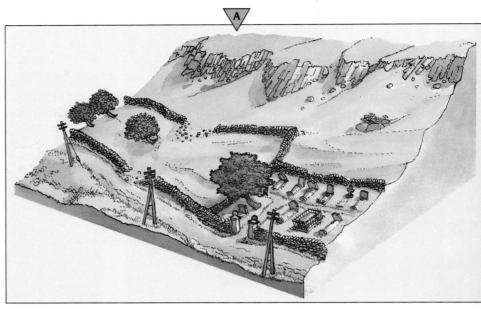

A

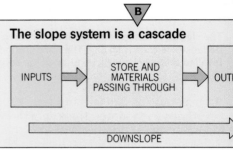

B

The slope system is a cascade

INPUTS → STORE AND MATERIALS PASSING THROUGH → OUTF

DOWNSLOPE

Mass movement

Not all slopes adjust themselves slowly. Some collapse suddenly and without warning. This MASS MOVEMENT can be triggered in several ways, e.g.
● the slope becomes too steep for the materials to hold together,
● the slope materials are weakened,
● extra weight is added to the slope.
The two main types of mass movement are *rockfalls* (Source C) and *landslides* or *earthflows* (Source D).

3   What has caused the Devil's Post-pile shown in Source C?
4   Estimate the size of the boulders in Source C.

C

The Devil's Postpile, Mammoth, California

The cliff is a thick dyke of hard igneous rock, formed from liquid magma which cooled and solidified into columns.

a   Weathering opens up gaps between the columns.

b   The cliff becomes weaker.

c   Parts of the cliff collapse suddenly as a rockfall, shattering into blocks.

d   The rock field grows as more and more of the cliff collapses.

The Portuguese Bend landslides of Palos Verdes, California

Palos Verdes is one of the wealthiest suburbs of Los Angeles. The houses fetch very high prices because the hills rise above the smog of the Los Angeles Basin, and because many have spectacular views over the Pacific Ocean. Some of the residents now know that they live on the site of an ancient landslide. They became aware of this only in the 1950s and 1960s when part of the area began to move again, destroying more than 150 houses. Engineers then discovered that the excavations and buildings on already weak slopes had triggered the series of landslides. Source D shows that it is the combination of natural processes and human activities that has caused the problem.

Study the diagram in Source D to answer these questions:

5 What are the two main rock types?
6 Why should the direction in which the shales are dipping make landslips easier?
7 **a)** In what weather conditions are landslips most likely?
   b) What other factors could cause landslips?
8 List all the factors which come together at Portuguese Bend to cause the unstable conditions.

D

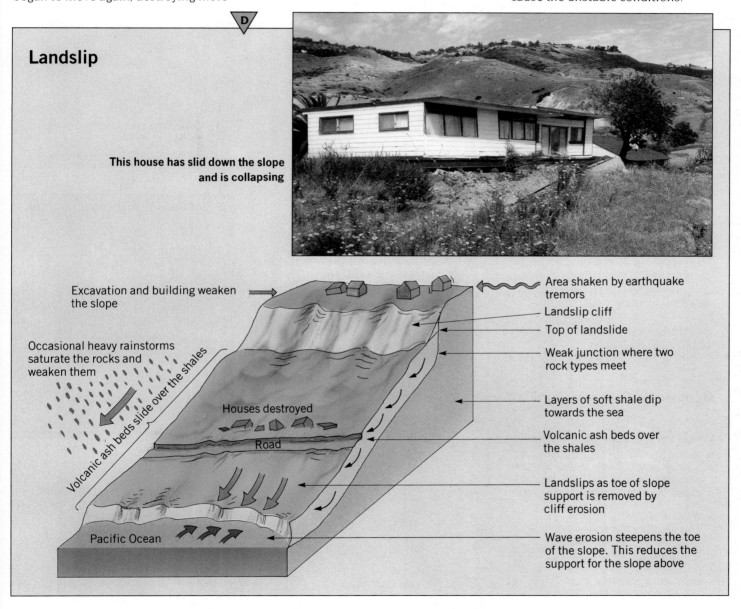

Landslip

This house has slid down the slope and is collapsing

Excavation and building weaken the slope

Occasional heavy rainstorms saturate the rocks and weaken them

Volcanic ash beds slide over the shales

Houses destroyed

Road

Pacific Ocean

Area shaken by earthquake tremors

Landslip cliff

Top of landslide

Weak junction where two rock types meet

Layers of soft shale dip towards the sea

Volcanic ash beds over the shales

Landslips as toe of slope support is removed by cliff erosion

Wave erosion steepens the toe of the slope. This reduces the support for the slope above

9 Work in small groups. Civil engineers have considered the following six ways of reducing landslip risk. For each method, work out how to do it:
   a) Stop the waves eroding the sea-cliffs.
   b) Lower the angle of slope (gradient).
   c) Strengthen the materials of the slope.
   d) Reduce the load on the slope.
   e) Reduce the volume of water percolating through the volcanic ash beds and the shales.
   f) Increase the vegetation cover, especially of deep-rooted plants.

11.7 DANGEROUS MOVES

Armero, Colombia

'Just one big beach of mud.' This was how a local man described the town of Armero after it had been buried by a massive mudflow up to 5 metres thick on 13 November 1985. The photograph in Source A shows what he meant. Several thousand people were killed.

Armero (population 22,500) was a market town in the middle of a fertile agricultural plain at the foot of one of the Andean mountain ranges (Source B). In the Andes, great volcanoes are common, but Nevado del Ruiz, the nearest to Armero, was 50 km away. In the autumn of 1985, the people knew the volcano was erupting, but thought they were safe. They forgot about one of the most dangerous products of the lithosphere at work: the mudflow or LAHAR. These are masses of water, ash and rock fragments that mix together to form sticky mud or slurry and roar down hillsides and valleys at up to 90 km an hour. Ironically, the fertile soils on which the people of Armero grew such good crops came from a mudflow in 1845!

Use the diagrams in Source C to work out what happened.

A

From mountains

Mudflow fans out over plain

Most of the town is buried in mud

1 Why was there such a sudden input of water?
2 What were the two sources of solid load for the mudflow?
3 What made the slopes of the Langunilla valley so unstable?
4 Make a list of the events and inputs which came together to wipe out Armero.

B

Location of Armero, Colombia

CARIBBEAN SEA
Panama
10°N
Venezuela
Nevado del Ruiz
Armero **Bogota**
PACIFIC OCEAN
Colombia
SOUTH AMERICA 0°
Ecuador
Brazil
Peru
0 500km

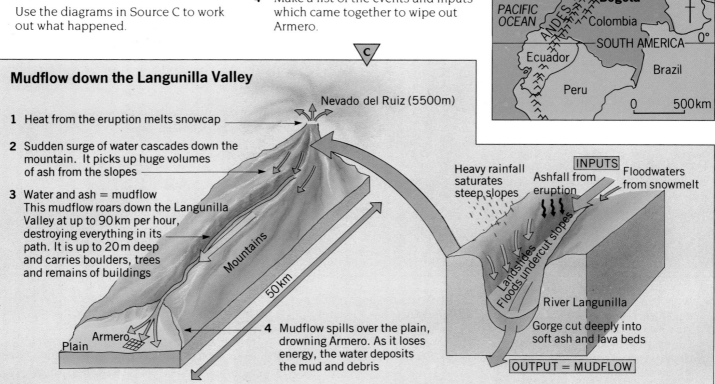

C

Mudflow down the Langunilla Valley

Nevado del Ruiz (5500m)

1 Heat from the eruption melts snowcap

2 Sudden surge of water cascades down the mountain. It picks up huge volumes of ash from the slopes

3 Water and ash = mudflow
This mudflow roars down the Langunilla Valley at up to 90 km per hour, destroying everything in its path. It is up to 20 m deep and carries boulders, trees and remains of buildings

Mountains

50 km

Armero

Plain

4 Mudflow spills over the plain, drowning Armero. As it loses energy, the water deposits the mud and debris

Heavy rainfall saturates steep slopes

INPUTS Floodwaters from snowmelt

Ashfall from eruption

Landslides
Floods undercut slopes

River Langunilla

Gorge cut deeply into soft ash and lava beds

OUTPUT = MUDFLOW

After a disaster happens, the danger does not go away

The Armero mudflow was very similar to those which occurred in the great 1980 Mt St Helens eruption (see pages 132–3). We can look at the Mt St Helens example again to illustrate a very important understanding: major events such as earthquakes, eruptions, landslides and mudflows, often leave behind them very unstable landscapes. This means that, in populated areas, the environment needs managing very carefully for a long time, until it settles into a new state of balance.

The pressures of Spirit Lake, USA
Study Sources D and E.

5 Are the materials of the landslip likely to be strong or weak? Why?
6 Why are the engineers so worried about the landslip materials across Spirit Lake?
7 What are the engineers trying to do?

Mudflow roared down the Toutle Valley, clogging it with mud and debris

Valley of Toutle River, the normal outlet for Spirit lake

Landslide and mudflow deposits block the exit from Spirit Lake. But they are not strong materials

Main landslide from the volcano, plus later mudflows

The landslide and mudflow dam Spirit Lake

Engineers create drainage channels and pump out water to reduce pressure on the mud dam

Great pressure by water

The level of Spirit Lake is raised by new 'dam'

The debris is thousands of dead trees

The Spirit Lake hazard

D

E

Mt St Helens lies in its own smoke haze, 5 km away on the horizon. The broad, bare floor of the Toutle valley shows how the huge volume of mud and ash filled this once deep valley. If the Spirit Lake mud dam fails, the floodwaters will pour down this valley. So the engineers are building low control dams.

The dangers of unstable slopes
Look at Source F.

8 What makes these slopes so unstable?
9 What signs of EROSION can you see?
10 What advantages would there be in leaving the dead trees covering the slopes?
11 Why are people down the valley worried about the loggers removing the dead trees?

F

Logging road cut

Steep slopes of loose ash, 1–5m thick

Forest was flattened by the eruption blast. Loggers haul out the dead timber. This lays the surface bare

Machinery churns up the surface

Logging in the blast zone

11.8 VARIED ROCKS, VARIED LANDSCAPES

Ingleborough, Yorkshire

On pages 106–7 we studied the erosion caused by walkers in the Three Peaks area of Yorkshire. Hiking across these uplands is like walking up and down a series of large, uneven steps (Source A). Ingleborough is built up of a set of rock layers (STRATA) piled on top of each other and gently tilted, like a stack of books. We now know (pages 136–7) that materials vary in their strength. So some rock strata are stronger and harder than others: they are more resistant to weathering and stand out as the steps.

Each layer of rock used to cover the whole area, but millions of years of weathering and erosion have removed all the rock, except for these hills.

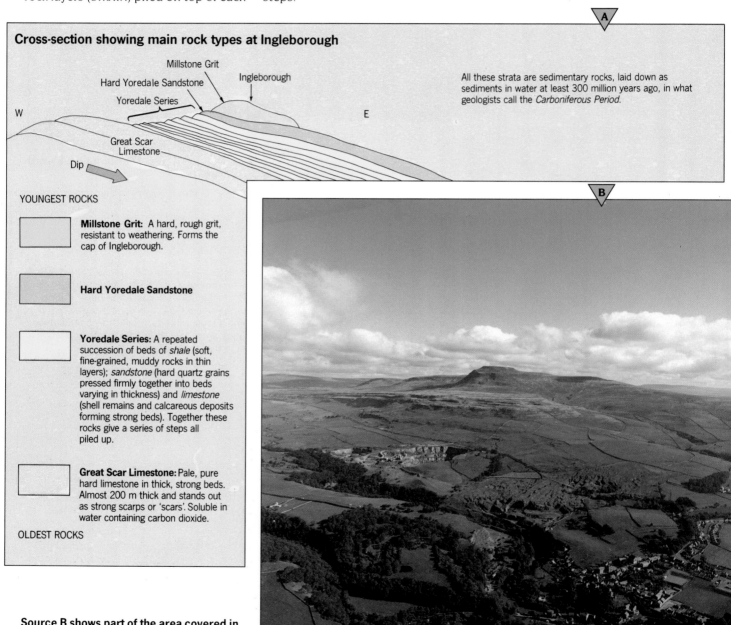

A

Cross-section showing main rock types at Ingleborough

Millstone Grit

Hard Yoredale Sandstone

Yoredale Series

Ingleborough

W

E

Great Scar Limestone

Dip

All these strata are sedimentary rocks, laid down as sediments in water at least 300 million years ago, in what geologists call the *Carboniferous Period*.

B

YOUNGEST ROCKS

Millstone Grit: A hard, rough grit, resistant to weathering. Forms the cap of Ingleborough.

Hard Yoredale Sandstone

Yoredale Series: A repeated succession of beds of *shale* (soft, fine-grained, muddy rocks in thin layers); *sandstone* (hard quartz grains pressed firmly together into beds varying in thickness) and *limestone* (shell remains and calcareous deposits forming strong beds). Together these rocks give a series of steps all piled up.

Great Scar Limestone: Pale, pure hard limestone in thick, strong beds. Almost 200 m thick and stands out as strong scarps or 'scars'. Soluble in water containing carbon dioxide.

OLDEST ROCKS

Source B shows part of the area covered in Sources C and D. The settlement is part of the small town of Ingleton which lies just off the map near point (a). Use the large quarry and Ingleborough peak to work out the direction the photographer was facing.

1. Use the contour map (Source C) to draw an altitude cross-section from point **a** to point **b**. (Make sure your x axis is the same as the distance from **a** to **b**.)

2. On tracing paper placed over Source D, construct a geological cross-section. Use Source A to help you and use different colours for each rock type.

3. **a)** Place your geological cross-section over the altitude cross-section and describe what relationships you see. For instance, where do the main steps and steep slopes occur?
   b) Use Sources A and B to explain these relationships.

4. Suppose you decide to walk from Ingleborough Summit (grid ref 741746) to Trow Gill (grid ref 755716). Describe your walk in as much detail as possible. (Drawing another cross-section may help.)

Scale 1:50,000
(2 cm = 1 km)

N

Contour map of the Ingleborough area

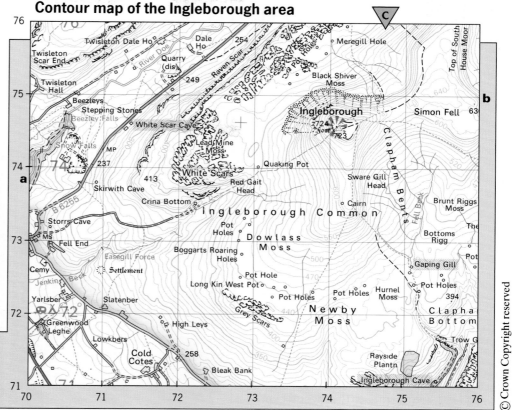

Geological map of the Ingleborough area

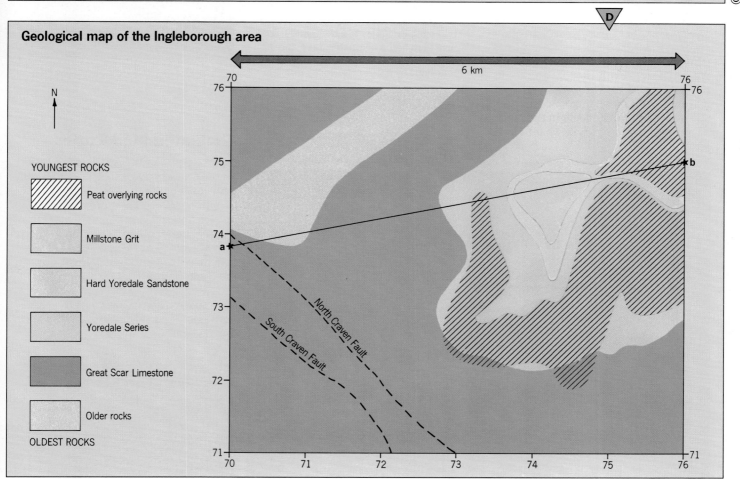

6 km

N

YOUNGEST ROCKS

Peat overlying rocks

Millstone Grit

Hard Yoredale Sandstone

Yoredale Series

Great Scar Limestone

Older rocks

OLDEST ROCKS

North Craven Fault

South Craven Fault

'Did ice do all this?'

Ice and the water melting from it have created some of the most beautiful landscapes in the world. In every continent, mountain environments show what ice-sheets and glaciers have done and how powerful they are.

The people in the photograph (Source A) are admiring the steep rock walls and great waterfalls in the Yosemite valley, California, one of the USA's most popular National Parks (Source B). In the British Isles, too, our favourite National Parks are glaciated landscapes (such as Snowdonia, Lake District, Yorkshire Dales) and millions of people visit them.

During the Earth's long history, there have been several ice ages: periods when average temperatures dropped and ice-sheets spread. The most recent cooling occurred within the last 2 million years, and is known as the PLEISTOCENE PERIOD. At one stage, ice-sheets covered the British Isles as far south as a line from the Severn Estuary to the Wash. The ice finally disappeared from our mountains, and from Yosemite, less than 10,000 years ago. So we can still see many of its effects in the landscape, but only if we know what to look for!

The Yosemite Valley is a U-shaped trough, more than half a kilometre deep and 12 kilometres long, carved into tough, granite mountains by a powerful valley glacier.

The Athabasca Glacier, Canada

Glaciated landscapes

Source C shows the Athabasca Glacier in the Canadian Rockies. Look carefully and you will see:
- both ice and water are involved;
- ice and MELTWATER cause erosion and deposition.

Any feature of a glaciated landscape can be placed into one of the four boxes in Source D.

GLACIAL LANDFORMS are caused by ice. FLUVIO-GLACIAL LANDFORMS are caused by meltwater.

Glaciated landscape features		
Agent	Process	
	Erosion	Depos
Ice		
Meltwater		

What to look for

The diagram (Source E) shows features found in a typical glacial valley, in areas like Snowdonia or the Lake District. The Assignment on page 148 aims to help you recognise and understand them when you see them. Remember:

- You may not find all of the features in any one valley.
- Features may occur in different places in different valleys.
- Vegetation, such as forests in Yosemite (Source B), may make features less easy to see.

Work in pairs.

1 Study Source E and find one feature for each box in Source D.
2 Which features labelled on Source E can you see on Source B? Draw a labelled sketch of Source B.

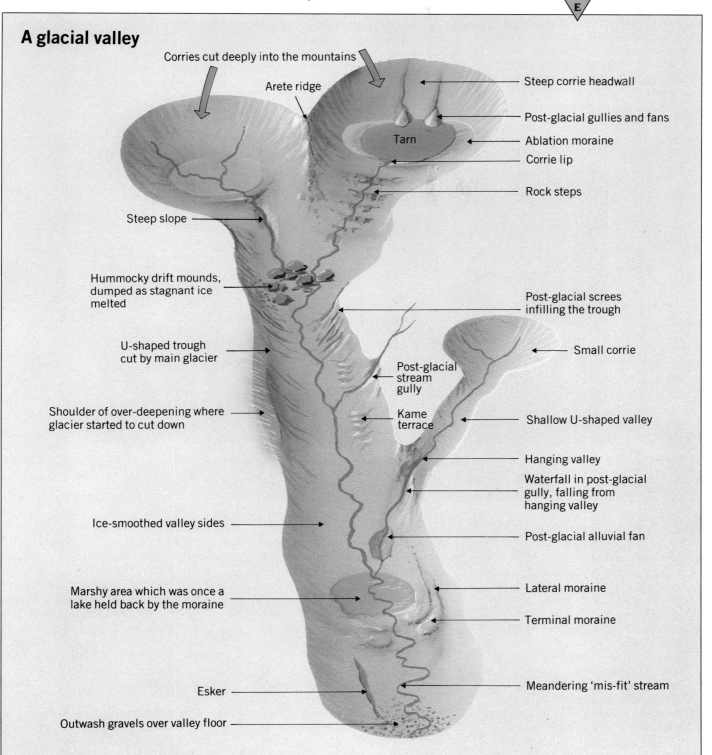

E

A glacial valley

Corries cut deeply into the mountains

Arete ridge

Steep corrie headwall

Post-glacial gullies and fans

Tarn

Ablation moraine

Corrie lip

Rock steps

Steep slope

Hummocky drift mounds, dumped as stagnant ice melted

Post-glacial screes infilling the trough

U-shaped trough cut by main glacier

Small corrie

Post-glacial stream gully

Shoulder of over-deepening where glacier started to cut down

Kame terrace

Shallow U-shaped valley

Hanging valley

Waterfall in post-glacial gully, falling from hanging valley

Ice-smoothed valley sides

Post-glacial alluvial fan

Marshy area which was once a lake held back by the moraine

Lateral moraine

Terminal moraine

Esker

Meandering 'mis-fit' stream

Outwash gravels over valley floor

11 LEARNING ABOUT THE WORK OF ICE

We can enjoy beautiful landscapes more if we understand what we are looking at. So, in many National Parks, there are displays, self-guiding trails, information boards to help us. The Rangers and other park managers see this education and interpretation service as an important part of their work: to encourage use and understanding, while conserving and preserving the environment.

Planning a self-guiding trail

The glacial trough on page 147 (Source E) was cut by a valley glacier which finally disappeared about 9,000 years ago. Since then, streams, wind, freezing and thawing have been changing the landscape which the ice left behind. So what we see today tells us about: (a) the work of ice and the meltwaters from it, and (b) what has been happening since the ice disappeared.

The valley is about 4 km long. It lies in a National Park, and the Rangers want to open it up to visitors. Their aim is to lay out a self-guiding trail. A self-guiding trail should do two things: first, allow visitors to walk easily and safely through an area; second, point visitors towards distinctive, interesting features, and tell people about these features.

Information sign in the Yosemite National Park

Work in pairs or in small groups.
1   On a copy of Source E (page 147) plot the route of the trail. Mark locations at which you would give information (*not more than 10* locations – as you do not want visitors to lose interest!).
2   For each location, set out what information you would display on a board: labelled sketch or diagram; written information; what direction to look, etc. (You need to plan the *design* of each display.)
3   Produce a pamphlet for the visitor to carry, including: map; background information, e.g. about the valley glacier and the work of ice;

information about the walk; information about the selected locations. Include any diagrams and illustrations you think would be helpful.

How to go about it
●   Use any physical geography textbooks you have available to find out:
    a) how valley glaciers work;
    b) how the features shown on page 147 were formed.
    Remember: First, some features were formed while the ice was present and other features have been developing since the ice disap-

peared. Second, features can be formed by either erosion or deposition.

●   You need to understand how ice works and how the various landform features were made before you can select your key features, choose the best route and locations for the trail, design the display boards on the trail, and produce your pamphlet.

●   Display boards and the pamphlet must be clear, attractive and brief. They should guide, describe and explain.

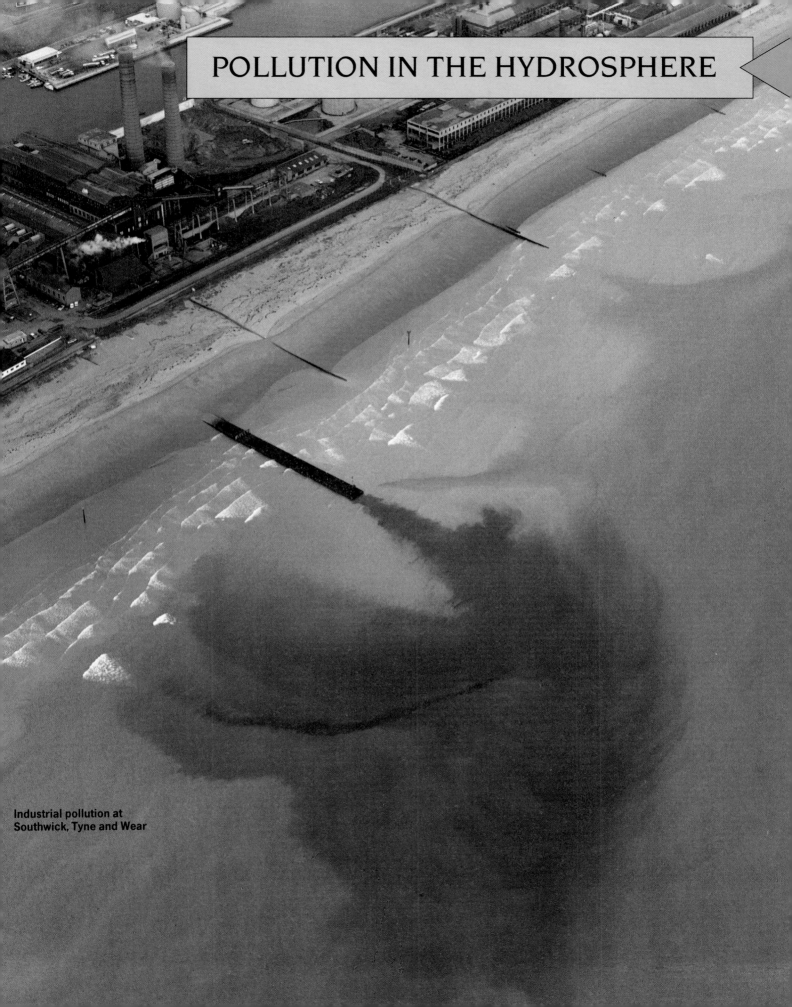

Industrial pollution at
Southwick, Tyne and Wear

Water, water everywhere, yet not a drop to drink

The chemical formula for water is H_2O: two atoms of hydrogen to each atom of oxygen, combined to give a clear, sparkling liquid. It sounds simple, but things are not quite what they seem. Pure H_2O is very rare in our environment. This Unit helps you to see why, and to understand the difference between activities which do good, and those which cause damage. The key questions for this Unit are:

What do we mean by water pollution?
What causes it?
What can we do about it?

1 Look at the photograph on page 149 and write down your feelings about it.

In pairs, study the diagram (Source A) carefully.
2 **a)** Make a list of all the ways in which water is being polluted.
   b) Now try to divide your list into pollution caused naturally, and pollution caused by human activity.
3 Describe the routes that the pollutants follow to the river. Try to use the terms that you have learnt from Unit 5.
4 How does pollution in the atmosphere lead to pollution in the hydrosphere?
5 How does the amount of pollution affect the animal life found in the river?

What is pollution?
6 From the examples shown in Source A, and from the photograph on page 149, write your own definition of the word *pollution*. Try to use systems language, e.g. INPUTS, STORES, and OUTPUTS. Compare your definition with others in your class. In what ways are your definitions similar, and in what ways do they differ?

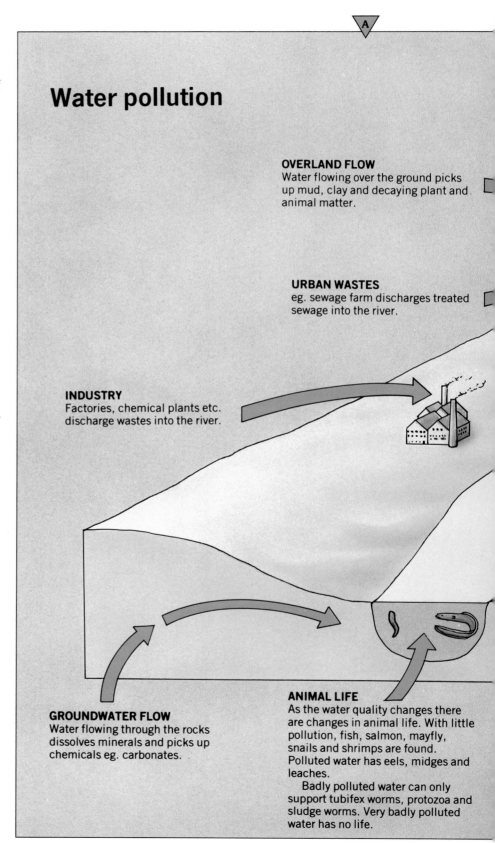

A

Water pollution

OVERLAND FLOW
Water flowing over the ground picks up mud, clay and decaying plant and animal matter.

URBAN WASTES
eg. sewage farm discharges treated sewage into the river.

INDUSTRY
Factories, chemical plants etc. discharge wastes into the river.

GROUNDWATER FLOW
Water flowing through the rocks dissolves minerals and picks up chemicals eg. carbonates.

ANIMAL LIFE
As the water quality changes there are changes in animal life. With little pollution, fish, salmon, mayfly, snails and shrimps are found. Polluted water has eels, midges and leaches.
Badly polluted water can only support tubifex worms, protozoa and sludge worms. Very badly polluted water has no life.

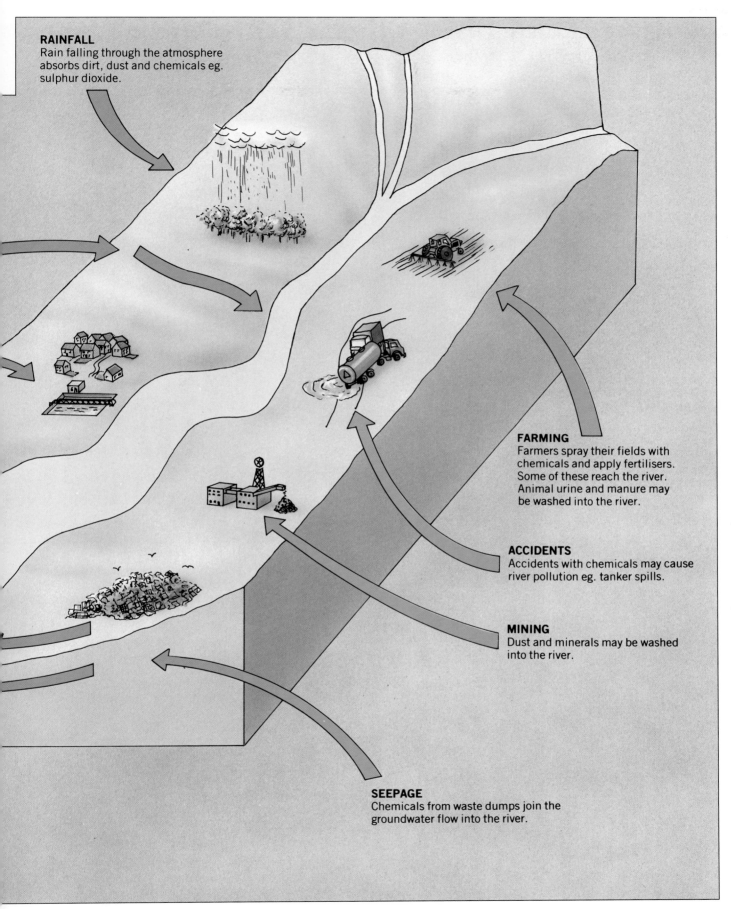

RAINFALL
Rain falling through the atmosphere absorbs dirt, dust and chemicals eg. sulphur dioxide.

FARMING
Farmers spray their fields with chemicals and apply fertilisers. Some of these reach the river. Animal urine and manure may be washed into the river.

ACCIDENTS
Accidents with chemicals may cause river pollution eg. tanker spills.

MINING
Dust and minerals may be washed into the river.

SEEPAGE
Chemicals from waste dumps join the groundwater flow into the river.

Water managers

Until 1990 the supply of high-quality water was the responsibility of the government (see Source B). They also managed the quality of water in rivers, canals and estuaries. Since 1990, water supply has been in the hands of private companies based upon the same regions. Water quality is now the responsibility of the National Rivers Authority, a government body.

As you know, maintaining water supply and quality is not easy. In 1985 a report showed how well the Water Authorities had done. Sources A and B show three levels of water quality (good, fair and poor). Source C shows what these mean.

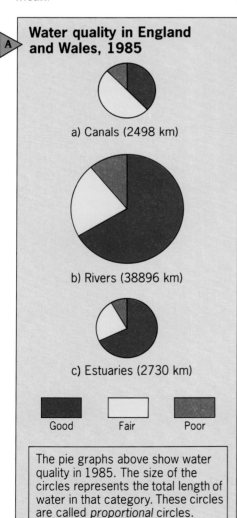

A Water quality in England and Wales, 1985

a) Canals (2498 km)

b) Rivers (38896 km)

c) Estuaries (2730 km)

| Good | Fair | Poor |

The pie graphs above show water quality in 1985. The size of the circles represents the total length of water in that category. These circles are called *proportional* circles.

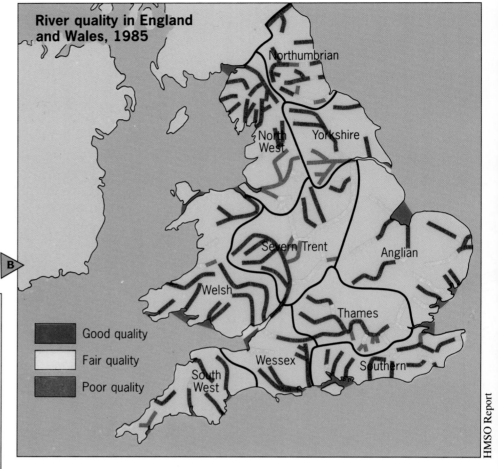

B River quality in England and Wales, 1985

- Good quality
- Fair quality
- Poor quality

HMSO Report

1 **a)** From the pie graphs (Source A) rank the water quality of canals, rivers, and estuaries from *best* to *worst*.
b) What proportion of each pie graph is *poor*?
c) Suggest reasons for the differences.
2 **a)** From the map (Source B) list the Water Authorities which had stretches of *poor*-quality water.
b) Which region seems to have had the most poor-quality water, and which the least?
c) Compare your answers with a partner and suggest reasons for the differences between regions. (Refer to maps of CONURBATIONS, cities, industries, and farming types, and check back to pages 150–1.)

Water quality classification scheme

C

Description	Possible use
Good quality	Waters of high quality and suitable for supply to humans; game and high-class fisheries. High amenity value, e.g. for leisure
Fair quality	Waters suitable for human use after advanced treatment; support reasonably good fisheries; moderate amenity value, e.g. leisure.
Poor quality	Waters are polluted to an extent that fish may be absent; may be used for low-grade industrial use. Further use if cleaned up.

A closer look at the regions

The graphs in Source D give more accurate figures than Source B, so that we can compare regions.

3 a) Rank the regions from best to worst in water quality. (Use the *good-quality* columns).
b) Which regions had above-average good-quality water?
c) Which two regions had the worst quality? (Explain how you used the columns to make your decision.)

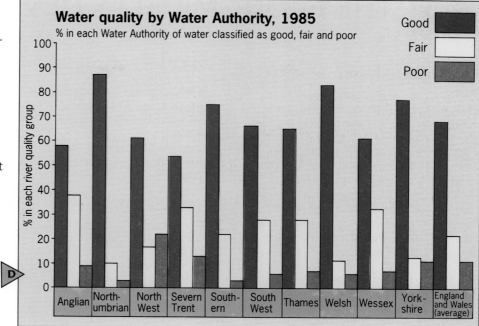

Water quality by Water Authority, 1985
% in each Water Authority of water classified as good, fair and poor

Good / Fair / Poor

% in each river quality group

Anglian, Northumbrian, North West, Severn Trent, Southern, South West, Thames, Welsh, Wessex, Yorkshire, England and Wales (average)

Did things get better?

Change in the quality of rivers and canals in England and Wales between 1980 and 1985.

(Figures as a percentage of the total length of rivers and canals for each authority).

Anglian	+6.0	Thames	−1.0
Northumbrian	+2.5	Welsh	+1.5
North-West	−7.5	Wessex	+15.5
Seven-Trent	+3.0	Yorkshire	−3.0
Southern	−1.5	England and	
South-West	−41.0	Wales	−2.3%

A + sign means that water quality has improved.
A − sign means water quality has declined.

Where did the problems come from?

These figures for the Mersey Basin in the North-West Region show the problems the Water Authority faces.
Water quality changes, Mersey Basin, 1983–6

Pollution source	Improvements (km)	Deterioration (km)	Change (km)
Sewers	27	10	+17
Industrial discharges	18	6	+12
Agricultural chemicals	1	43	−42

4 a) On an outline map of England and Wales draw in the boundaries of the Regional Water Authorities. Using the information in Source E, showing 1980–85 changes, shade each region in colour using the four categories below:
i) Slight improvement in water quality (+0.1 to +5.0).
ii) Good improvement in water quality (more than +5.1).
iii) Slight decline in water quality (−0.1 to −5.0).
iv) Large decline in water quality (more than −5.0).
b) Where did water quality decline and improve?
c) Use Source G to suggest reasons for the changes in water quality shown on your map. Choose *three* Water Authority regions in your answer.

5 a) Use Source F to describe the changes in pollution in the Mersey Basin during 1983–86.
b) What were the reasons for changes in water quality in the Mersey Basin? (Use Source G.)

6 If you live in England or Wales, for your own water supply region (in Source B) find out what are likely to be the two most important factors improving water quality, and the two factors most likely to cause water quality to decline.

Factors which cause improvements in water quality
1) Money spent on new or improved sewage treatment works.
2) Improvements made by industry in treating their discharges.
3) Closing of factories and mines.
4) Polluting discharges diverted and treated by water businesses.
5) Ministry of Agriculture encourage farmers to reduce pollution.
6) New laws are passed and higher standards are required.

Factors which cause water quality to decline
1) Sewage treatment plants become overloaded and lower-quality treated water is let out.
2) Intensive farming methods, and changes of land use, bring more pollution.
3) Discharges from fish farms.
4) Waste from working and abandoned mines.
5) Overflows from storms.
6) Pollution accidents increase.

The Ganga, India

The quotation in Source A comes from a Hindu religious poem. Unfortunately, *the promise has not been kept.*

The River Ganga (Ganges) in northern India is of major importance to India's people. It is a holy river to the Hindus, visited by millions of pilgrims who come to bathe in its waters (Source B). Apart from its religious importance, the river is also a source of water for drinking, washing and IRRIGATION.

The pressure of rapid population growth, and the poverty of many of the people, have resulted in the Ganga becoming badly polluted. In the more industrialised parts of the world industrial and agricultural pollution are the main concerns, but the Ganga is polluted mainly by sewage.

On these pages we will try to answer the following key questions:
- What are the sources of water pollution in developing countries?
- Are the problems similar or different to water pollution issues in Britain?
- How does the MONSOON affect the discharge and quality of river water over the year?
- How can pollution be reduced?

1 Using Source C, describe the mean discharge of the Ganga over the year.
2 In pairs, discuss how the sources of pollution of the Ganga (Source D) compare with those in Britain. (See pp. 152–3.)

A

“ Ganga was unwilling to come to Earth. But Bhagirath persisted until Ganga, exasperated, cried out, 'If I go down to Earth, sinners will want to purify themselves by bathing in my waters. I will be left tainted and polluted. No one will care.'

And Bhagirath replied, 'Mother, I promise the religious and the pious of future generations will take care of you. They will preserve your purity.' ”
(Shrimat Bhagavat Purana)

B

The Ghats at Varanasi

C

Mean discharge of the Ganga at Farakka

Rate (000m³/s)

0 2 4 6 8 10 12 14 16 18 20 22 24 26 28 30 32 34 36 38 40 42 44 46 48 50

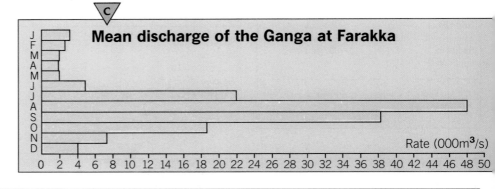

Sources of Ganga pollution

D

1 *Urban waste.* Storm water mixes with sewage, human, cattle and kitchen wastes and is carried by drains to the river. Of the 80 million people living in the towns and cities along the Ganga, only 27 million people have a sewerage system. Very few towns have sewage treatment plants. Sewage causes 75% of the Ganga pollution.

2 *Industrial liquid waste.* There are 132 big factories and many small factories along the Ganga.

3 *Surface runoff from cultivated land* carrying chemical fertilisers, pesticides, insecticides and manures. About 142 million people live in the rural areas of the Ganga Basin.

4 *Surface runoff from urban areas* carrying urban and industrial solid wastes direct from tips etc, into the Ganga.

5 *Religious ceremonies.* People bathe in the holy waters of the Ganga, and it is a ritual for dead bodies to be burnt alongside the river in holy places called *ghats*. Many half-burnt corpses find their way into the river. No one knows how many bodies enter the river, but in the city of Varanasi alone the figure is about 200 per day. Very poor people may not be able to afford to buy the wood to cremate their loved ones. Bodies may simply be weighted down and thrown into the river.

The Ganga Basin: water quality

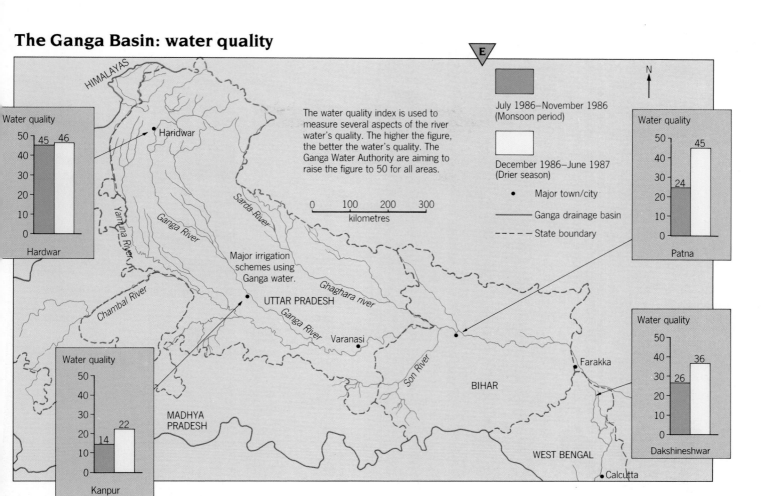

The water quality index is used to measure several aspects of the river water's quality. The higher the figure, the better the water's quality. The Ganga Water Authority are aiming to raise the figure to 50 for all areas.

E

July 1986–November 1986 (Monsoon period)

December 1986–June 1987 (Drier season)

● Major town/city

— Ganga drainage basin

- - - State boundary

Water quality — Hardwar
45, 46

Water quality — Patna
24, 45

Water quality — Kanpur
14, 22

Water quality — Dakshineshwar
26, 36

HIMALAYAS · Haridwar · Yamuna River · Ganga River · Sarda River · Chambal River · Major irrigation schemes using Ganga water. · UTTAR PRADESH · Ghaghara river · Ganga River · Varanasi · Son River · MADHYA PRADESH · BIHAR · Farakka · WEST BENGAL · Calcutta

0 100 200 300 kilometres

3 Find the Himalayas in Source E. Follow the Ganga from its source to its mouth in the Bay of Bengal.
a) Describe the water quality for each of the four stations shown on the map: Hardwar, Kanpur, Patna and Dakshineshwar.
b) What changes occur in water quality downstream?
c) How does water quality vary between July and November (the monsoon season) and December–June? (Refer to p 119 for details of the monsoon climate.)
4 Now try to explain the water quality

changes downstream, and over the year. To help you with this, look at the list of sources of pollution (Source D) and consider the following factors:
a) Increasing pollution occurs as the river moves downstream and more pollutants enter the water.
b) The monsoon rains cause large amounts of overland flow into the river.
c) The location of the towns and cities.
d) Tributaries of the Ganga add cleaner water to the river.

e) Irrigation schemes divert much of the river water and concentrate the pollution in what is left.
5 In pairs, discuss by what means the Indian Government is aiming to tackle the pollution problem.
6 Where along the river would you recommend that the Ganga Action Plan (Souces E and F) begins to control pollution first? Why?
7 Why may the task of the Ganga Action Plan be made more difficult by the poverty of the people and the large population involved?

F

The Ganga Action Plan

"This programme, starting at Varanasi here today, will reach out to every corner of our land and to all our rivers. In the years to come, not only the Ganga, but all our rivers will be clean and pure as they were thousands of years ago."

The above is a quote from Indian Prime Minister Rajiv Gandhi, launching the Ganga Action Plan at Varanasi, 14 June 1986.

The Ganga Action Plan is a major Indian Government survey and investment of money into improving the water quality of the Ganga. The aim is to bring the water quality index up to at least 50 in all areas.

Source E shows the figures for July 1986 to June 1987. This will be achieved by:

1 Involving universities in understanding the river and its pollution.

2 Installing and repairing sewers to prevent flow into the Ganga.
3 Building new sewage treatment plants.
4 Low-cost sanitation schemes to prevent human wastes reaching the river.
5 Building electric crematoria.
6 Schemes to prevent runoff during the monsoon from carrying waste to the river.
7 Educating the local people.

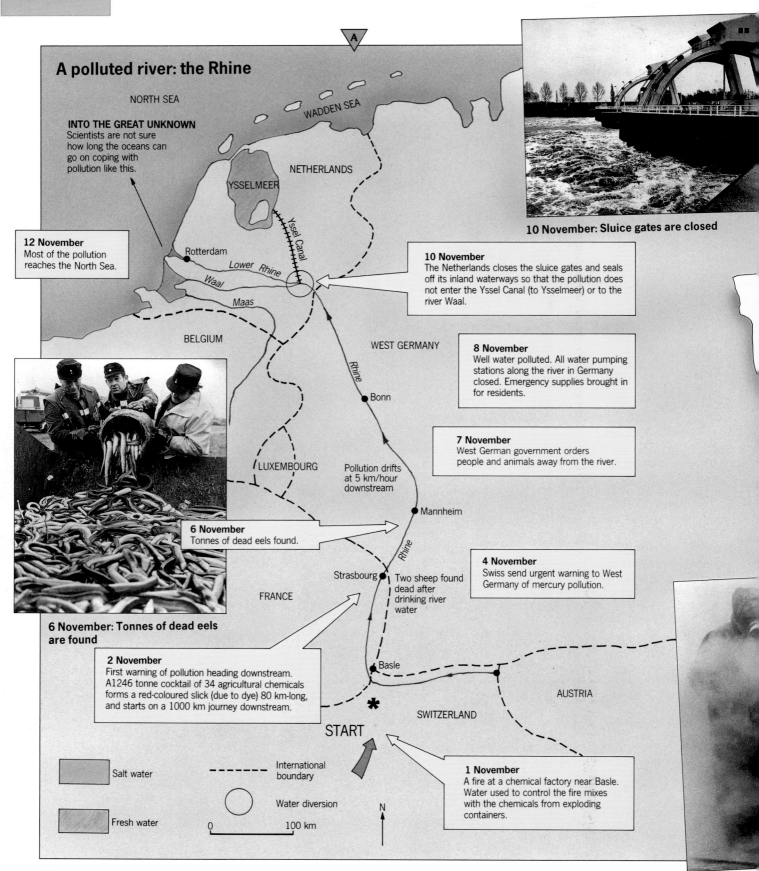

A polluted river: the Rhine

NORTH SEA

WADDEN SEA

INTO THE GREAT UNKNOWN
Scientists are not sure how long the oceans can go on coping with pollution like this.

NETHERLANDS

YSSELMEER

Yssel Canal

12 November
Most of the pollution reaches the North Sea.

Rotterdam

Lower Rhine

Waal

Maas

BELGIUM

10 November
The Netherlands closes the sluice gates and seals off its inland waterways so that the pollution does not enter the Yssel Canal (to Ysselmeer) or to the river Waal.

10 November: Sluice gates are closed

WEST GERMANY

8 November
Well water polluted. All water pumping stations along the river in Germany closed. Emergency supplies brought in for residents.

Rhine

Bonn

7 November
West German government orders people and animals away from the river.

LUXEMBOURG

Pollution drifts at 5 km/hour downstream

6 November
Tonnes of dead eels found.

Mannheim

4 November
Swiss send urgent warning to West Germany of mercury pollution.

Rhine

Strasbourg

Two sheep found dead after drinking river water

FRANCE

6 November: Tonnes of dead eels are found

2 November
First warning of pollution heading downstream. A1246 tonne cocktail of 34 agricultural chemicals forms a red-coloured slick (due to dye) 80 km-long, and starts on a 1000 km journey downstream.

Basle

AUSTRIA

SWITZERLAND

START

1 November
A fire at a chemical factory near Basle. Water used to control the fire mixes with the chemicals from exploding containers.

	Salt water	- - - - -	International boundary
		◯	Water diversion
	Fresh water		

0   100 km

N

The Basle incident

In November 1986, a stretch of the River Rhine from Basle in Switzerland to Mannheim in West Germany was declared ecologically dead. All animal life, from micro-organisms to fish and river birds, had been killed. Estimates suggest that it will take ten years for the Rhine to recover.

What was the cause of all this destruction? Follow the events on the map (Source A) to find out. Find the 'start here' sign.

The River Rhine example allows us to find out some of the causes of river pollution. Since the Rhine flows through four countries, we can study some of the problems involved in pollution control and international management of the world's major rivers.

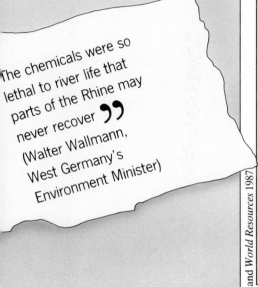

"The chemicals were so lethal to river life that parts of the Rhine may never recover"
(Walter Wallmann, West Germany's Environment Minister)

1 November: Fire at a chemical factory near Basle

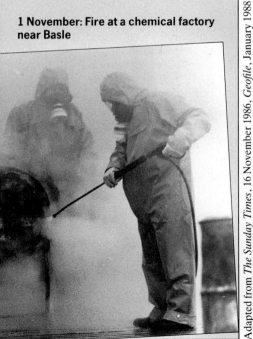

Adapted from *The Sunday Times*, 16 November 1986, *Geofile*, January 1988 and *World Resources* 1987

The River Rhine: key facts

* The Rhine provides drinking water for 20 million people
* The river is over 1200 km long.
* Rhine basin population: 40 million.
* Netherlands: 66% of the water supply is from the Rhine.
* West Germany: 70% of the country's factories and industrial cities are along the Rhine.
* Pollution is a long-term issue.
* 1977 on the Dutch–German border the river contained:
  1) 7 million tonnes salt (359 mg/litre)
  2) Smaller amounts of arsenic, mercury, lead, copper, zinc, chromium. These all are a hazard to life as they build up through the FOOD CHAIN.
  3) Large amounts of organic waste.
  4) THERMAL POLLUTION – a rise in water temperature due to industrial processes.

International agreements

The international nature of the river means that there have been many international agreements to try to control pollution in the interests of all the countries involved. Pollution from one country can cause problems in other countries as the pollutants travel downstream.

Some of the important agreements are:

* **1963:** International Commission for the Protection of the Rhine against Pollution.

* **1976:** Protection of the Rhine against Chemical Pollution. This had some success. The levels of pollutants have fallen, especially of metals (until the 1986 spill at Basle). However, nitrate pollution from agriculture has increased.

* **1976:** Rhine Salt Convention. This has had limited success. 33% of the salt in the river comes from the Alsace Region of France. The countries agreed to share the cost of disposing of the salt elsewhere. The share of costs was agreed as shown below.
Netherlands – 34%; Germany – 30%; France – 30%; Switzerland – 6%.

* **1987:** Within two months of the Basle spill, international organisations had begun to focus attention on accidental pollution:
OECD (Organisation for Economic Co-operation and Development)
UNEP (United Nations Environment Programme)
ECE (Economic Commission for Europe)
EEC (European Economic Community)

The key question for the future is: Has the Basle spill helped to create the will to fight pollution of the Rhine and other European rivers?

1 Which four countries 'share' the River Rhine?
2 The incident of November 1986 is just one of many. For years the Rhine has been called 'Europe's sewer'. Describe the pollutants found in the river. Use an atlas and Source B to suggest why the river should be so polluted.
3 Which one of the four countries will be most affected by pollution from everyday activities on the River Rhine? Why? (See Source B.)
4 What is the evidence that the river system could not cope with the sudden input of chemicals from the Basle fire?
5 In pairs, discuss why the Basle fire may be a good thing for the long-term improvement of the pollution problem on the River Rhine.
6 How did the effects of the pollution accident at Basle vary in time and space (downstream)?
7 In groups, discuss why international co-operation on the Rhine is so important. (See Source C.)

8 Study the 1976 Rhine Salt Agreement, and how the costs are to be shared. Why do you think that West Germany and the Netherlands are prepared to pay so much, and Switzerland pays so little? How do you think that the costs should be shared? Give reasons for your answer.

North-West Europe's dustbin

What types of pollution are affecting the North Sea? Why is there now increasing cause for concern about the long-term effects of toxic chemicals and other pollutants? Read on to find out.

The marine environment is so huge that wastes can usually be broken down and dispersed without long-term effects. Indeed, as we saw on pages 156–7, when the River Rhine pollution spill reached the North Sea, it was estimated that pollutants would be cleared by 1996.

The North Sea is a shallow sea surrounded by eight industrial nations. It has been used to dispose of waste for many years (Sources A and B).

The North Sea: location, currents and pollution sources

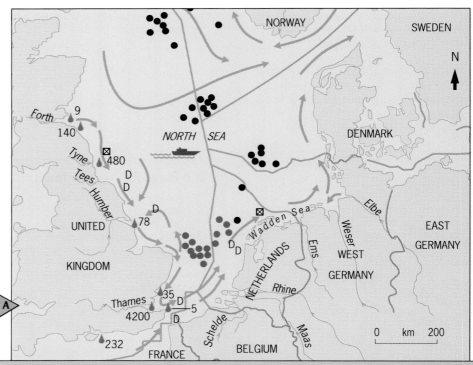

A

Pollution sources

——— Boundary of national sectors of seabed	💧 Sewage sludge (in thousands of tonnes in 1984)
⟶ Water circulation (currents) in the North Sea	→ Major rivers flowing into the North Sea
	⬤⬤ Offshore oil fields
	⬤⬤ Offshore gas fields

⊠ Incineration and dumping of toxic wastes

D Liquid waste from industry (e.g. acids) dumped from tankers International sea transport. North Sea is busiest shipping route in the world

---

1 You are to write a report for Greenpeace about pollution in the North Sea. In order to compile your report, use the information on this page. You may also use a ship to study the North Sea in detail. You will set sail from the Firth of Forth in Scotland, and will then sail around the North Sea, heading southwards down the coast of the United Kingdom, and eastwards along the coastline of France, Belgium, Netherlands and Denmark. After that, you will turn northwards towards Norway and then back to the Forth. Follow the route on the map (Source A).

In your report include:
a) Why the North Sea has been used as a rubbish dump for so long.
b) The types of the pollution.
c) The amounts of pollution and

how they vary on your journey (use Sources B and C).
d) The areas into which the pollution is washed by currents in the North Sea.

e) The possible effects of pollution on marine creatures.
f) The location of areas at high risk from the effects of marine pollution.
g) Conclusions and recommendations for the future.

B

River pollution of the North Sea

River	Mercury (tonnes per year)	Cadmium (tonnes per year)	Nitrogen (thousand tonnes per year)	Phosphorus (thousand tonnes per year)
Forth	0.1	2.0	1	–
Tyne	1.4	1.3	1	0.2
Tees	0.6	0.6	2	0.2
Humber	0.7	3.5	41	0.6
Thames	1.1	1.5	31	0.1
Scheldt	1.0	7.4	62	7.0
Rhine	3.9	13.8	420	37.0
Ems	0.4	0.7	22	0.7
Weser	1.1	2.9	87	3.8
Elbe	7.3	8.4	150	12.0

The Wadden Sea

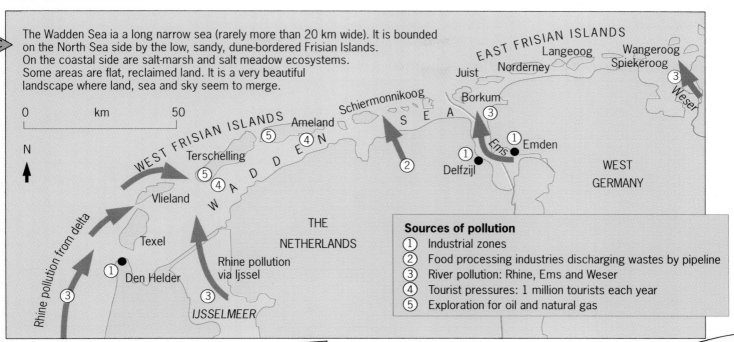

C The Wadden Sea ia a long narrow sea (rarely more than 20 km wide). It is bounded on the North Sea side by the low, sandy, dune-bordered Frisian Islands. On the coastal side are salt-marsh and salt meadow ecosystems. Some areas are flat, reclaimed land. It is a very beautiful landscape where land, sea and sky seem to merge.

EAST FRISIAN ISLANDS
Langeoog   Wangeroog
Norderney   Spiekeroog
Juist
Borkum
Schiermonnikoog
Ameland   WADDEN   SEA
WEST FRISIAN ISLANDS
Terschelling
Vlieland
Texel
Den Helder
Delfzijl
Emden
Ems
Weser

0   km   50
N

THE NETHERLANDS

Rhine pollution from delta
Rhine pollution via Ijssel
IJSSELMEER

WEST GERMANY

Sources of pollution
1. Industrial zones
2. Food processing industries discharging wastes by pipeline
3. River pollution: Rhine, Ems and Weser
4. Tourist pressures: 1 million tourists each year
5. Exploration for oil and natural gas

---

2 What are the sources of pollution in the Wadden Sea? (Use Sources A and C.)

3 Why is the Wadden Sea a popular area with tourists?

4 Use Source D to draw a diagram of the FOOD CHAIN in the Wadden Sea. Add notes to your diagram to show the effects of pollutants on the different stages of the food chain.

5 In pairs, discuss how the Wadden Sea is important to life in the North Sea.

6 Imagine you are one of the Wadden Sea fishermen in the photograph (Source D). Describe the effects of pollution on your fishing catch. What are your views concerning the future of the Wadden Sea?

7 a) Why is pollution in the North Sea (including the Wadden Sea) an international problem?
b) How does this make it more difficult for action to be taken?

8 Why might companies be unwilling to stop dumping harmful wastes in the North Sea?

Germans seek help for an endangered sea

D

Wadden Sea fishermen at work. They say up to a third of their catch is so badly affected by pollution that it must be thrown away.

The Wadden Sea runs some 450 km along the continental North Sea coast. This long, narrow, strip of tidal sand-banks, mud-flats and salt-marshes is considered to be one of the only original ecosystems in Europe.

It is a cradle of life for the North Sea – the home or breeding ground for some 4,000 of its 7,000 species. Nine million birds breed, feed, moult or rest there each year, yet both the sea and the birds are in grave danger – their survival threatened by the millions of tons of poisons and oil poured into the sea.

Underfoot it is teeming with life. It is full of micro-organisms, bacteria, plankton, algae and larvae. These are food for tiny crabs, shrimps, worms and shellfish and a myriad of other tiny creatures who in turn are hunted by fish, and by the birds. The fish also feed the only mammal inhabitants, the seals.

The salt-marshes, an ecosystem of their own, support 2,000 different varieties of interdependent plant and animal life.

The Wadden Sea, according to a West German scientist is extremely delicate, irreplaceable and in danger. The currents which wash the silt and the larvae of fish and shellfish to these parts also bring sewage, dangerous chemicals and heavy metals, garbage and oil.

From the other side, the Rhine, the Elbe, the Weser and the Ems spew in effluent from the industries and households of half Central Europe.

The tiny organisms absorb the poisons and metals, but do not generally suffer themselves. Instead many concentrate the poisons so that they become more potent as they pass up the food chain. It is the bigger creatures who are affected: the mussels and fish.

When so much is at stake German demands for a total halt to the dumping of harmful wastes in the North Sea by 1990, a 50 per cent reduction in river pollution by 1995, a stop to the burning of waste on ships by the same year and a reduction in air pollution would seem to be urgent.

159

Integrated sewage utilisation scheme

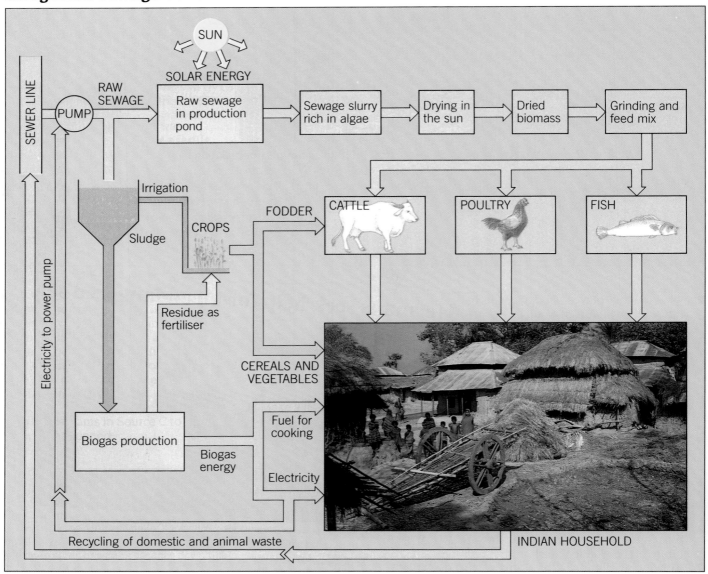

The integrated sewage utilisation scheme forms part of the Ganga Action Plan. It should turn human and animal wastes into useful materials by using the gases produced to give fuel (BIO-GAS), and the solid wastes can be used as part of animal feed. Follow the arrows from the sewage line to see how the household would benefit. You will see that the sewage utilisation scheme works like a natural SYSTEM. There are flows, stores, and material (BIOMASS) is recycled.

In areas with no sewer lines, extra equipment will be used to take waste to the sewage collection points. It will benefit the local people, and the pollution of the Ganga River will be reduced. Remember that 75% of the Ganga pollution is due to sewage.

1   What are the two main products of the sewage utilisation scheme?
2   How will the scheme benefit crops, and animal rearing for the household?

3   How will the household benefit from biogas production?
4   How does the system maintain itself once it has been set up?
5   Draw a summary diagram of the sewage utilisation scheme, showing inputs, stores and outputs. Add an arrow to show the FEEDBACK into the system.
6   Suggest the problems the Ganga Authority will face in starting up the integrated sewage utilisation scheme.

Air pollution in Cubatão, Brazil

> **"** Some days it is so bad you can't breathe. If you go outside, you will vomit. **"**

This was said by a person living in Cubatão in Brazil, where the photograph on page 161 was taken. Cubatão may be the most polluted town on earth, but in all parts of the world there is concern about the quality of the atmosphere that we all breathe.

The atmosphere has always been a temporary STORE for gases and solids produced naturally, so why is there so much concern about pollution today?

Work with a partner or in a small group to answer these questions. Use Source A and Source B.

1. Make a list of all the natural INPUTS and OUTPUTS shown in Source A.
2. Modern industrial societies use the atmosphere store as a huge dump for their waste materials (the outputs they do not want). Why do societies do this? Where else could waste material be dumped? Could making the waste be avoided? What would this cost?
3. What do we mean by *pollution*? Discuss it within your group and write a definition. Then compare it with those of other groups. (Use systems language if you can.)
4. Present the data in Source B as four pie graphs. What are the largest sources of pollution in the UK?
5. Look at the two photographs (Source C). What pollutants are being emitted in each case? (Use Source B to help you.)
6. Add the inputs which come from human activity to the list of natural inputs and outputs you made in answer to question 1. Use a different colour to show human inputs. As you work through this Unit add any other inputs and outputs to your list.
7. Make a list of signs you have heard about which suggest that the atmosphere is not coping with human-made inputs. Compare your answers with those of other groups.

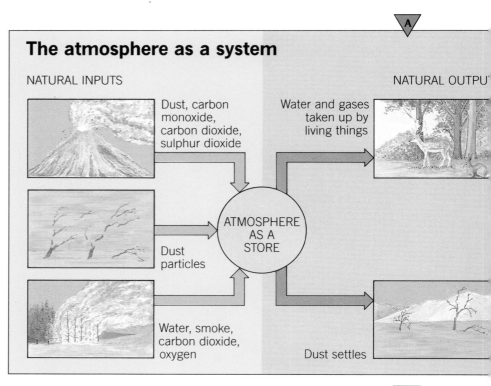

The atmosphere as a system

A

NATURAL INPUTS

NATURAL OUTPU[T]

Dust, carbon monoxide, carbon dioxide, sulphur dioxide

Dust particles

Water, smoke, carbon dioxide, oxygen

ATMOSPHERE AS A STORE

Water and gases taken up by living things

Dust settles

Main sources of air pollution in the United Kingdom for 1984
(Shown as percentages of the total for each gas)

B

Source	Sulphur dioxide	Nitrogen oxides	Carbon dioxide	Hydro-carbons
Homes and commercial	9	5	8	3
Power stations, and gas leakage	70	37	2	25
Industries	19	13	2	38
Transport	2	45	88	34
Amount in million tonnes	3.5	1.7	5.2	1.6

Unnatural inputs

C

162

Where it comes from, where it goes

One of the most important things to understand about pollutants is that they can travel and change in character on the way.

8 Look at Sources D and E.
 a) What are the two main types of pollutant?
 b) At what distance from the source region are they found?
 c) Suggest why PRIMARY POLLUTANTS are deposited nearer to the source region than SECONDARY POLLUTANTS.

9 Which areas of the United Kingdom would you expect to have the highest levels of atmospheric pollution? Use an atlas to help you.

10 Use the diagram (Source E) to explain the difference between dry and wet deposition.

11 a) Will the United Kingdom suffer much wet deposition from its own sources of pollution?
 b) Use an atlas to suggest areas in the UK which might suffer from wet deposition. Find the main centres of population and industry and use the scale accurately.

12 What effects might the pollution have on the lives of the people in village X on Source E? Why might they be particularly angry?

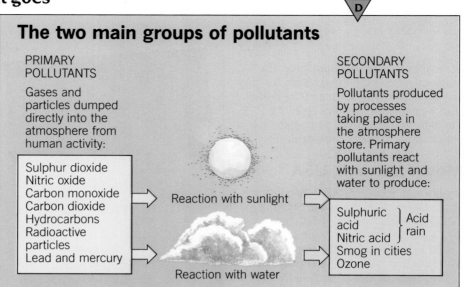

The two main groups of pollutants

PRIMARY POLLUTANTS

Gases and particles dumped directly into the atmosphere from human activity:

Sulphur dioxide
Nitric oxide
Carbon monoxide
Carbon dioxide
Hydrocarbons
Radioactive particles
Lead and mercury

Reaction with sunlight

Reaction with water

SECONDARY POLLUTANTS

Pollutants produced by processes taking place in the atmosphere store. Primary pollutants react with sunlight and water to produce:

Sulphuric acid ⎱ Acid
Nitric acid ⎰ rain
Smog in cities
Ozone

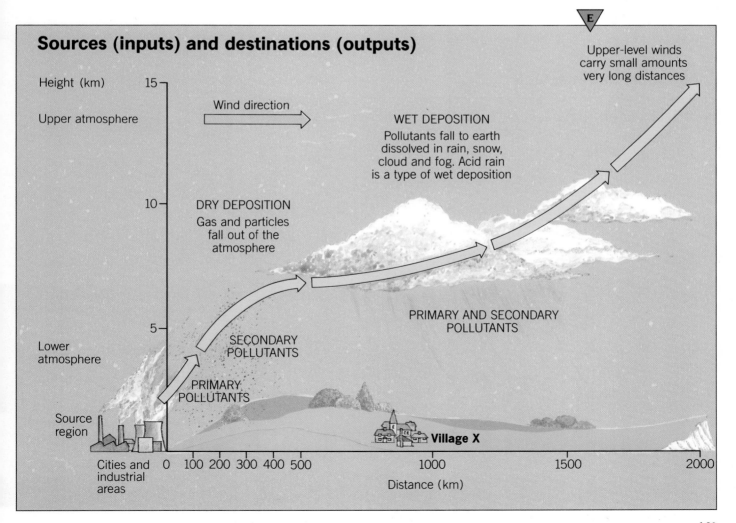

Sources (inputs) and destinations (outputs)

Height (km)

Upper atmosphere

Wind direction

Upper-level winds carry small amounts very long distances

WET DEPOSITION
Pollutants fall to earth dissolved in rain, snow, cloud and fog. Acid rain is a type of wet deposition

DRY DEPOSITION
Gas and particles fall out of the atmosphere

PRIMARY AND SECONDARY POLLUTANTS

Lower atmosphere

SECONDARY POLLUTANTS

PRIMARY POLLUTANTS

Source region

Cities and industrial areas

Distance (km)

15
10
5

0 100 200 300 400 500   1000   1500   2000

Village X

163

Atmospheric pollution can have dramatic effects on the biosphere a long way away from the source of the pollution. ACID RAIN or mist is a type of wet deposition that causes damage to forests in many parts of the world.

Mount Mitchell, USA

1 Look at Source A. What, according to Dr Bruck, is the cause of damage to the trees on Mount Mitchell?
2 Study the three bar graphs in Source A. Read off the figures to show the changing percentages of red spruce trees in each of the four categories.
3 How does the type of pollution found on Mount Mitchell show that the mountain is far from the source of the pollutants? Refer to Source E on p. 163 for help.
4 Why is Dr Bruck so concerned for the future? What will happen?

Damaged trees

World Resources, 1987

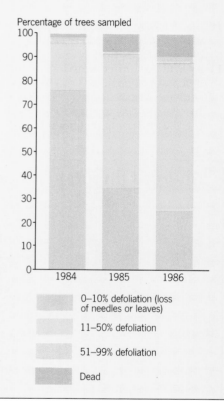

A

Mount Mitchell in North Carolina is the highest peak in the eastern USA. It is a long way from the big cities and is covered by a lush CONIFEROUS FOREST. However, according to Dr Robert Bruck it will soon be 'bald'. The trees are having to suffer an 'alphabet soup' of pollutants that spills over the mountain every day. High levels of OZONE and lead have been recorded on the mountain. The clouds, mist and fog that cover the mountain on most days have very high levels of acidity. The graph shows the rapid decline of red spruce on Mount Mitchell between 1984 and 1986.

Percentage of trees sampled

0–10% defoliation (loss of needles or leaves)

11–50% defoliation

51–99% defoliation

Dead

Ecosystems under attack

B

The effects of atmospheric pollution on the forest ecosystem

WET DEPOSITION (ACID RAIN) AND DRY DEPOSITION

Sign
Process

Tree is weakened - more likely to be affected by pests, frost, diseases and drought

Needles and leaves show chlorosis or yellowing

Seedlings do not grow

Coniferous forest soils are naturally acid, especially near the surface

Release of toxic heavy metals by acid rainwater, such as aluminium and cadmium to groundwater

Damage to crops and wildlife

Tree crown becomes thinner and dies back

Needles, leaves and bark damaged by direct contact with pollutants - sulphur and nitrogen oxides

Leaves and needles are shed at a high rate

Less undergrowth

Decomposition of leaf litter is slower

Higher acidity nearer the surface and at depth

Tree poisoned

Soil is naturally thin and low in alkaline minerals (such as lime) which could neutralise the acid rain

The natural process of leaching of nutrients is increased

Loss of nutrients especially calcium and magnesium

Source B shows the effects of acid rain and other air pollutants on coniferous forest ECOSYSTEMS.

5 Use Source B to explain what is happening to:
   a) the BIOMASS store (vegetation), and
   b) the soil store, as acid rain falls on the forest. Base your answers on changes in inputs, contents of the store and outputs.
6 What effect is acid rain having on the CYCLES of ORGANIC and MINERAL NUTRIENTS through the forest ecosystem?

Trees under stress

Under natural conditions the forest ecosystem is in a state of balance. Atmospheric pollution indirectly affects the forest ecosystem by upsetting this natural balance.

7 Compare the two photographs in Source C. Describe the differences between the two trees.
8 Look at the diagrams in Sources D and E and explain how pollution causes trees to be damaged more easily by natural hazards, such as drought, frost or disease.

Below left: A healthy coniferous tree
Below right: A tree damaged by chlorosis

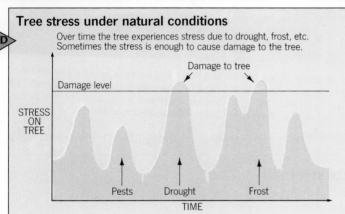

D

Tree stress under natural conditions

Over time the tree experiences stress due to drought, frost, etc. Sometimes the stress is enough to cause damage to the tree.

Damage to tree
Damage level
STRESS ON TREE
Pests Drought Frost
TIME

New Scientist

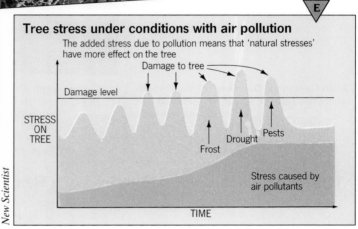

E

Tree stress under conditions with air pollution

The added stress due to pollution means that 'natural stresses' have more effect on the tree

Damage to tree
Damage level
STRESS ON TREE
Frost Drought Pests
Stress caused by air pollutants
TIME

New Scientist

Is it getting worse?

9 Use the table of statistics in Source F and draw six bar graphs, similar to those in Source A, to show the percentages of needle/leaf loss between 1984 and 1986. Choose one species of tree from each country.
10 What happened to the amount of tree damage between 1984 and 1986?
11 Which country is the worst affected?
12 Are all species of tree suffering damage from pollution, or is it just coniferous trees?
13 Working in pairs imagine that you are newspaper reporters who have just been given the information on these pages. Under an eye-catching headline, write a brief, but lively 'alarm' article for your newspaper.

F

Forest damage assessment in three European countries

(C) CONIFEROUS tree (D) BROAD-LEAVED deciduous tree	Percentage needle leaf loss							
	0–10% healthy		11–25% slight damage		26–60% medium to serious damage		61–100% dying/dead	
	1984	1986	1984	1986	1984	1986	1984	1986
United Kingdom Norway spruce (C)	71	32	26	36	3	31	1	1
West Germany Norway spruce (C)	49	46	31	32	19	20	2	2
Beech (D)	50	40	39	41	11	18	1	1
Oak (D)	57	39	35	41	9	19	0	1
Switzerland Pine (C)	50	34	31	43	16	19	1	4
Beech (D)	74	52	23	40	3	7	0	1
Oak (D)	71	37	28	50	1	11	0	2

Forestry Commission Bulletin, no. 70

13.3 OVERCOMING ACIDITY

Loch Fleet, Scotland

Can the damage caused by acid rain and pollution in the atmosphere be repaired? This case study shows how some researchers are trying to do this by restoring balance and richness to an ecosystem.

1 Look at the photograph in Source A. Describe the land and vegetation of the loch's CATCHMENT AREA.
2 Look at the diagram (Source B). Follow the arrows through the diagram and explain why Loch Fleet's ecosystem is poorer today than in the past.
3 Why do you think the water in the loch is crystal clear? What effect does acid rain have on plant and animal life?

Loch Fleet in the Galloway region of south-west Scotland, the site of a major acid lake restoration project

Restoring a lake in south-west Scotland

The photograph above is an aerial view of Loch Fleet and the catchment area which supplies it with water in the Galloway region of Scotland. The loch is clear, and the bed has a rich carpet of algae and moss. But there are no fish or other animals. The loch has become more acid, probably from air pollution and acid rain.

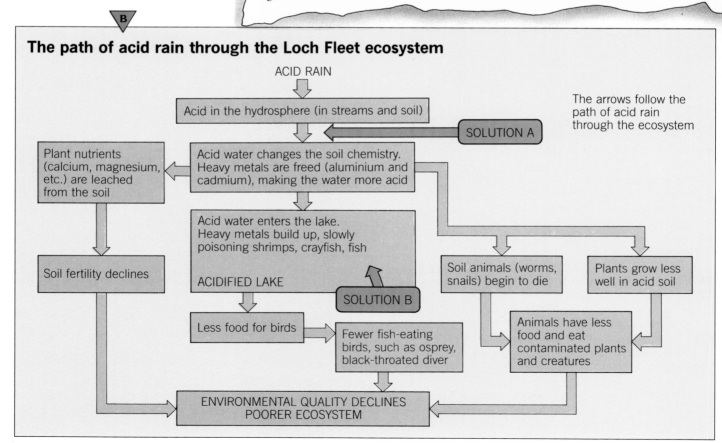

The path of acid rain through the Loch Fleet ecosystem

The arrows follow the path of acid rain through the ecosystem

ACID RAIN

Acid in the hydrosphere (in streams and soil) ← SOLUTION A

Plant nutrients (calcium, magnesium, etc.) are leached from the soil ← Acid water changes the soil chemistry. Heavy metals are freed (aluminium and cadmium), making the water more acid

Acid water enters the lake. Heavy metals build up, slowly poisoning shrimps, crayfish, fish

ACIDIFIED LAKE — SOLUTION B

Soil fertility declines

Soil animals (worms, snails) begin to die

Plants grow less well in acid soil

Less food for birds

Fewer fish-eating birds, such as osprey, black-throated diver

Animals have less food and eat contaminated plants and creatures

ENVIRONMENTAL QUALITY DECLINES
POORER ECOSYSTEM

166

The Loch Fleet project

The aim of the Loch Fleet project is to restore the lake so that it will support fish once more. The money for the research is coming from British Coal, the Central Electricity Generating Board, the South of Scotland Electricity Board and the North of Scotland Hydro-Electric Board.

4 Why is dropping lime directly into the lake (solution B in Sources B and D) only a short-term solution?

5 **a)** Why does adding lime to the catchment area (Solution A in Sources B and D) have a wider impact on the ecosystem.
   b) Why is this solution more likely to last longer?

6 **a)** Look carefully at the map (Source C) and list what methods the scientists are using to collect information.
   b) Why are they using different methods?

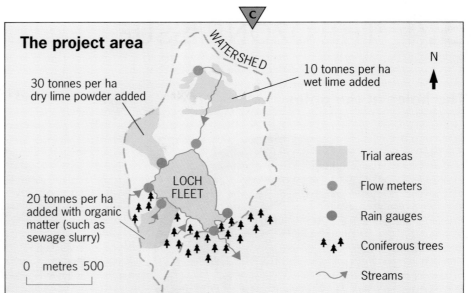

The project area

WATERSHED

30 tonnes per ha dry lime powder added

10 tonnes per ha wet lime added

N

LOCH FLEET

20 tonnes per ha added with organic matter (such as sewage slurry)

0 metres 500

Trial areas
Flow meters
Rain gauges
Coniferous trees
Streams

Two solutions

Liming by helicopter in Sweden

In Sweden, where thousands of lakes have suffered from acid rain, scientists have used lime (calcium carbonate) to repair the damage. Lime is alkaline and helps to neutralise the acid. There are two ways of doing this:

Solution B:
The simplest method is to drop lime directly into the lake (as in the photograph). Look at Source B.

This method enters the flow diagram of the ecosystem where the Solution B arrow is marked.

Solution A:
The Loch Fleet scientists are adding lime to the catchment area. In 1986, 300 tonnes of lime were added to three trial areas, using three different methods. More will have to be added in future years.

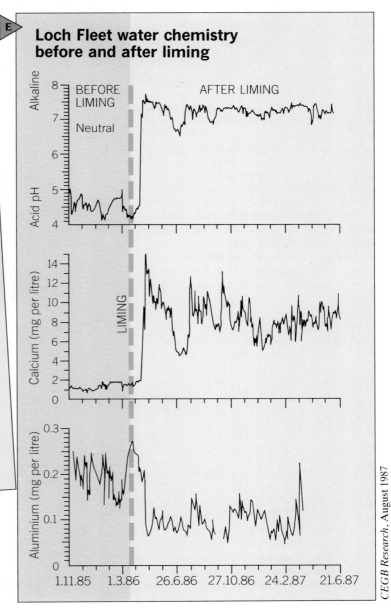

Loch Fleet water chemistry before and after liming

BEFORE LIMING   AFTER LIMING
Neutral
LIMING

Alkaline
Acid pH

Calcium (mg per litre)

Aluminium (mg per litre)

1.11.85   1.3.86   26.6.86   27.10.86   24.2.87   21.6.87

CEGB Research, August 1987

7 Use Source E to explain why the scientists are pleased with their first results.

8 The money for this research is coming from the industries which have been blamed for causing acid rain. What else do you think the coal and electricity industries could do to keep Loch Fleet healthy?

13.4 THE OZONE ISSUE

The holes at the poles

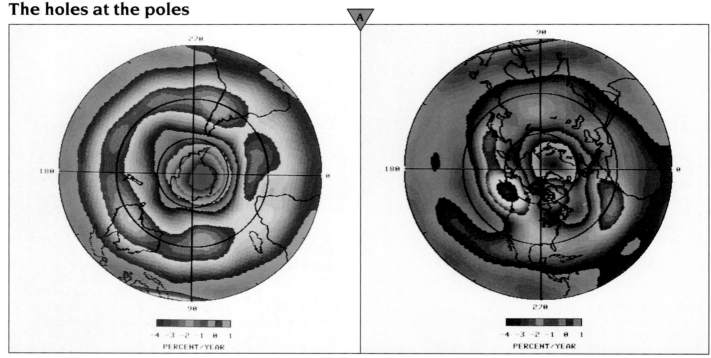

Satellite image of the atmosphere over the Antarctic

Satellite image of the atmosphere over the Arctic

The problem

The two images in Source A were taken by the Nimbus 7 satellite and show that ozone is decreasing in some parts of the atmosphere. Ozone (O_3) is a minor gas in the atmosphere's make-up. Near the earth's surface it can be a pollutant – so what is all the fuss about?

The so-called 'ozone layer' is found 15–35 km above the earth's surface. Ozone is only one of the gases in this layer, but it does an important job in protecting life on earth. It acts as a shield against ULTRAVIOLET RADIATION from the sun. Scientists are worried because holes are appearing in this shield.

1 Use Source A to describe the changes in ozone levels between 1978 and 1984.
2 Where are the three 'holes' that are worrying scientists? Look for the areas where the fall in ozone levels has been greatest.
3 Look at the graph in Source B. Describe the changes shown by the graph.

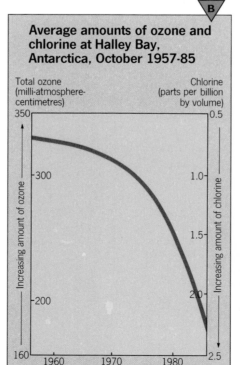

Average amounts of ozone and chlorine at Halley Bay, Antarctica, October 1957-85

4 Use an atlas and the map in Source C to describe the size of the ozone holes.

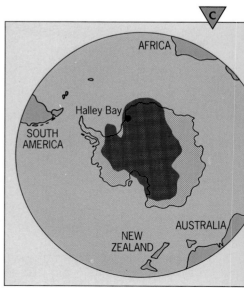

The area shaded grey represents the hole in the ozone layer above Antarctica at its greatest extent in October 1987

Who is to blame?

Nobody knows for sure why holes in the ozone layer are growing. Some scientists say it is part of the earth's natural rhythms, and that perhaps in thousands of years the balance will be restored. Others say that the holes over the Antarctic grow a few weeks after the main burning season in the Amazonian rainforest. However, we can identify one main reason.

Chlorofluorocarbons

5 Look at the diagram in Source D Explain what is happening by describing:
   a) the job of the ozone layer;
   b) what may happen if it gets thinner or disappears.
6 What do you understand by the term CFCs? Give some examples of the use of CFCs in daily life.
7 How does the evidence in the graph in Source B support the idea that CFCs releasing chlorine may be to blame?

8 Chemical companies producing CFCs took the scientists' message seriously and reduced their production of CFCs during the 1970s. But what has happened in the 1980s? Use Source E to help you.
9 Source F is an advertisement produced by Friends of the Earth, an environmental pressure group. In the advertisement:
   a) what do they say the problem is, and
   b) what do they suggest should be done?

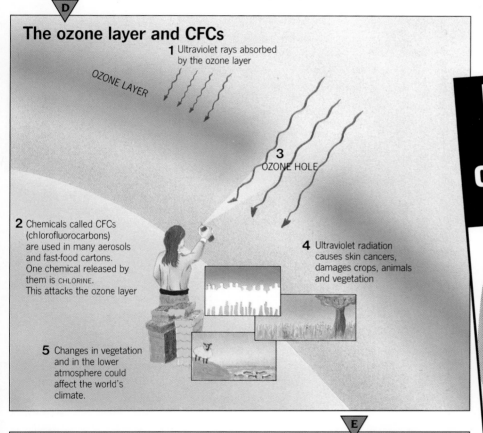

D

The ozone layer and CFCs

OZONE LAYER

1 Ultraviolet rays absorbed by the ozone layer

3 OZONE HOLE

2 Chemicals called CFCs (chlorofluorocarbons) are used in many aerosols and fast-food cartons. One chemical released by them is CHLORINE. This attacks the ozone layer

4 Ultraviolet radiation causes skin cancers, damages crops, animals and vegetation

5 Changes in vegetation and in the lower atmosphere could affect the world's climate.

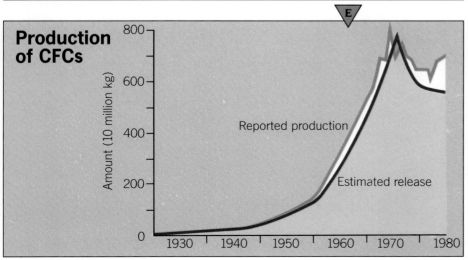

E

Production of CFCs

Amount (10 million kg)

Reported production

Estimated release

1930 1940 1950 1960 1970 1980

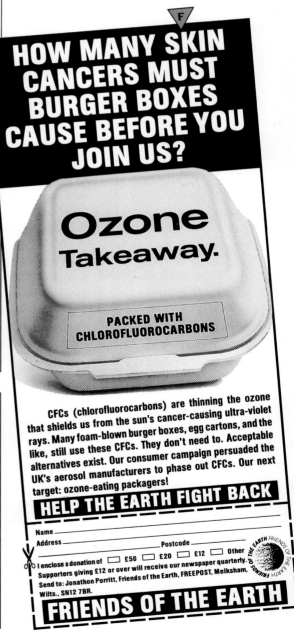

F

HOW MANY SKIN CANCERS MUST BURGER BOXES CAUSE BEFORE YOU JOIN US?

Ozone Takeaway.

PACKED WITH CHLOROFLUOROCARBONS

CFCs (chlorofluorocarbons) are thinning the ozone that shields us from the sun's cancer-causing ultra-violet rays. Many foam-blown burger boxes, egg cartons, and the like, still use these CFCs. They don't need to. Acceptable alternatives exist. Our consumer campaign persuaded the UK's aerosol manufacturers to phase out CFCs. Our next target: ozone-eating packagers!

HELP THE EARTH FIGHT BACK

Name
Address _____ Postcode _____

I enclose a donation of ☐ £50 ☐ £20 ☐ £12 ☐ Other
Supporters giving £12 or over will receive our newspaper quarterly.
Send to: Jonathon Porritt, Friends of the Earth, FREEPOST, Melksham, Wilts., SN12 7BR.

FRIENDS OF THE EARTH

What is the problem?

A possible reason for the increase in icebergs breaking away from Antarctica (Source A) is the warming of the atmosphere. This has been called the GREENHOUSE EFFECT. One of the main pollutants which may cause this is carbon dioxide (CO_2). Carbon dioxide is a natural part of the atmosphere, but it is the *increase* in carbon dioxide that is the problem. In 1850 the amount of CO_2 in the atmosphere was 280 ppm (parts per million). Today it is 350 ppm.

Look at Source B to help discover the causes of the increase in CO_2.

1 Redraw the diagram of the CARBON CYCLE (Source B) as a FLOW DIAGRAM. Show the four carbon stores as boxes, and the transfers of carbon as labelled arrows. Use one colour for the natural transfers of carbon, and a second colour for the transfers due to human activity.

2 **a)** How do trees and other plants help balance the amount of carbon dioxide in the atmosphere?
   b) What could be the effects of DEFORESTATION on this balance?

The big heat

" I have been watching the world's biggest iceberg – 62 km long, 16 km wide and 1100 m thick – which has broken loose from Antarctica. There has been 13 others so far this year. Perhaps there is something going on which maybe we should be worrying about. "
Dr Chris Sear, British Antarctic Survey, 1987

3 In which of the four stores do you think carbon remains longest? Why?

4 Name the two stores *from* which carbon transfers have been speeded up by human activity.

5 Which store has *gained* the most carbon due to human activity? The figures in Source B may help you work this out.

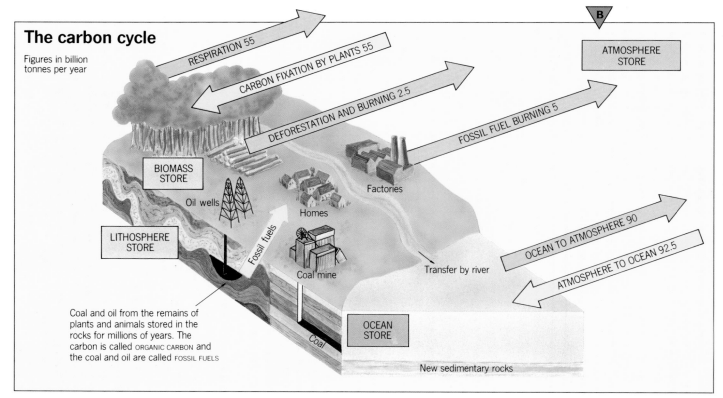

The carbon cycle

Figures in billion tonnes per year

RESPIRATION 55

CARBON FIXATION BY PLANTS 55

DEFORESTATION AND BURNING 2.5

FOSSIL FUEL BURNING 5

ATMOSPHERE STORE

BIOMASS STORE

Oil wells

Homes

Factories

LITHOSPHERE STORE

Fossil fuels

Coal mine

Transfer by river

OCEAN TO ATMOSPHERE 90

ATMOSPHERE TO OCEAN 92.5

Coal and oil from the remains of plants and animals stored in the rocks for millions of years. The carbon is called ORGANIC CARBON and the coal and oil are called FOSSIL FUELS

Coal

OCEAN STORE

New sedimentary rocks

How is the problem caused?

In the last 250 years we have mined and used almost 150,000 million tonnes of organic fuel, such as coal, oil and gas. The burning of wood for fuel and through deforestation has also released carbon. Some of this carbon passes into the atmosphere as carbon dioxide gas.

6 Use Source C to describe the Earth's energy balance.
7 Compare Sources C and D and explain how the increase in carbon dioxide levels has altered this balance.
8 **a)** How could this 'greenhouse effect' cause more icebergs to break away from the Antarctic ice sheet and melt?
   b) What might be the long-term effect on world sea-levels?

What will be the impact?

Read the extracts in Source E.

9 List some of the possible impacts of the greenhouse effect mentioned in Source E.
10 Some scientists say that the 1988 DROUGHT in Indiana, USA, was due to the greenhouse effect. Describe what happened to Howard Wreitzel's crops.

11 Many of the results of the greenhouse effect will happen slowly over the next 50 years. In a group, discuss the following questions about what could be done.
   a) How could the people of the Earth prepare for these changes?

Think about what Howard Wreitzel would have to do to prepare for the future.
   b) Will all countries be able to prepare equally well?
   c) What could be done to reduce the causes of the greenhouse effect?

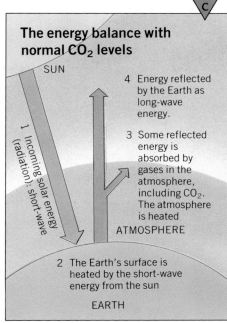

C

The energy balance with normal CO₂ levels

SUN

1 Incoming solar energy (radiation): short-wave

4 Energy reflected by the Earth as long-wave energy.

3 Some reflected energy is absorbed by gases in the atmosphere, including CO_2. The atmosphere is heated

ATMOSPHERE

2 The Earth's surface is heated by the short-wave energy from the sun

EARTH

D

The energy balance with increased CO₂ levels

SUN

1 Incoming solar energy (radiation): short-wave

4 Less energy reflected by the Earth (long-wave)

3 More reflected energy is absorbed due to the increase in CO_2 and the atmosphere warms – this is the greenhouse effect

ATMOSPHERE

2 The Earth's surface is heated by the short-wave energy from the sun

EARTH

E

Guardian, 16 June 1988

...iver deltas flooding threat

THE most dramatic impacts of the greenhouse effect could be on the world's great river deltas.

If ocean levels rise by one metre in the next 50 years, 12 to 15 per cent of Egypt's arable land would be flooded. Eight million people – about 16 per cent of the population – would lose their homes.

These figures were spelled out by Dr Irving Mintzer, director of the energy and climate project of the World Resources Institute in Washington.

In Bangladesh, a one metre rise in sea level would affect land on which 9 per cent of the population live, he said.

"Such a sea level rise would cause flooding in many coastal areas, increase salt water intrusion in aquifers, inundate vital wetlands and destroy commercially important fishing grounds," Dr Mintzer said.

The patterns of winds and currents, timing and distribution of rainfall would change. With the shift of ocean currents, countries such as Ireland and Britain might cool as others warmed.

Dr Mintzer said: "The homes and lives of millions of people living in the deltas of the Ganges, the Nile, the Mekong, the Yangtze and the Mississippi could be at risk."

Record drought grips America's grain belt

IN Howard Wreitzel's 33 years of farming he has never seen a spring like this one. His corn, stunted by one of the earliest droughts on record stands not even half as tall as it should be by mid-June. Some of his soybeans still have not sprouted. Those that have are weed-like.

The ground on his west central Indiana farm is dry, "brick-hard." When Wreitzel drives a tractor along the rows of weakened plants, the soil rises in dusty brown clouds that waft ominously across the fields, turning the otherwise clear day hazy beneath a frying sun.

Mr Wreitzel and hundreds of thousands of other Mid-west farmers are helpless this spring, as one of the worst droughts of the century tightens across America's grain belt.

Facing up to drought: insurance claims by farmers have fallen on barren ground

Los Angeles Times, 28 June 1988

Long-term effects

Scientists are using computers to work out what the greenhouse effect could mean, but their results do not yet agree. Some scientists say that the complex global SYSTEM will adjust and there will be no noticeable effect. Others predict that averge temperatures will rise by 2–3°C, climatic regions will change and sea levels will rise by 0.15–1.5 metres. A temperature rise of only 1°C would make the world warmer than it has been for 120,000 years. In fact, since the last Ice Age, when the British Isles were iced over, average temperatures have risen by only 4°C!

13 ACID RAIN: TESTING HYPOTHESES

The pH scale

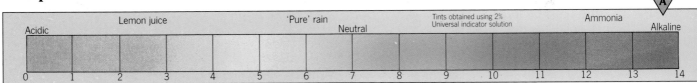

▽ **A**

Acidic   Lemon juice   'Pure' rain   Neutral   Tints obtained using 2% Universal indicator solution   Ammonia   Alkaline

0   1   2   3   4   5   6   7   8   9   10   11   12   13   14

Acidity and alkalinity are measured on a PH SCALE (Source A). This scale runs from 0 (very acid) to 14 (very alkaline). A pH value of 7 means neutral (neither acid nor alkaline).

The pH scale is logarithmic. This means that each step on the scale represents a *tenfold* increase or decrease. For example, rain with a pH of 6 is *ten times* more acid than rain with a pH of 7.

Rainfall polluted by sulphur dioxide and nitric oxide has a lower pH than 'pure' rainwater. This lower pH means it is *more* acid, and so it is called acid rain.

Acid rain: the global pattern

▽ **B**

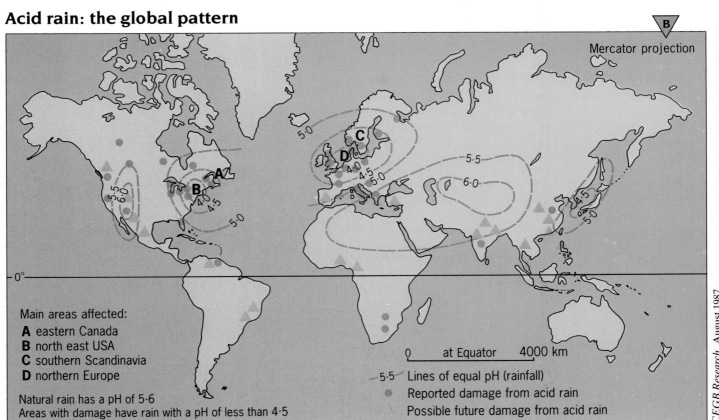

Mercator projection

Main areas affected:

A eastern Canada
B north east USA
C southern Scandinavia
D northern Europe

Natural rain has a pH of 5·6
Areas with damage have rain with a pH of less than 4·5

0   at Equator   4000 km

— 5·5 — Lines of equal pH (rainfall)
● Reported damage from acid rain
▲ Possible future damage from acid rain

CEGB Research, August 1987

Source B shows the world pattern of acid rain.

1 On an outline map of the world, mark the four areas labelled A, B, C and D. Put a dot for the centre of each area.

2 a) From the centre of each area draw two circles 1000 km and 2000 km in radius.
b) Shade the areas *between* the two circles (this is where wet deposition mainly occurs).

c) Using an atlas, suggest where the source areas could be for each of A, B, C and D. Look for densely populated and industrial regions in your shaded areas.

3 Using an atlas and what you learnt in this Unit, test these four hypotheses for areas affected by acid rain:
a) They are all in rich countries of the Northern Hemisphere.
b) They are all downwind of major industrial areas.
c) They are all upland areas with

high amounts of precipitation (rain or snow).
d) All these areas have many lakes, rivers and forests.

4 Source B also shows the areas that environmental groups think will have 'possible future damage from acid rain'.
a) Describe the location of these areas.
b) How does their location compare with areas A, B, C and D as described in question 3?

Dian Fossey studying gorillas in the wild

Humans rule – OK?

In this book you have learned that all the parts of the global SYSTEM depend on each other. They must work together and maintain a balance if life on earth is to survive. Today the global structure is changing: humans have become the dominant species. The key question is: *Does this power give us new responsibilities?*

Gorillas

The photograph on page 173 shows a scientist with a group of mountain gorillas, in their HABITAT on their terms. Yet they, and the rainforests they depend on, are still there, only because governments have decided they can stay and because scientists and conservationists have protected these animals and their environment.

Fewer than 300 mountain gorillas remain, in their last stronghold, the Virunga Volcanoes of Central Africa (Source B). The National Park gives protection, but human populations are growing and need land. Also, the rare gorillas fetch high prices. The scientist in the photograph on page 173, Dian Fossey, was killed in 1985, probably by poachers.

1 Give an example of each of the four components in the diagram (Source A) where humans are ecological dominants.
2 Describe the location and landscape of the Virunga Volcanoes NATIONAL PARK (Source B).
3 What are the pressures on the National Park?
4 Use Source C to describe the migration of the gorilla group.
5 What area of land does the group (made up of ten individuals) need to survive?
6 Scientists say that a *minimum* population of 500 gorillas is needed, i.e. 50 groups like that in Source C. If the population could be built up from 300 to 500 gorillas, how much forest habitat would be needed?
7 In Source C, you will notice that the gorilla group's area is right next to cultivated land. What problems could this cause?

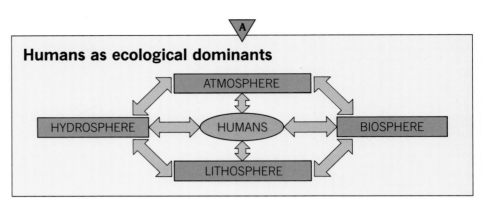

A

Humans as ecological dominants

ATMOSPHERE

HYDROSPHERE — HUMANS — BIOSPHERE

LITHOSPHERE

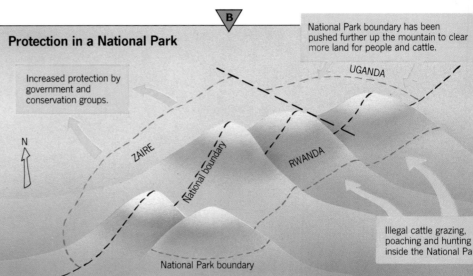

B

Protection in a National Park

National Park boundary has been pushed further up the mountain to clear more land for people and cattle.

Increased protection by government and conservation groups.

UGANDA

ZAIRE

National boundary

RWANDA

N

National Park boundary

Illegal cattle grazing, poaching and hunting inside the National Pa

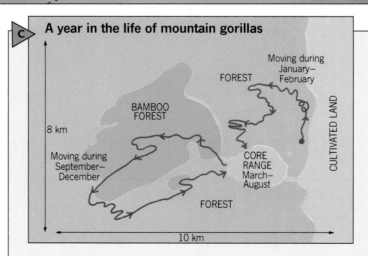

C

A year in the life of mountain gorillas

Moving during January–February

FOREST

BAMBOO FOREST

8 km

Moving during September–December

CORE RANGE March–August

CULTIVATED LAND

FOREST

10 km

Key problems

- small numbers
- space needs
- loss of habitat

There are too few gorillas in the wild to remove some of them for breeding in zoos. Their only chance is in the forests. Gorillas live in groups of 6–20 individuals and have huge appetites: an adult may eat 30 kg of leaves, shoots etc. a day. So, as the map shows, they migrate across a large territory. As each group tries to avoid contact with others, living densities are low – the groups take up a lot of space.

Making space

Letting creatures live and natural ECO-SYSTEMS work is now seen as a major global issue. In 1980, the United Nations Organisation launched its World Conservation Strategy. This aims: first, to conserve the full variety of the world's ecosystems, e.g. tropical rainforests, TEMPERATE FORESTS and wetlands. Second, it aims to develop resources in a way that allows the natural systems to function and be used by people today and into the future. (This is called managing resources for SUSTAINED YIELD.)

A biosphere reserve?

An important part of this Strategy is the WORLD BIOSPHERE RESERVE (Source D). A biosphere reserve is a natural ecosystem in which use is strictly controlled, either by complete protection from humans, or by using it in a way that does not damage or destroy the environment.

The 'biosphere reserve' idea will only be useful if reserves are set up in all the major ecosystems (BIOMES). This idea is part of the United Nations Environmental Programme (UNEP), where different countries are working together.

8   Look at Source D.
   a) Measure the width of the three zones of the biosphere reserve.
   b) How does the size of the core area compare with the two zones around it?
   c) What are the functions of the buffer and transition zones?
   d) Why are these zones necessary?
9   Refer to the Virunga National Park and the gorillas (Sources B, C and E).
   a) How would a buffer zone around the National Park help the conservation of the gorillas?
   b) What problems might occur in setting this up?
10 **a)** Why is it important to have a world-wide network?
   b) From this book, list as many types of ecosystems as you can.
   c) Why is the role of the United Nations particularly important in the World Conservation Strategy?

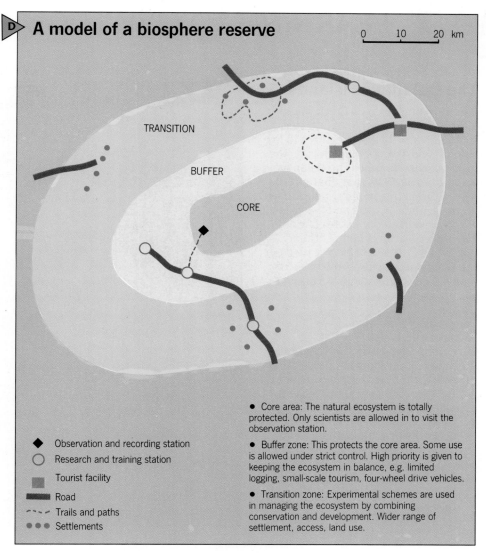

A model of a biosphere reserve

0   10   20 km

TRANSITION

BUFFER

CORE

◆   Observation and recording station
◯   Research and training station
▣   Tourist facility
▬   Road
- - -   Trails and paths
●●●   Settlements

● Core area: The natural ecosystem is totally protected. Only scientists are allowed in to visit the observation station.

● Buffer zone: This protects the core area. Some use is allowed under strict control. High priority is given to keeping the ecosystem in balance, e.g. limited logging, small-scale tourism, four-wheel drive vehicles.

● Transition zone: Experimental schemes are used in managing the ecosystem by combining conservation and development. Wider range of settlement, access, land use.

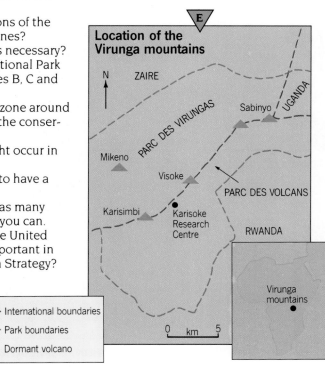

Location of the Virunga mountains

N
ZAIRE

PARC DES VIRUNGAS

Sabinyo   UGANDA

Mikeno

Visoke

PARC DES VOLCANS

Karisimbi

Karisoke Research Centre

RWANDA

Virunga mountains

- - - - -   International boundaries
- - - - -   Park boundaries
▲   Dormant volcano

0   km   5

Responsibility

11 In a small group, think about the case study of the mountain gorilla and discuss these questions:
   a) Humans are the dominant species, so do we have the right to use the Earth's resources as we wish?
   b) Because we are so powerful, do we have a duty to respect and protect the right of all species to live now and into the future? If so, must individuals, nations and organisations change their attitudes and values?
   c) As some individuals, groups and nations are more powerful than others, does this give them a very special responsibility to all species, including other humans?

The Galapagos Islands

If there is one place on Earth where efforts should be made to find space for humans and other creatures to live side by side, then perhaps it is on the group of islands called the Galapagos. It was here, in 1835, that Charles Darwin recorded the amazing, specialised animals, birds, insects and fish from which he worked out his THEORY OF EVOLUTION. Darwin's famous theory, published in 1859 in a book called *On the Origin of Species*, is the basis of many of our understandings about environments.

The study of the Galapagos will help us to understand:

● how species evolve and adapt to their environments.

● how the different parts of an eco-system work together to make up a balanced whole.

● how changed INPUTS and OUTPUTS can upset an ENVIRONMENTAL SYSTEM.

Study Source A:

1   How far are the Galapagos Islands from South America?
2   How far apart are the main islands?
3   How big are the main islands?

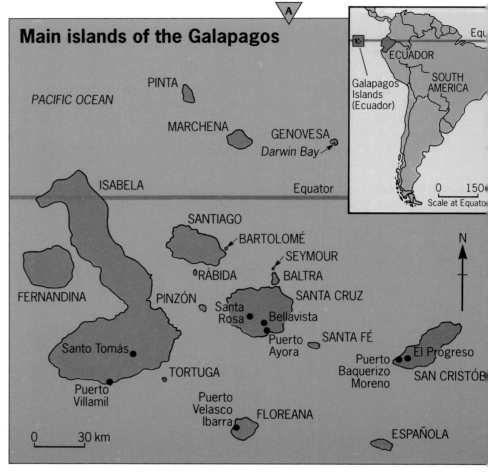

Main islands of the Galapagos

A

PACIFIC OCEAN

PINTA

MARCHENA

GENOVESA
Darwin Bay

ISABELA

Equator

SANTIAGO

BARTOLOMÉ

SEYMOUR

RÁBIDA

BALTRA

FERNANDINA

PINZÓN

Santa Rosa

Bellavista

SANTA CRUZ

Puerto Ayora

SANTA FÉ

Santo Tomás

Puerto Baquerizo Moreno

El Progreso

SAN CRISTÓBAL

TORTUGA

Puerto Villamil

Puerto Velasco Ibarra

FLOREANA

ESPAÑOLA

N

0   30 km

ECUADOR

SOUTH AMERICA

Galapagos Islands (Ecuador)

Equ

0   150

Scale at Equato

4   Look at Source B. How did animals such as tortoises and iguanas reach the Galapagos Islands thousands of years ago?
5   Why are the animals so amazing and specialised?

B

Iguana

'Galapagos' is the Spanish word for 'tortoise'. Once there were 250,000, but today there are only 15,000. Three sub-species are extinct.

Changes in the species

The giant tortoises and iguanas are the 'superstars' of Galapagos. Like all the other land animals their ancestors were carried on rafts of vegetation from the South American mainland by the cold Peru Current. Once the animals were dispersed across the 19 islands, they evolved separately, over thousands of years.

So, when Darwin arrived, he saw that the tortoises, iguanas etc. of each island were different: they had become *sub-species*. Darwin recorded 14 sub-species of giant tortoise because the environments of each island are different. There are also land and marine iguanas, with totally different habitats.

ISOLATION + TIME + EVOLUTION = SPECIATION AND SPECIALISATION

Coping with people and their animals?

Until 1800 there were no people on the Galapagos. When Darwin arrived in 1835, there were 250. In the 1930s there were still fewer than 1000, but in 1987 there were 10,000 people living on four of the islands, in eight small towns. Hundreds more arrive each year, driven from mainland Ecuador by poverty (the cheapest boat ticket costs only £52). They hear tales of jobs and wealth to be found in cattle ranching and tourism on Galapagos, but many find only more poverty.

Perhaps as dangerous for the fragile Galapagos ecosystems are the animals introduced by humans. Many have escaped, and thousands of horses, cattle, pigs, mules, goats, cats, rats and mice roam wild. For example, Santiago Island has no people, but in 1982 it had 100,000 goats and 10,000 pigs. They compete with the natural Galapagos wildlife for space and food.

Puerto Ayora, the capital and economic centre, has a population of about 4000

---

6 Study Source C.
a) What are the threats to the Galapagos Islands?

b) Why have these occurred in recent years?

Protecting the Galapagos

The Galapagos are as protected as possible: they are a World Biosphere Reserve. In 1959 the Ecuador government made 97% of the area a National Park (all inhabitants must live in the other 3%), and the rich waters around the islands are a Marine Resources Reserve.

The key ideas for the future are:
- control of immigration by the government.
- working together by the National Park managers and the scientists at the Darwin Research Station, to balance the demands for tourism and agriculture with the conservation needs of the wildlife (Source D).

Close encounters on the Galapagos

Tasks for the scientists

Get rid of introduced animal and plant species	Restore and protect natural habitats	Breed endangered species at the research station and release them to their restored habitats	Maintain the balance between food supply and species numbers

Tasks for the National Park managers

Park managers must limit and control the numbers of tourists. In 1987, they planned the capacity for 25,000, but 26,000 arrived, so they plan to slowly increase capacity to 45,000. Most visitors arrive by air, stay on boats (not in hotels) to reduce impact and help movement between islands. All tourists must travel with a trained guide, stay on marked trails and not touch the animals. The isolation which allowed the species to evolve also makes them vulnerable – they show no fear of humans!

Success
- By 1987, Santiago Island had only 5000 pigs.
- By 1987, 900 giant tortoises from eight endangered sub-species had been bred and released on their islands.

7 In groups, discuss the key points for the future management of the Galapagos.

8 Write a brief report entitled 'Valuing the Galapagos', which answers these key questions:
a) What makes the Galapagos so valuable?
b) What are the main threats?
c) Who owns the Galapagos and how are they trying to combine conservation and development?

The letter in Source A was writtten by a young forester working in Nepal

1 **a)** What problems is she trying to tackle in Nepal?
b) How are the problems being tackled?

Population pressure

In 1987 the population of Nepal was 16 million, and growing at 2.3% a year. About 15 million people live in the countryside, over half of them in the steeply sloping hill zones between the Ganga Plain and the high Himalayas. The natural vegetation of these hills is forest. In 1955, half of Nepal was forested; in 1985, a fifth. Since then, it has been estimated that 40,000 hectares are lost every year. Yet the forests are vital: they provide fuel, feed for animals, timber, fibres, medicines, dyes and glues.

A

Eastern Nepal

Dear Neil,

I now know why the job specification for my work as a VSO forester in Nepal included the immortal words: "...it is essential that he or she should be healthy and fit and must enjoy walking and be prepared to put up with physical hardship."

Visiting the deforested areas needs all the climbing energy I've got!

But it's only by seeing for myself the extent of the damage that I've been able to appreciate fully the scale of the problem.

In some areas whole hillsides are completely barren, though the old people here can remember them being covered with trees.

The gullies that scar the landscape where erosion has set in are a sight I'll never forget.

But the new tree nurseries and community forestry programmes are now gradually beginning to make an impact. The key to their success is the fact that, for the first time, the local people feel properly included in all the forestry protection schemes. When you can see the new saplings growing, it gives you hope that we can succeed...

B

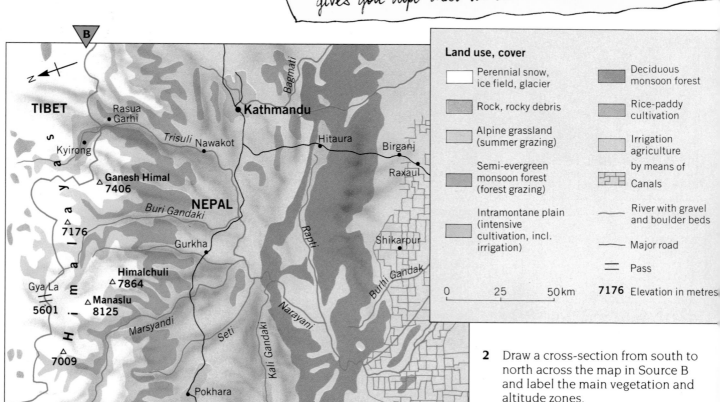

Land use, cover

⬜ Perennial snow, ice field, glacier	Deciduous monsoon forest
Rock, rocky debris	Rice-paddy cultivation
Alpine grassland (summer grazing)	Irrigation agriculture
Semi-evergreen monsoon forest (forest grazing)	by means of
	Canals
Intramontane plain (intensive cultivation, incl. irrigation)	River with gravel and boulder beds
	── Major road
	═ Pass

0   25   50km   **7176** Elevation in metres

2 Draw a cross-section from south to north across the map in Source B and label the main vegetation and altitude zones.

3 What uses do people make of the forests?

Soil erosion

As population grows, people cultivate every usable space. The terraces in Source B are built by hand labour. The narrow terraces on the higher, steeper slopes are called *baari* land, used for maize and millet. The rainwater seeps down to the lower, flatter terraces, called *khet*, where wheat and rice are grown. Once the forests are removed from the steep slopes, SOIL EROSION can be rapid, even where there are terraces. One estimate says that Nepal loses 6 billion tonnes of topsoil a year.

4 Why are the forests being removed?
5 Draw an annotated sketch of Source C. Label the terraces; areas of different crops; water and soil movement down the slope.

Making the most of the slope, Nepal

Trees for the people

Nepal is handing its forests back to the villagers who depend on them. Progress is slow, not just because trees take time to grow, but also because attitudes must change

New Scientist 10 September 1987

Common ownership

With the best intentions, the Nepal government nationalised the forests in 1957. They hoped that central control would manage the precious resource efficiently. It did not work, mainly because the villagers felt they had been robbed of *their* forests. So, instead of caring for the forests as they had done for hundreds of years, they simply took out whatever they could.

In 1977, the government saw their mistake and passed new laws. Each district, or *panchayat*, of about 3000 people, now decides the policy for its local forests (Source D). This is called COMMUNITY FORESTRY and is becoming popular in other economically developing countries.

The role of women

Wood provides 85% of Nepal's energy. Each person uses an average of 600 kg a year, but the forests grow only 80 kg per person per year. So, each year women have to walk further to collect wood. In 1980, a survey found that in many districts, women spend 6 hours a day collecting wood.

So why not let women decide?
As women do the work in the forest, except for the felling, one *panchayat* has its forest committee made up entirely of women. In their first year, they stopped illegal wood collecting, organised the selling and fenced off the tree nursery.

Watering seedlings in a tree nursery, Nepal

Forest management

Many people had lost their forestry skills, during the period of nationalisation, so a number of groups and projects are helping and working with the villagers. They help with such questions as:
● Where to plant the trees?
● Which species will grow best and suit the needs of the environment?
● How can the forest be managed to give sustained yield over many years?
● How can the Nepalese environment be *used* and *conserved*?

6 Why did the Nepalese government's nationalisation plan fail?
7 What is a community forest? Why were these set up?
8 Why are women so actively involved in forest management (Source E)?
9 What is the role of the forest groups and projects?
10 Group research: An urgent problem is to reduce the demands made on the forests. Make a set of suggestions which would work at a local level. Think of the uses of the forest: energy, fodder, etc. Are there other ways these needs could be met?

Who, what and why?

Campaigns to conserve environments can be large or small. They can be organised by individuals, communities, action groups, governments, international bodies.

For each of the examples on these pages, answer the following questions. Use the rest of this book and other references to help you.

1 What is the campaign about?
2 Who is organising it?
3 Who are they hoping to influence?
4 Which environments or species are they concerned about? Why?
5 How do they want to change things?

Villagers campaign

A

International and national bodies protest

B

One dam thing after another

THE FUTURE of the huge Narmada Valley Dam project in India is in doubt. The World Bank is considering pulling out of this proposed $450 million investment. It is two years since the loan agreement was signed and no funds have yet been made available. The World Bank has yet to make any official announcement.

Some 350,000 hectares of land would be inundated when the scheme is completed. This includes 45,000 hectares of rich rain forests—11 per cent of the Narmada Valley forests—and 40,000 hectares of fertile agricultural land, grazing lands and orchards.

The greatest concern, however, is the human cost. People in 236 communities, in the shadow of the Sagar Sarover dam in three states—Madhya Pradesh (180); Maharashtra (36) and Guarat (19)—would have to be relocated. According to the National Institute of Urban Planning an estimated one million people, mostly tribal people, from 435 villages and the major township of Harsud, would need resettlement.

Environmental groups have insisted that the scheme may also have serious long-term ecological consequences. Some of India's best deciduous forests will be completely destroyed. Although the Madhya Pradesh government has promised to afforest twice the area of land submerged in their announced compensatory afforestation plan—90,000 hectares, costing 162 million rupees—it would take 12 years to plant the area and over 40 years before the trees mature.

In the meantime, increased pressure would be put on the adjoining forests which could lead to silting in the river and so shorten the dam's life span. According to the Indian Science Institute, almost 40 per cent of the area—100,000 hectares of black cotton soil—would suffer from chronic waterlogging, which increases salinity and renders soil infertile.

But the grimmest environmental warning was issued by seismologists at the National Geophysical Research Institute at Hyderabad who forecast that the dams would increase the risk of earthquakes in the seismologically active river valley.

Guardian, 11 July 1987

Action groups protest

C

GREENPEACE

Greenpeace campaigns to save the whales · to stop nuclear weapons tests · to protect seals, dolphins, porpoises and sea turtles · to stop the disposal of radioactive waste and dangerous chemicals at sea · to close down nuclear power stations and nuclear reprocessing plants · to stop ACID RAIN and protect the atmosphere · to reduce the trade in endangered species products.

Greenpeace campaigns for stricter control over chemical waste disposal on land and to declare Antarctica a World Park – free of military and industrial exploitation.

Blocking a toxic waste outfall

A journalist campaigns

In 1988, Brian Jackman of *The Sunday Times* wrote an article about the plight of tigers, an endangered species. In China, for instance, there are only 10–20 tigers left.

The photograph shows a scene in a Taiwan market. The tiger is about to be killed and parts of it sold for very high prices: blood for £28 a bottle, the heart for £75. The rest will be made into a special soup for expensive banquets in Canton and Hong Kong.

There are international laws that aim to stop people killing rare animals. However, in practice this is very difficult to achieve.

A superstar shouts out

Stop the destruction of the rainforest!

In December 1987, Sting played a concert in Brazil. He was asked whether he would be willing to fly into the jungle in a small plane to meet the Brazilian Indians whose home, the tropical rainforest, is being cleared in order to obtain timber, land for cultivation and for mining.

The rainforest is being destroyed very fast. What is left behind is bare earth, dust and ash. By staying in the forest and getting publicity for their situation, the Indians can stop some of the clearance work. They have managed this successfully only in the Xingu national park. Elsewhere, Indians are being driven out of the rainforest or killed.

Sting was very moved by what he saw. Since then, he and his girlfriend have been campaigning to bring the world's attention to this issue and try to stop the destruction before it is too late. It is a sad fact that newspapers are more willing to listen to a pop superstar than to Indian chiefs.

14 JUST LOOK AROUND YOU!

Wherever you live, you will find schemes going on to improve how the environment looks and works. The two examples on this page show that everyone can be involved.

Projects to protect and improve the environment are organised by government bodies, local groups and some companies.

A The main national body looking after the British countryside is the Countryside Commission. It is funded by the government. This is how it describes its job:

> **To conserve the landscape beauty ... and to encourage the development of facilities for information, recreation and access to the countryside. The Commission has to achieve many of its objectives by working closely with its 'partners' private individuals and organisations, local authorities and public and voluntary bodies.**

Volunteers at work on a Countryside Commission scheme

B

... from little acorns

Brocton Coppice remains a fairly secret place on an otherwise busy Cannock Chase. It is close to a network of public roads but is not visible from any of them. It is an important wildlife habitat and site of special scientific interest; a place where plants and animals have first priority.

The youngest of the oaks in the coppice dates from the mid 18th century and the oldest from the early 16th century. They grow along with a dense stand of silver birch, in marked contrast to the more typical open heathland of the Chase, and are probably the last remnant of the ancient forest of Kank (or Cank), which covered tens of thousands of hectares.

This is an ideal haven for deer, providing food and rutting stands; grey squirrels are common and there is a colourful and varied bird population. A survey has shown that Brocton Coppice is home to a number of rare and local species of beetle which are found only in primary woodland, i.e., that which has never been cleared and replanted.

But this valuable woodland is not regenerating. Large quantities of acorns are still being produced but they are quickly snapped up by deer, squirrels and mice. Some of the older trees are dying; the majority will not last 50 years.

But a scheme now in hand ensures that the wood will survive. Up to 10,000 acorns are collected each year by cubs, schoolchildren and the Watch group of the Stafford Nature Conservation Trust. The acorns are grown for two years at a local nursery then many of the young trees are transferred to plantations at Brocton Coppice.

The plantations are carefully sited to allow the beetles to move from the old trees to the new trees when the time is right, and so as not to interfere with the deer. So the Brocton Coppice oaks will continue.

"The children love it. They are helping to make trees which the beetles won't use for 200 years; it gives them a sense of working for the future," said project officer Jo Daniels.

1 Look at the photograph in Source A.
a) What do you think the people are doing?
b) Why do you think they are doing this?
2 **a)** Who is involved in the project in Source B?
b) What is the problem and how would it be solved?
c) Why do you think these people are involved?

In small groups:
3 As a follow up, check out your local district and build up a list of what is going on, and who is involved.
4 Look back at Sources A–E on pages 180–181 and come to a group decision about which campaign or project you would like to support. Decide how you could raise money for it and design publicity materials, e.g. posters or leaflets.

Countryside Commission News, November 1987

GLOSSARY

Adiabatic cooling   The cooling which takes place in a mass of air when it expands, usually by rising.

Afforestation   The organised planting of trees.

Agroforestry   The growing together of tree and ground crops. It is useful in protecting the soil from erosion.

Air masses   Large bodies of air with relatively homogeneous properties of temperature and humidity.

Air pressure   The 'weight' of a vertical column of air, measured in millibars.

Airstream   An air mass in motion.

Anemogram   A chart showing changes in wind speed over a period, measured by an instrument called an *anemometer*.

Aquifer   A layer of rock or soil which can hold or carry a lot of water.

Arid (environments)   Dry environments where there is always a shortage of water, i.e. a permanent water budget deficit.

Atmosphere   The gaseous component of the global system, containing also moisture and solid particles.

Bankfull discharge   The volume of water moving along a river when the river channel is full to the top of the banks.

Barometric pressure   Air pressure is measured by a *barometer*. It is commonly expressed in millibars and mapped as isobars.

Base flow   The flow in a stream which is fed from the groundwater store.

Benioff zone   Another name for subduction zone.

Biogas   Gas produced from organic matter by biological processes.

Biomass   The total mass of living organisms in an ecosystem.

Biomes   Major ecosystems or living realms of the world.

Biosphere   The living component of the global system.

Biosphere reserve   A large area set aside by a government to conserve the area's special ecological characteristics and protect certain species.

Blanket peat   Peat is partially-decomposed plant material. In cool, damp conditions it may build up to cover large areas in a 'blanket'.

Broadleaved (trees)   Trees which have wide, flat leaves (rather than needles).

Brown forest earth   Soils found under temperate deciduous forests, the brown colour being humus (organic matter).

Carbon   A chemical element with the symbol C. It is a vital part of all natural systems.

Carbon cycle   The circular movement of carbon through the components of the environment.

Carrying capacity   The amount of use, or the level of demand, that a particular environment can sustain.

Catchment area   The area which is drained by a river and its tributaries.

Channel precipitation   Rainfall that falls directly into the river channel.

CFCs (chlorofluorocarbons)   Chemicals used in the manufacture of some aerosols, fast-food cartons and refrigerators, and harmful to the ozone layer.

Climate   Weather conditions averaged out over long periods.

Climatic climax vegetation   The assemblage of plants which evolves over time to be in balance with the environmental conditions. The ideal plant community for that environment.

Closed forest   Woodland where the overhead canopy is complete.

Community forestry   Forests managed and looked after by local communities to suit their own needs and wishes.

Coniferous (trees)   Trees which produce cones.

Conurbations   Large urban areas created by the growing together of several towns.

Convection   Transfer of heat which takes place when a heated substance moves. Convection currents cause warm air or liquid rock to circulate in the *atmosphere* or *lithosphere*.

Critical growth threshold   The minimum temperature at which growth in plants begins. For many temperate plants this is around 6°C.

Cycle   The circular movement of energy or matter through the components of a system.

Deciduous (plants)   Plants which lose their leaves seasonally because of cold and/or lack of moisture.

Deciduous broadleaved forest   Woods that consist of trees which have broad leaves rather than needles, and which shed their leaves seasonally.

Decomposers   Bacteria and other tiny organisms that eat and break down dead tissue.

Deforestation   The removal of forest cover.

Desertification   The spread of desert conditions in a region which was not previously a desert.

Dew point temperature   The air temperature at which condensation takes place, i.e. when the moisture in the atmosphere changes from a gas to a liquid.

Discharge   The rate at which water is being moved down a river. It is usually expressed as the volume which passes a point in a certain time.

Dormant   In a non-growth, non-active state because of the lack of certain inputs, such as heat or moisture.

Drainage basin   The network of streams and the land they drain.

Drought   Periods when rainfall is significantly below the average. Unusual dry spells.

Earthquake swarm   A series of minor earth tremors which occur over a short period and signal that magma or crustal fragments are moving somewhere locally within the Earth's crust.

Ecological capacity   The level of use an environment can take before there is obvious damage to plants, animals, soils etc.

Ecosystem   A system that shows the relationships between a community of living things (plants and animals) and their non-living environment.

EEC   The European Economic Community, now increasingly known as the European Community (EC). A grouping of 12 countries in Europe which have formally agreed to have close economic links with each other.

Environmental system   An environment seen as a set of linked parts (components) which work together as a whole.

Erosion   The wearing-away of surfaces and rocks by chemical, physical and biological processes.

Evaporation   Loss of water when it changes from a liquid into a vapour.

Evapotranspiration   Combined water loss from *evaporation* and *transpiration*.

Evergreen (plants)   Plants which keep their leaves all year.

Fallow (land)   Land which is being rested between periods of cultivation.

Faults   Lines or zones caused by the breaking or shearing of rocks as a result of enormous forces.

Feedback   The response in the rest of the system to a change in one component of it.

Fertility   The level of plant nutrients in a soil.

Fissures   Long, narrow cracks in the earth's crust.

Flow diagram   A diagram of boxes and arrows which represents the components and pathways of a system. It is used to show the movement or flow of energy and matter through a system.

Fluvio-glacial landforms   Features in the landscape which are the result of erosion and deposition by meltwaters associated with glaciers.

Food chain   The feeding succession, starting with producers and leading through the various consumers. This forms a series of links along which energy passes through a system.

Food web   A set of interlinked food chains.

Front   The forward edge of an advancing mass of cold or warm air.

Glacial landforms   Features in the landscape which are the result of erosion and deposition by ice.

Graben   A block of land which has dropped down between two faults.

Greenhouse effect   Carbon dioxide in the atmosphere allows short-wave solar radiation to pass through, but it prevents part of the re-radiated longer-wave radiation from returning to space. Thus, it acts like a greenhouse: letting heat in, but preventing some of it from escaping.

Groundwater flow   The movement of water below the surface.

Groundwater store   The water held below the surface of the land.

Groyne   A barrier built out into the sea to stop the longshore drift of sand, and so cause the beach to grow.

Gust speed   The speed of the most powerful surges of wind.

Habitat   The place were an organism normally lives.

Horizon   A layer in a soil profile.

Hydroelectric power   Electricity generated by the force of water turning turbines.

Hydrograph   A graph which shows the rate of water discharge in a stream.

Hydrological cycle   The circular movement of water through the various stores of the environment.

Hydrosphere   The water component of the global system.

Impermeable   Does not allow water to pass through.

Infiltration   Gradual penetration of water into soil or rock.

Infiltration capacity   How much infiltration is possible.

Infiltration rate   The rate at which water can seep into a surface.

Input   Energy or matter which enters a system or moves from one part of a system to another.

Intercept   Interrupt the movement of matter. This often refers to vegetation interrupting the fall of raindrops.

Interplant   To plant additional crops between rows of crops already growing, or under trees.

Irrigation   The controlled addition of water to the land.

Isobars   Lines of equal pressure drawn on weather maps.

Lahar   A mudflow associated with volcanic eruptions. It is often made up of ash and water melted from snow and ice by the heat of the eruption.

Laterite   A red soil left after rock weathering and leaching under humid tropical conditions. Sometimes called 'brick earth', because it sets hard as brick when it dries out.

Latitudes   Lines round the Earth drawn parallel to the Equator. They are measured in degrees north or south of the Equator, and this represents the angular distance of each line from the Equator.

Leaching   Washing of mineral and organic nutrients out of a soil by the movement of water.

Levée   A natural or artificial bank along a river.

Lithosphere   The crust of the Earth.

Loam   A permeable soil with an even mixture of sand and clay particles. This makes the soil hold water well and plough easily.

Loess   Sediments that have been carried by the wind and deposited

Magma   Molten rock within the Earth's crust. It may be extruded (squeezed out) at the Earth's surface as lava.

Mass movement   Downhill movement of a slope. It is caused by weathering and can be a sudden landslide or a gradual process.

Meltwater   Water which has melted from glaciers.

Meteorologist   A scientist who specialises in the study of weather.

Mid-latitude depression   Area of low pressure occurring in middle latitudes. Also known as a trough of low pressure, or low-pressure system.

Mineral nutrients   Minerals useful to plants as part of their food intake.

Monsoon   The rainy season in tropical regions, especially in the Indian subcontinent. The word comes from an Arabic word meaning 'season'.

National Parks   Areas of special environmental qualities set aside by governments to preserve and conserve these qualities and to provide access to them.

Niche   The specific place that an organism occupies in an ecosystem.

Nutrients (plant)   Materials which plants need and use for food.

Open forest   Woodland where there are gaps in the overhead canopy.

Organic nutrients   Organic matter used by plants as food.

Output   Energy or matter which leaves a system or moves out of one store in a system.

Overland flow   Movement of water over the land surface.

Ozone   A form of oxygen (O_3) found in tiny quantities high in the atmosphere. It protects the Earth's surface from ultraviolet rays. However, ozone is a pollutant at ground level.

Perceptual capacity   The number of people that can take part in activities at a location before their satisfaction level begins to fall, i.e. the point at which people find the location is overcrowded.

Permeable   Allows water to pass through.

pH scale   A scale used to measure how acid or alkaline a substance is.

Photosynthesis   The process in which green plants take in sunlight, carbon dioxide and water to produce oxygen, tissue and energy.

Physical capacity   The number of people or vehicles that can physically get on to a location.

Plantations   Areas of trees which are planted for particular uses.

Plates   Huge segments of the Earth's crust and upper mantle.

Plate tectonics   The theory which states that the Earth's crust is made up of a series of huge plates which move slowly, driven by mighty convection currents deeper within the Earth.

Pleistocene period   The last great Ice Age when global temperatures fell. It began more than 2 million years ago, and ended approximately 10,000 years ago.

Podsol   A soil formed in cool, seasonally humid environments where leaching is strong and so the soils have a pale colour.

Porosity   The ability of a soil or rock to absorb water.

Porous   Able to hold water in the pore spaces.

Precipitation   Rain, snow, hail, sleet, frost: outputs of moisture from the atmosphere.

Pressure gradient   A measure of the rate of pressure change over distance. The more rapid the pressure change over distance, the steeper the pressure gradient – and the closer together are the isobars on a weather map.

Primary consumers   Herbivores which eat the producers (green plants).

Primary forest   The untouched, natural forest of a region.

Primary pollutants   Harmful gases and solid particles from human activity dumped directly into the atmosphere, e.g. sulphur dioxide.

Processes   Activities going on in an environment.

Producers   Green plants which produce energy by photosynthesis and store it in plant tissue.

Rainfall intensity   How much rain falls in a certain period.

Range of tolerance   The amount of change or stress that an environment, or component of an environment, can stand before it begins to change rapidly.

Regime   The rhythm of some environmental component such as river flow, rainfall, temperature.

Regolith   The soil and weathered debris layer above the bedrock.

Relief of the area   The differences in height and the shape of the land surface.

Richter scale   A scale used to measure earthquake strength. Each higher step on the scale represents a tenfold increase.

Runoff   The part of rainfall that runs into streams as surace water (rather than being absorbed into the ground or lost by evapotranspiration).

Salinisation   The build-up of salts in the soil.

Savanna   Tropical grasslands, usually with a scattering of trees. They lie between the tropical rainforests and hot deserts.

Scrub   Vegetation consisting mainly of bushes and shrubs.

Secondary consumers   Animals (including humans, birds, insects) which eat herbivores (primary consumers).

Secondary forest   Forest which regrows after the primary forest has been removed.

Secondary pollutants   Pollutants produced in the atmosphere by the reaction of primary pollutants with water and sunlight. New pollutants are formed, e.g. acid rain.

Sediment loss   Removal of sediment by the river as the end result of weathering, erosion and mass movement.

Shifting cultivation   Agriculture where vegetation is cleared, crops are grown for a few years and then the plot is left to rest while other plots are cleared and used.

Soil cohesion   The strength with which individual soil particles hold together.

Soil creep   The slow movement of soil down a slope.

Soil horizons   Layers in a soil profile.

Soil profile   A vertical section through a soil.

Solar energy   Energy (e.g. heat, light) produced by the sun.

Speciation   The evolution of distinctive characteristics by species.

Stemflow   Water running down the stems of plants.

Steppe   A type of temperate grassland found in continents that have long, cold winters and short, warm summers with rain.

Store   A component of a system in which energy and matter are held.

Storm hydrograph   A graph showing the discharge of a stream as the result of water input from a storm.

Strata   Layers of rock identifiable by their character.

Subduction zone   The zone at the margin of two plates where one crustal plate is being dragged beneath another and its material destroyed. Earthquakes and magma formation occur along this zone. It is also called a Benioff zone.

Succession   The sequence of plant types which occupy an area through time.

Succession of feeding   The sequence of consumption through a food chain.

Suspended load   Particles carried in the body of the water in a stream, rather than rolling along the stream bed.

Sustained yield   Productivity retained over long periods due to careful use and management of the environment.

Synoptic chart   A map showing atmospheric and weather conditions at a certain moment.

System   A set of parts (components) linked together by pathways. Energy and matter pass along these pathways to make the system work as a single unit.

Taiga   Huge belt of coniferous forest in the USSR.

Temperate forest   Woodland found in middle latitudes, where temperatures are neither very hot nor very cold.

Tertiary consumers   Animals (including humans, birds, insects) which eat secondary consumers.

Theory of evolution   The theory proposed by Darwin in the 19th century to explain how living organisms have evolved (adapted, specialised and advanced).

Thermal pollution   Pollution caused by the addition of heat to the atmosphere and hydrosphere as a result of human activities.

Threshold   The point when an environment begins to change rapidly because of altered conditions.

Throughflow   Movement of water through the soil or rock.

Throughput   The movement of energy or matter through a system.

Topography   The shape of the land

Tornado   A rapidly rotating column of air spiralling around a very intense low-pressure centre.

Transpiration   The loss of moisture by plants through their stomata (pores).

Tundra   Stony or marshy land with moss, lichen and dwarf shrub vegetation. It is found in regions that have long, cold winters and short, mild summers.

Ultraviolet radiation   A kind of radiation present in sunlight and harmful to living organisms.

Water budget   The relationship or balance between water entering a drainage basin and water leaving the basin.

Watershed   The boundary of a catchment area.

Water table   The surface of the saturated layer in the soil and bedrock, i.e. the top of the groundwater store.

Weather   Short-term events and characteristics of the atmosphere at work.

Wind chill factor   The cooling effect of wind moving over a body, causing heat loss from any exposed skin surfaces. This is why it *seems* colder when the winds are blowing, because the heat loss from the body is greater.

INDEX

Designed by Hilary Norman
Edited by Kate Harris, Nicole Lagneau and Ela Ginalska
Picture research by Caroline Thompson
Production by Lorna Heaslip
Maps and diagrams by John Booth, Jerry Fowler, Jillian Luff, Malcolm Porter, s + m Technical Services, Gillian Tyson
Cartoons by Mike Gordon
Other artwork by Gay Galsworthy and Annette Olney

The authors and publishers are grateful to Fiona Burgess for her detailed comments on the manuscript.

Typeset by Tradespools Ltd, Frome, Somerset
Printed in Hong Kong by Wing King Tong Ltd

Acknowledgements

Every effort has been made to contact the holders of copyright material but if any have been inadvertently overlooked the publishers will be pleased to make the necessary arrangements at the first opportunity.

Maps on pp. 52, 61 and 145 are reproduced from the 1989 Ordnance Survey 1:50000 Landranger map with permission of the Controller of Her Majesty's Stationery Office © Crown Copyright.

Photographs The publishers would like to thank the following for permission to reproduce photographs on these pages:

Key: T = Top C = Centre B = Bottom R = Right L = Left

Aerofilms, 144, 149; Allsport (UK), 109L, 117T; David Cannon/Allsport (UK), 122; Dr Philip Amis, 84; Paul Amos, 126; Heather Angel, 30TLR&BR, Ardea London, 31BL&R, 97T, 114CL&R, 115; Argus Foto Agentur, 159; Associated Press, 110T, 120, 156T; David R. Austen, 74, 75; Patrick Bailey, 112; The Bettmann Archives, 113T; Biophoto Associates, 136BL; Dr John Boardman, 19; Des Bowden, 43; The J. Allan Cash Photolibrary, 20, 54, 55, 58, 117BL, 127, 134; Central Electricity Generating Board, 166; Martyn Chillmaid, 17R; Bruce Coleman, 12T; Bob Campbell/Bruce Coleman, 173; Dieter & Mary Plage/Bruce Coleman, 177; Diana Hunt/Colorific! 69; Fred Ward/Colorific!/Black Star, 101T&B; Ted Spiegel/Colorific!/Black Star, 161; Shepard Sherbell/Colorific!/Picture Group, 171; Charles Meecham/Countryside Commission, 107TR; Mike Williams/Countryside Commission, 182R; Dr J.L. Daniels, 182L; Deutsche Prsss-Agentur, 156B, 156–7; Dr Robert Dolan, 113B; University of Dundee, 123T; Gary Rosenquist/Earth Images, 133; Steve Simon/Edmonton Journal, 123B; Mark Edwards, 82, 85, 86T, 93; Chris Fairclough Colour Library, 154; Forestry Commission (Research Division), 165; Friends of the Earth, 169; GAMMA, 103, 142; GeoScience Features Picture Library, 136BR; Adam Ginalski, 1; Goddard Space Flight Center/NASA, 48; Sally & Richard Greenhill, 70, 146TL; Greenpeace/Morgan, 180B; J. Christianson/Susan Griggs Agency, 132; Denis Thorpe/*Guardian*, 105T; Robert Harding Picture Library, 25, 117TR, 170; Juliet Highet, 104TL&C; Holt Studios, 3R, 12B; Eric & David Hosking, 14CR, 34, 176R; The Hutchinson Library, 8R, 45CR, 102, 104TR; Mark Boulton/ICCE, 162L; Icelandic Photos & Press Service, 131; Impact Photos, 97B, 181T; Julian Calder/Impact Photos, 38; Frank Lane Picture Agency, 51; Kjell-Arne Larsson, 167; Loren McIntyre, 47C; Alberto Venzago/Magnum Photos, 37, 181B; Bruce Barbey/Magnum Photos, 47B; Steve McCurry/Magnum Photos, 81, 86B; Fred Mayer/Magnum Photos, 129; John Mannion, 30BL, 56; Mary Evans Picture Library, 17L; Dr Peter Moore, 98; NASA, 168; Nature Conservancy Council, 95; National Trust/Simon Rose, 107TL; Nature History Photographic Agency, 9, 14TLCR&BL, 18, 31TL&C, 41BR, 52, 117BRCL&B, 164; Neilson Leisure Group, 111; Peter Newark's Western Americana, 13; Jeremy Hartley/OXFAM, 90, 179; Terry Heathcote/Oxford Scientific Films, 3L; Partridge Films/Oxford Scientific Films, 41BL; Michael Fogden/Oxford Scientific Films, 41TL&R; Peter Ryley/Oxford Scientific Films, 176L; Paul Harison/Panos Pictures, 87; Ann & Bury Peerless Slide Resources & Picture Library, 160; Picture House, 107B; Picturepoint, 162R; Jonathan Scott/Planet Earth Pictures, 14C; Sean Avery/Planet Earth Pictures, 14BR; Peter Poulides, 39, 46; Dr R. Prosser, 22, 65, 66, 67, 73, 101C, 106, 109TC&B, 136T, 139, 140, 141, 143, 146TR&B, 148, 180T; Tim Bauer/Retna Pictures, 2R; Rex Features, 110B, 114T; P.A. Jacobberger/Smithsonian Institution, 94; Smithsonian Institution, 27; Society for Cultural Relations with the USSR, 15, 32; Marion Morrison/South American Pictures, 8L, 45CL; Peter Fry/Survival International, 44, 45T; Swiss National Tourist Office, 2L; *Telegraph* Colour Library, 88; Professor D.E. Walling, 78, 79; Simon Warner, 105B; Janet & Colin Board/Wales Scene, 8C; ZEFA, 100, 138.

Front cover photograph: Panos Pictures
Nepal: the steep terraced land is vulnerable to erosion and landslides.